EDWARD TIVNAN

THE LOBBY

JEWISH POLITICAL POWER AND AMERICAN FOREIGN POLICY

SIMON AND SCHUSTER   **NEW YORK**

Published by Simon and Schuster
A Division of Simon & Schuster, Inc.
Simon & Schuster Building
Rockefeller Center
1230 Avenue of the Americas
New York, New York 10020
SIMON AND SCHUSTER and colophon are registered trademarks of
Simon & Schuster, Inc.
Designed by Karolina Harris
Manufactured in the United States of America

3   5   7   9   10   8   6   4   2

Library of Congress Cataloging-in-Publication Data
Tivnan, Edward.
The Lobby: Jewish political power and American
foreign policy.

Bibliography: p.
Includes index.
1. United States—Foreign relations—Israel.
2. Israel—Foreign relations—United States.
3. Zionism—United States. 4. Jews—United States—
Attitudes toward Israel. 5. American Israel Public
Affairs Committee. 6. United States—Foreign
relations—1945–   . 7. United States—Ethnic
relations. I. Title.
E183.8.I75T58   1987   327.7305694   86-31432
ISBN: 0-671-50153-4

FOR MY PARENTS,
EDWARD J. AND AGNES B.

CONTENTS

PREFACE

In the fall of 1984, Arye L. Dulzin, the chairman of the World Zionist Organization and head of the Jewish Agency, leaned across his desk in his Tel Aviv office and, in an almost conspiratorial whisper, asked me, "Are they as powerful as they say they are?"

It was a good question—the same question in fact that had provoked me to begin research on this book more than a year before. The idea had emerged during a conversation with my friend Steve Schwartz, a New York lawyer and entrepreneur with a well-informed interest in U.S. foreign policy: Was the so-called "Jewish lobby" as powerful as everyone (including Jewish lobbyists) said it was? We were discussing the nasty battle that had taken place in the Senate in 1981 over the Reagan Administration's proposal to sell five intelligence-gathering planes—AWACS—to Saudi Arabia. American Jewish organizations, with the support of the Israeli government of Menachem Begin, had fought the sale aggressively, amidst charges in the press, on Capitol Hill, and from former U.S. Presidents that the Israelis were interfering in U.S. policy, that the Jewish lobby had become too powerful, that the "special relationship" between the U.S. and Israel was skewing U.S. policy in the Middle East. There were countercharges that such criticism smelled of anti-Semitism.

We wondered how the Middle East debate had descended into name-calling. And what did it mean for a lobby to be "too powerful" in a political system where the pleadings of "special interests" were as American as the *Federalist Papers* that had allotted such "factions" an integral role in the U.S. Constitutional system? Wasn't that what lobbies were supposed to do—influence policy? Were only Jewish lobbies too powerful? How did a community of only 6 million Americans become so politically influential? Were U.S. interests and Israel's interests the same? Could American Jews support Israel but dissent from policies of a particular Israeli government? The answers, we concluded, might make a book.

In my preliminary research, I discovered that though the subject of Jewish influence in the making (or unmaking) of U.S. Middle East policy was much grumbled about in various corners of Washington, surprisingly little had been written about it. Most commentators danced nimbly around the effects of the "Jewish vote" and "Jewish money" in American politics. Diplomatic histories and political tracts on the Middle East tended to mention the effects of "domestic politics" on U.S. policy only to skip quickly to other matters. The few things written specifically on the Jewish lobby were so bad or so biased—from the pro-Israel or pro-Arab point of view—that they were not worth reading. Some people even denied the existence of a Jewish lobby.

Clearly, there was a need to take a fresh look at the subject. I decided to attempt to put this particular instance of "special interest" lobbying within the wider historical context of the evolution of U.S.-Israeli relations since the creation of the Jewish state in 1948. How did the American Jewish community and its leadership fit into this "special relationship"? What were the attitudes of American Jews toward Zionism and its greatest achievement?

The answers were not as obvious as either the critics or fans of the Jewish lobby would have it. Even the title "Jewish Lobby," I quickly discovered, needed some fine-tuning; what was most at issue, as the lobbyists themselves insisted, was the influence of the "pro-Israel lobby." Indeed, how the Jewish lobby had become primarily a pro-Israel lobby, one so aggressive, omnipresent and influential on matters relating to the Middle East that the denizens of Capitol Hill refer to it simply as "the lobby," became a focal point of my research.

That I was onto a good story few disagreed. But there was one problem: "Nobody will talk to you," I was informed over and over again. The subject was too hot, too touchy, too politically dangerous for all concerned. Jewish leaders, the lobbyists, their friends—and enemies—in Congress preferred to keep this subject under wraps. I was told that if I was to be as fair as I claimed, I would have to be critical of Israel and the American Jewish community (even my well-informed Jewish friends conceded that was a given) and the slightest criticism of either was bound to invite the charge that I was "pro-Arab" or "anti-Israel" or, worse still, "anti-Semitic."

Others had a darker view. Former career foreign-service officers and ex-ambassadors to Arab countries warned that "no New York publisher will publish such a book." When I explained I already had a commitment from a major New York publisher, they waved a hand and explained that distributors would reject it or that local Jewish groups would pressure bookstores to remove it from the shelves. One ex-ambassador, who had recently been cited by a Jewish organization as a major figure in the "anti-Israel camp," went so far as to suggest tha if my book did eventually get published Jewish groups would buy up all the copies to keep it from wider circulation. (As a freelance writer with a long list of creditors, this notion, I must admit, intrigued me.)

As it turned out, virtually every Jewish leader I asked—and every Israeli politician—was willing to talk, positively eager, in some cases. On the cautious side, yet still cooperative, was Thomas A. Dine, the current head of the American Israel Public Affairs Committee (AIPAC), the only registered lobby for Israel on Capitol Hill and the "spearhead," as Dine likes to call it, for support for Israel in Washington. AIPAC's success has won it a host of critics, including leaders of the nation's oldest Jewish organizations. Though many warned me that Dine would not grant me an interview, he gave me several, proving to be generous with his time and candid in his explanations, on and off the record. So were a few of his subordinates, present and past, as well as several other former AIPACers of previous regimes including Dine's controversial predecessor Morris Amitay. All spoke candidly about the rise of Jewish political power over the past decade and the changes in American and Jewish politics that have helped boost AIPAC's own level of influence in the Arab-Israeli-U.S. calculus.

Other Jewish leaders also welcomed my inquiries; indeed, some seemed to find our sessions therapeutic. Six years of Menachem Begin as prime minister of Israel had left many of them frustrated and embittered by a vision of Israel that clashed with their own; Israel's invasion and occupation of Lebanon in 1982–83 had left some of Israel's most loyal supporters, inside and outside the Jewish community, feeling betrayed. A few were willing to report their reservations for the record; most were at least willing to discuss in private the

consequences of Begin's policies for Israel's future. The result is a
number of unattributed quotations, and any number of blind sources
is too many.

Nevertheless, this willingness to be interviewed and unwillingness
to be quoted by name is also part of the story; it is also one answer to
the question posed by Arye Dulzin: the lobby is powerful enough to
engender fear among dissenters in the uppermost levels of American
government and the American Jewish community. The consequences
of such power—what AIPAC likes to call "Jewish muscle"—for
Israel, American foreign policy in the Middle East, and for the American Jewish community is another matter, and another part of the
story I set out to tell.

This book is the result of nearly two hundred interviews in the
U.S. and Israel and three years of reading, discussing, writing, and
revising. The lobby's most hostile critics have denounced its activities as an example of "foreign influence" in the making of U.S. foreign policy. On the contrary, the story of the pro-Israel lobby's role in
the American political system is a very American story—so American, in fact, that Israelis, including top Zionist leaders such as Dulzin, are as mystified by the source of Jewish power in the U.S. as are
their Arab counterparts. It is also a tale of how the American system
works, for better or for worse, and how one group has exploited it on
behalf of its own interests (and not always in the interests of Israel).

It is also a story that begins long before there was an Israel, when a
Jewish state was the wild dream of a group of nineteenth century
European political activists who, as it happened, had little support
among the Jews of America.

Edward Tivnan, 1986

INTRODUCTION

BEFORE Israel existed as a state, it existed as a political lobby first in the capitals of Europe and then in Washington. Zionism was the romantic dream of a band of nineteenth-century European ideologues who often could agree on only one thing: that to achieve a "normal" life in an anti-Semitic world, Jews required a "Jewish state." Zionist leaders worked tirelessly to convince the rest of the world to help them make that dream a reality. They met with hostility and skepticism. Foremost among their doubters and critics were the Jewish leaders of America.

The founder and prime mover of "political Zionism" was the well-known Viennese journalist Theodor Herzl. Like many Jews of his bourgeois background—his father was in the clothing business—Herzl, who had earned a doctorate in Roman law and had failed as a playwright, was an assimilated Jew with no Jewish education and without concern for religion or Jewish matters. That changed in 1893 when Karl Lueger was elected mayor of Vienna on an anti-Jewish platform. The following year the reporter's mind focused again on the future of Europe's Jews when as the Paris correspondent of the Viennese daily *Neue Freie Presse* he was covering the trial of Alfred Dreyfus, a Jewish French army officer charged with treason. In spite of his claims and evidence of innocence, Dreyfus was convicted and sentenced to Devil's Island. The Dreyfus Affair stirred up deep divisions between the political right and left in Paris against a backdrop of a virulently anti-Semitic press and demonstrations against Dreyfus.

Herzl was profoundly shocked at this surge of anti-Jewish hatred and became convinced that anti-Semitism was so ingrained in European society that the Jews would never be allowed to blend in. The only answer to "the Jewish Question," Herzl concluded, was a Jewish state. The central idea of his classic work on Zionism, *Der Judenstaat*, was that to solve Europe's Jewish problem "we must first of all establish it as an international political problem to be discussed and settled by the civilized nations of the world."

The goal of Herzl's Zionism was to rescue Jews from their alien status in the world and restore them to "normalcy" within the confines of a Jewish state. If the hostility of the world toward its Jews was a natural phenomenon, then Zionism would remove the provocation. By giving the Jews their own nation, Zionism would become Europe's "peacemaker." As the historian of Zionism Arthur Hertzberg has pointed out in his book *The Zionist Idea*, earlier Zionist thinkers had stirred up a revolution in Jewish thought by suggesting that the crucial dialogue was not between Jews and God but between Jews and the rest of the world. The central tenet of Judaism—that salvation rested in the coming of a Messiah—was replaced with Zion, the coming of a new Israel that would bestow on the Jews the political liberty and the economic and social justice that the progressives of the nineteenth century had promised to the rest of the world. To the other national movements that populated the dreams of nineteenth-century political thinkers throughout Europe, Herzl added the Zionist Dream.[1]

Yet there was an important difference between Jewish nationalism and the other struggles for national self-determination: Jewish identity was not based on an already existing national land or spoken language. Herzl was the leader of a new nation without a homeland, and thus his primary goal became to find a place for the Jews to establish their state and the money to finance the exodus. Herzl began calling upon the wealthy Jews of the world. They saw him as a dreamer and sent him away empty-handed. After meeting Herzl for the first time, Jacob Schiff, the New York financier who was a powerful leader of the American Jewish community at the turn of the century, reported that Zionism was a "sentimental theory" without a future.[2]

Religious Jews found the idea preposterous, if not blasphemous. Salvation awaited the coming of the Messiah and not the political aspirations of Doktor Herzl, the famous journalist and man-about-Vienna, who, in an ideal world, would have preferred to have been assimilated. Even fellow Zionists wondered about Herzl's program. Ahad Ha'am, the founder of "cultural Zionism," which saw a new Israel as the spiritual and cultural center of the Jewish Diaspora, first encountered Herzl at the First Zionist Congress in Basel in 1897 and saw, in the historian Walter Laqueur's blunt phrase, "little more than a confidence trickster." Ahad Ha'am warned his own readers that "the salvation of Israel will come through prophets, not through diplomats."[3]

Yet it would take something of a "confidence trickster" and a master international diplomat, which Herzl turned out to be, to push Zionism before the leaders of the world. Herzl shuttled from country to country exploiting his connections as a famous journalist to meet with the Turkish sultan, the German kaiser, the king of Italy, the pope, Britain's colonial secretary. Herzl had the right amount of self-confidence, messianic fervor, and public-relations genius to turn his idea into the dream of hundreds of thousands of Russian Jews who saw political Zionism as their refuge from the vicious and deadly anti-Semitism of their current homeland. The founder of Zionism believed that everyone—and above all the "sensible anti-Semites"— would eventually recognize that his solution was also the answer to their Jewish problem. In 1903—a year before his early death at age forty-four—Herzl even met with the czar's minister of the interior, Count Vyacheslav Plehve, the man Jews held responsible for some of the most bloody pogroms in Russian history. In return for removing the Jews from the tinderbox of Russian revolutionary politics, Herzl wanted Plehve to lift restrictions on Zionist activity in Russia, financial aid for emigration, and help with the Turkish sultan to gain a charter for a Jewish homeland in Palestine, then part of the Ottoman Empire.

But Zionism remained a European movement. Rabbi I. M. Wise, the founder of American Reform Judaism, which dominated Jewish religious life in the U.S. at the turn of the century, would declare in the name of his organization, "We are unalterably opposed to political Zionism. . . . Zion was a precious possession of the past . . . but it is not our hope of the future. America is our Zion."[4] Jewish leaders like Wise and Schiff preferred to protect the interests of their constituencies by following the medieval Jewish tradition of the *shtadlan*, or "court Jew," those influential and financially powerful Jews of old Europe who lived on the margin of gentile society and could influence it on behalf of the poor and uneducated masses they claimed to represent. In 1906, the grandees of the New York Jewish community institutionalized the notion of the court Jew in the form of the American Jewish Committee. The new group would deal with the political and social problems of the massive influx of Jewish immigrants from Eastern Europe at the turn of the century; the committee would also insure that its kind of American Jews, urbane, well educated, rich, and assimilated, would control Jewish life in America.

The new Jewish immigrants found their German cousins as inscrutable as the Fifth Avenue Protestants the German Jews did business with. These refugees from pogroms now living in teeming proximity on New York's Lower East Side were not the beneficiaries of nineteenth-century European liberalism. Herded into the Pale of Settlement, they had developed their own institutions isolated from the rest of their country, and the world. Imprisoned in their ghettos—and thus strangely secure—the oppression they had experienced only made them more conscious of their lives as Jews. They were the ripest candidates in America for Herzl's Zionism.

Most American Jews had remained unimpressed. By the outbreak of World War I, the Zionist movement in the U.S. numbered no more than 20,000 of the nation's 2.5 milion Jews. The Zionists lacked leaders who were as influential on the local political scene as the hidalgos at the American Jewish Committee; worse, the AJC leaders were dedicated anti-Zionists.

And then in 1912, suddenly and mysteriously, a brilliant and famous Boston lawyer, Louis Dembitz Brandeis, decided to become a Zionist. The son of Jews from Prague, Brandeis was born in Louisville, Kentucky, where he grew up, by his own account, "free from Jewish contacts or traditions." Graduated at the head of his class at Harvard Law School, he had made enough money at the Boston bar by age thirty-four to turn his attention to "public interest" law. Brandeis's Jewish consciousness was raised, so the story goes, by two events in his life: helping settle a strike in New York in 1910 in the garment district, which was dominated by Eastern European Jewish immigrants, and a conversation in 1912 with Jacob de Haas, an editor of a Boston Jewish paper and a former aide to Herzl.[5]

Whatever the occasion of the great man's surprising conversion, it was a PR man's dream. Zionism had acquired one of the most distinguished Jews in America—indeed, one of the most distinguished men in all of American life and a friend of the next President of the U.S. Woodrow Wilson. Brandeis agreed to become head of the infant

American Zionist movement, and from 1914 to 1918, he devoted a great deal of his time, energy, and money spreading the Zionist word throughout America. When Brandeis, in his fifties and living proof of how successful a Jew could be in America, embraced Zionism, he pushed that distinctly made-in-Europe and bred-in-the-Russian-Pale ideology onto the American political stage, and painted it with a distinctly American face. But the leaders of the American Jewish Committee remained unconvinced. They even persuaded Wilson not to give Brandeis a Cabinet post because he was not a representative American Jew.

Brandeis, however, toured America's Jewish communities arguing that joining the movement would not put one's loyalties in question; to the contrary, it was the only patriotic thing an American Jew could do. As he declared in a famous speech in 1915 to a conference of Reform rabbis:

> Let no American imagine that Zionism is inconsistent with Patriotism. Multiple loyalties are objectionable only if they are inconsistent. . . . Every American who aids in advancing the Jewish settlement in Palestine, though he feels that neither he nor his descendants will ever live there, will likewise be a better man and a better American for doing so. . . . There is no inconsistency between loyalty to America and loyalty to Jewry. The Jewish spirit, the product of our religion and experiences, is essentially modern and essentially American. . . . America's fundamental laws seek to make real the brotherhood of man. That brotherhood became the Jewish fundamental law more than twenty-five hundred years ago. America's insistent demand in the twentieth century is for social justice. That also has been the Jews striving for ages. Their affliction, as well as their religion, has prepared the Jews for effective democracy. . . . Indeed loyalty to America demands rather that each American Jew become a Zionist. . . .[6]

With Brandeis leading its newly formed Zionist Organization of America, Herzl's movement suddenly had a friend in the White House. As it turned out, Wilson, who would appoint Brandeis to the Supreme Court in 1916, was bound to be sympathetic to his friend's newfound passion; Zionism seemed to fit Wilson's own theory about the right of every people in the world for self-determination.

There were also pragmatic political reasons. The American Federation of Labor was endorsing the principle of a Jewish homeland, in spite of opposition from several Jewish trade unions who disliked both Wilson and Zionism. Theodore Roosevelt too saw votes in

backing the Jewish cause. But the appeal of Zionism to Woodrow
Wilson was more than a matter of politics or political theory. The son
of a Presbyterian minister and a daily reader of the Bible, the President was emotionally drawn to the plight of the Jews. As Peter Grose
points out in *Israel in the Mind of America*, there was a deep tradition
of sympathy for the dream of Zion in American Protestantism. Grose
cites Wilson as once saying, "To think that I, the son of the manse,
should be able to help restore the Holy Land to its people."[7]

IT was, however, another "Christian Zionist" who gave the Jews a
real hope of returning to Palestine. Arthur Balfour, Britain's secretary
of state for foreign affairs, was a devout Christian and also a student
of Roman and Jewish history who considered the Roman destruction
of Judea "one of the great wrongs of history" and was eager to right
that wrong. Balfour won his honored place in the history of the Jews
with a brief paragraph in a letter to Lord Rothschild in 1917 declaring
that "His Majesty's Government view with favor the establishment in
Palestine of a national home for the Jewish people" in that part of
Palestine that the British had recently captured from the Turks, Germany's ally during World War I.[8] Yet Balfour too had his political
reasons for supporting the Zionists. Britain was desperate for help
from the U.S. and Russia against the Germans. Balfour persuaded his
fellow Cabinet members that support for a Jewish homeland would
be "extremely useful propaganda" among American and Russian
Jews.[9]

The Balfour Declaration was Zionism's first major triumph in the
twentieth century, and to the beleaguered Jews of Russia, only twenty
years after Herzl had announced his program at the First Zionist Congress, that vague phrase "a national home for the Jewish people"
must have seemed like a miracle. But the real miracle of Zionism
would be to keep its warring factions from destroying the movement
from the inside.

The excitement of the Balfour Declaration had barely worn off
before a split erupted between Brandeis and Chaim Weizmann, the
Russian Zionist and Anglophile who had become Herzl's most brilliant heir as head of the World Zionist Organization. An "irresistible
political seducer," in the phrase of his friend Isaiah Berlin, the eminent Oxford philosopher and Zionist,[10] Weizmann, who had earned
enough as a chemist in Britain to devote himself tirelessly to the

movement, was responsible for winning over Britain's leading politicians to the Zionist cause. He had first met Balfour in 1906, and the two men became friends.

But Weizmann was no friend of Louis Brandeis. The American leader may have given Zionism a new respectability among his countrymen, but he did not win the respect of his fellow Zionists in Europe. The Zionist Dream could always be fashioned in the political image of the dreamer: Herzl had seen the Jewish state as a perfect version of *fin de siècle* Vienna; Weizmann saw it as a Jewish version of the British parliamentary system; and Brandeis seemed to see Zion as a utopian New England town set down in the Middle East. His critics charged that the American Zionist was extracting the ideology from Zionism; Weizmann and others called Brandeis's views "Zionism without Zion."[11] And with some justification. Brandeis, always the pragmatic American jurist, viewed the long speeches and ideological hairsplitting of Zionist congresses as a waste of time. There is no evidence that America's foremost Zionist had ever considered living in Palestine.

When Weizmann arrived in the United States in 1921 to help promote the founding of the Hebrew University in Jerusalem, he was quite blunt about Zionism Brandeis-style: "I do not agree with the philosophy of your Zionism," Weizmann informed the Americans. "We are different, absolutely different. There is no bridge between Washington and Pinsk."[12] The Downtown Jews seemed to agree, and two months later the American Zionists voted Justice Brandeis out of office. Scores of the brightest Jews in America, who had been attracted to Zionism by Brandeis, left the movement with their leader, including the future Supreme Court justice Felix Frankfurter, Stephen Wise, a talented Reform rabbi and social activist, and Abba Hillel Silver, another Reform rabbi who took refuge in a wealthy Cleveland synagogue. The anti-Zionists at the American Jewish Committee could not have written a better script for blunting the political influence of the Zionist movement in the United States.

That left only one rival to Weizmann's dominance of World Zionism, Vladimir Ze'ev Jabotinsky, an adamant hardliner for whom the straightest line to the Zionist Dream was mass immigration of European Jews to Palestine, which would present the British—and the Arabs—with a Jewish majority and thus the *fait accompli* of a Jewish state. To confront the Arab hostility that would inevitably result, Jabotinsky proposed an "iron wall" of Jewish military might around

Palestine. While Weizmann believed that the British and the Arabs would eventually support the Zionist state, Jabotinsky saw a battle shaping up. His version of Zionism contained no illusions that the Arabs would be won over by European technical expertise and culture. The Arabs were bound to resent the presence of the Jews, and thus would have to be treated without pity. Their claim to Palestine —and Jabotinsky did not dispute that claim—would have to take second place to that of the Jews. Besides, Jabotinsky argued, the Arabs of Palestine had other Arab countries nearby to move to. The Jews had none.[13]

When Jabotinsky opposed, in 1922, a British plan for a legislative assembly in Palestine that would include Arabs, he was forced to resign from the Zionist Executive. Three years later he tried to topple Weizmann from the leadership of the World Zionist Organization, and failed. He then quit the official Zionist movement and in 1935 founded his New Zionist Organization, also known as Revisionist Zionism. Jabotinsky claimed to be liberating Zionism from the "minimalism" and socialism of the current leadership and returning it to "the all absorbing mission of creating a state."[14] The only thing that was missing from his plan was Jews; from 1920 to 1929, the net immigration of Jews into British Palestine was 77,063. According to an official census two years later, there were 175,000 Jews in Palestine—17 percent of the population. A Jewish majority seemed unlikely. But the facts did not stop Jabotinsky and his disciples.

JABOTINSKY is the most controversial figure in the history of Zionism. "Jabo," as his Zionist colleagues called him, had been a European correspondent for a series of Russian dailies, but his great talent, his genius, was as a propagandist for Zionism, first the classic Herzlian line and then his own hardline. The NZO's main aims were "the redemption of Israel and its land, the revival of its sovereignty and language,"[15] "a Jewish state on both sides of Jordan," and "social justice without a class struggle."[16] Jabotinsky's opponents attacked him as a "reactionary" and a "bourgeois." Chief among his enemies was the ardent socialist David Ben-Gurion. Having emigrated from Russia to Palestine in 1906, Ben-Gurion helped found a Zionist labor movement in Palestine and created the economically and politically powerful Labor Party (Mapai). While Weizmann ran the World Zionist Organization, Ben-Gurion sat on its executive and headed the Jewish Agency, which was responsible for building the Jewish national home in Palestine with funds from World Jewry. Such power made Ben-Gurion Zionism's undisputed leader in Palestine and the closest thing to "the Establishment" in the yet unestablished Jewish state. Jabotinsky's attacks on socialism and the labor movement (and Ben-Gurion) provoked rioting in the streets.

Revisionist hostility toward the Arabs switched from words to action in 1936 when Jabotinsky's heavily armed disciples abandoned the official Zionist policy of "self-restraint" from retaliating against the civilian population. The Revisionists feared that the riots and bloodshed initiated by Arabs who resented the threatened Jewish dominance would scare off Jewish immigrants to Palestine. To end the conflict, the Irgun Zvai Leumi (the National Military Organization), the non-Socialist faction of the Haganah comprised of Jabotinsky loyalists, launched retaliatory attacks on Arab civilians. Instead of squashing Arab resistance, Jewish terrorism increased Arab violence against Jews.

In his historical analysis of Zionist attitudes toward the Arab-Jewish conflict in Palestine, the Israeli journalist Simha Flapan offers an unsettling comment on this turn of events:

It can be said that the Irgun established the pattern of terrorism adopted 30 years later by Al-Fatah [the Palestinian terrorist group headed by Yasser Arafat]. Among its actions were the wheeling of a vegetable barrow containing a bomb into an Arab market in Jerusalem, firing at a bus and throwing bombs into market places [Jerusalem, Haifa].[17]

Jabotinsky, the Irgun's nominal commander in chief as well as its ideological force, was not comfortable with the murder of Arab women and children; he implored the Irgun commanders to give fair warning so that the Arabs could evacuate the areas under attack. The leaders contended that such warnings could not be given without endangering the lives of the attackers, and thus the success of the terrorist operations.[18] Such intransigence was creating a dangerous fissure in Zionism. Ben-Gurion demanded that the Revisionists accept Zionist discipline, and set about arresting its members.

• • •

THE American Zionists were far from the shooting in Palestine, but
they too were caught up in internal wars and intrigue. Rabbi Stephen
Wise had taken over the leadership of the American branch in 1935.
The nation's best-known rabbi and a friend of President Franklin
Roosevelt, Wise soon gave the ZOA the visibility it had lost when
Brandeis departed. But he also had to confront the nagging question
of how hard American Zionists should be pushing for a state in Palestine when Hitler was now threatening the survival of Europe's Jews.
Fund raisers around the country were withholding donations to the
Zionists, lest the money be spent entirely on "Zionist politics" and
not on the refugee problem. The Zionists were anti-Nazi, but they
were also anti-Britain, and in England Arab nationalism was winning
support and checking the growth of the Jewish community in British
Palestine. Worse still, there was news that the German Zionists were
dealing with the Nazis in an effort to get as many Jews out of Germany as possible, along with their money, which was needed in Palestine.

Wise believed that his close ties to the Roosevelt Administration
would help in the fight to rescue and resettle Jews; he was also willing to sidestep Arab—and thus British—resistance to more Jews
arriving in Palestine by settling for another British colony, Kenya
perhaps, or Uganda. Herzl had raised the same idea and was attacked
by Zionist purists, who believed that a Jewish state outside the Biblical Land of Israel could not be the result of genuine Zionism.

Wise too was attacked. His main opponent was his old colleague
under Brandeis, Rabbi Abba Hillel Silver, who re-emerged in the
movement in 1940 to argue that a Jewish state in Palestine was still
Zionism's primary goal, regardless of what was happening in Europe.
He vowed to fight British restrictions on Jewish immigration into
Palestine, and ended an impassioned speech at a fund raiser for those
efforts in January 1941 with the words of the Irish rebel Daniel
O'Connell: "Agitate! Agitate! Agitate!" and topped them off with the
cry of the French revolutionary Danton: *"L'audace, encore l'audace,
toujours l'audace."*[19]

The following year, at an American Zionist convention at New
York's Biltmore Hotel, Silver's "maximalists" carried the meeting as
the American Zionists decided to abandon their gradualist policy of
seeking first a Jewish community in Palestine under a U.S. or British
protectorate and to press for a sovereign Jewish state. Concerned that
such an aggressive stand might jeopardize the whole movement,

Wise and Weizmann preferred a step-by-step approach, first a protectorate and then perhaps a state. They lost. The Zionist movement had taken on a new militancy. And Silver, its self-proclaimed O'Connell and Danton, vowed "to convert a club of well-intentioned but politically passive Zionist personalities into the nerve center of a revolutionary program with a mass following."

But there were efforts to gain the support of the non-Zionists. Before the Biltmore, Ben-Gurion had failed in an attempt to gain the support of the American Jewish Committee, still the most prestigious Jewish organization in the U.S. The Zionists quickly switched to romancing the B'nai B'rith, a Jewish fraternal organization founded in 1843 by German-American Jews, but by World War II its membership of 150,000 was comprised of Eastern European Jews. Throughout the 1920s and 1930s pro-Zionist sentiment had grown in the organization, though B'nai B'rith leaders intentionally stayed clear of battles between the Zionists and American anti-Zionists. But the organization's president during World War II, Henry Monsky, was eager to maintain a sense of unity among American Jews, and during 1942 met with Weizmann, Wise, and Nahum Goldmann, a German Jewish intellectual who had set up the World Jewish Congress in Geneva in 1936 at Wise's request. Goldmann and Wise overcame the reservations of their colleagues and worked out a plan for a major conference of American Jews that would support the Zionist enterprise and thus isolate the anti-Zionist American Jewish Committee.

In January 1943, delegates from thirty-two national Jewish organizations met in Pittsburgh to decide upon the role that the American Jewish community would play in representing Jewish demands after the war and helping to build Jewish Palestine. The result was the creation of an American Jewish Conference of sixty-four Jewish groups, including a skeptical American Jewish Committee, representing 1.5 million American Jews—the most representative gathering of American Jews ever. The first meeting took place in August with moderate Zionists eager to play down the maximalist goal of a "Jewish commonwealth" and concentrate on supporting Zionism through philanthropy. Silver erupted in an attack on Wise, and called for the delegates to endorse Biltmore. Upset, the delegates from the American Jewish Committee walked out. But the conference sided with Silver and he emerged from the meeting as the new leader of American Zionism. Silver called for "loud diplomacy."[20]

The American Jewish community now had a full-fledged "Jewish lobby." In 1943, Silver cranked up the Zionist Organization of America's one-man lobbying operation in Washington—renaming it the American Zionist Emergency Council (AZEC)—and began to mobilize American Jewry into a mass movement. Silver ordered local committees to be set up in every Jewish community in the nation. Instructions went out from Washington: "The first task will be to make direct contact with your local Congressman or Senator. . . ."[21] Local activists received tips for letter-writing and telegram campaigns; form letters went out that required only a signature before they were then mailed to the President and influential members of Congress. AZEC established ties in the Protestant community. Rallies and demonstrations on behalf of a Jewish state were organized. In 1944, labor unions, church groups, granges, Rotary clubs—three thousand organizations in all, none of them Jewish—passed pro-Zionist resolutions and sent telegrams to Congress. When AZEC received news of a British tactic that was bound to hurt the Zionist cause in the fall of 1945, the lobby booked Madison Square Garden, ordered up advertisements, and mailed 250,000 notices—the first day. There were demonstrations in thirty cities, a letter-writing campaign, and twenty-seven senators gave speeches about Palestine over a two-day period.[22]

Such attention from his Jewish constituents did not please the new President, Harry S. Truman. Roosevelt in his meetings with Zionist leaders had humored them, and then, in private, agreed with his foreign-policy and defense advisers that a Jewish state in the region would be disastrous for Western interests. Truman too was surrounded by naysayers—the "striped pants fellers" he called them—but the good news for the Zionists was that the President was deeply concerned about the problem of Displaced Persons. He was not, however, enthusiastic about all the mail he was receiving at the urging of Silver's Zionist lobby. "I don't believe there is any way we can satisfy our Jewish friends," he once told a Democratic leader. He told another friend that he had received "35,000 pieces of mail and propaganda" on the issue of Palestine, "piled it up and put a match to it."[23]

But the mail kept coming, and Silver kept gaining power. At the World Zionist Congress in 1946, the Cleveland rabbi, with the help of David Ben-Gurion, staged a *coup d'état*. As the remnant of Europe's Jews sat confused and skeletal in DP camps and American Jews suffered from the guilt of perhaps not having done enough to have saved them, Weizmann's pleas against moving too fast toward statehood, that it threatened everything he and Herzl had achieved, seemed irrelevant. The membership retired Chaim Weizmann from leadership of the World Zionist Organization. Silver himself would now officially replace Stephen Wise as the leader of the American branch. "Jewish muscle" had won out.

But there was one problem: Harry Truman could not stand Abba Hillel Silver. The rabbi supported the President's Republican opponents; he had humiliated the two Zionist leaders Truman respected; and on a summer day in 1946 the *audace* of the head of American Zionism stirred him to pound on the President's desk.[24] Truman never received Silver at the White House again.

"TERROR and Silver are the contributing cause of some, if not all, of our troubles," the President complained, still genuinely concerned about the fate of those 500,000 Jews languishing in DP camps in Europe in conditions little better than Hitler's death camps. While Silver's troops were armed with postcards and the White House address, in Palestine, the Zionists were still shooting. During the summer of 1946, Ben-Gurion ordered the official Jewish underground army, the Haganah, to desist in attacking the British and turn its ingenuity to the DP problem. But not all members of the underground obeyed. The most ungovernable and vicious faction, Fighters for the Freedom of Israel—known as Lechi for its Hebrew initials and as the Stern Gang for its founder, Avraham Stern, an admirer of Mussolini—carried out one hundred acts of sabotage and murder against the British over the next two years.[25]

Jabotinsky's ideological heirs, the Irgun, by then an independent band of two thousand armed ideologues who had broken away from Ben-Gurion's Haganah, increased its own terrorist attacks. Their leader was a thin, bespectacled Polish lawyer in his mid-thirties devoted to Jabotinsky's belief that only armed force would insure the Jewish state against Arab hatred—Menachem Begin. On July 22, 1946, a band of armed Irgun members entered the King David Hotel in Jerusalem where the British government occupied an entire wing with offices. They planted milk cans filled with explosives, set the time fuses, and departed. The explosion left ninety-one dead, British, Arabs, and Jews. The British ordered punitive measures against the entire Jewish community, and Ben-Gurion, furious, urged Jews to turn in members of the Irgun. The Jewish terrorism was hurting Zion-

ism's cause in world opinion. Begin continued his attacks against the
British.

Jewish terror, however, seemed to be working, as was Ben-
Gurion's less violent alternative of sneaking boatloads of Jews into
Palestine. By the fall of 1946, the British were clearly exhausted by
the violence and their efforts to block the illegal immigration, and
wanted out. In February 1947, Foreign Secretary Ernest Bevin informed the House of Commons that the government was unable to
find a workable solution between the Arabs and the Jews for governing Palestine; the matter was being turned over to the United Nations.

The following November, a 33 to 13 majority in the U.N. General
Assembly voted for a plan to partition Palestine into two states, Jewish and Arab. The Jewish Agency immediately accepted the plan; so
did the American Zionists, though Silver had been reluctant. Begin
denounced the partition plan, still unwilling to share Palestine with
the Arabs. The Arabs too were unwilling to share what they perceived as their own land, and rejected the plan outright. The anti-
Zionists in the State and Defense departments were not much happier
about the U.N. solution, recognizing that a Jewish presence in the
area would hardly be the end of Arab-Zionist conflict but only a new
beginning. While Jews around the world rejoiced at the prospect of
an official Jewish presence in Palestine, others had their doubts. Dr.
Judah Magnes, president of the Hebrew University in Jerusalem and
a vigorous supporter of a binational state of Arabs and Jews in Palestine, summed up their fears when he told *The New York Times* after
the vote, "It looks like trouble to me."[26]

The morning after the vote, Palestinian Arabs called a three-day
strike and Jews were the victims of attacks throughout the country.
The prospect of more violence jeopardized American support of partition. But the juggernaut was now rolling, and the probability was
high that regardless of Arab, U.N., or U.S. support there would be a
Jewish state. One question, however, remained: Could it last without
the recognition of Harry Truman?

The Zionists, in spite of Silver and terror, still had several things
going for them in Washington: the President's empathy for the DPs,
his affection for aged Chaim Weizmann, and Nahum Goldmann and
David K. Niles. Goldmann had been actively working behind the
scenes for Ben-Gurion to counter Silver's mischief in Washington.
Niles, a former aide to Roosevelt, was the Zionists' secret weapon in
the White House. Truman gave no speech or authorized any docu-

ment on the issue of Palestine or the DPs without Niles's counsel.[27]

With Niles keeping the anti-Zionist "striped pants fellers" from the State Department at bay and isolating the President from Silver's lobbying crusade, Goldmann went to work on Truman's anti-Zionist friends at the American Jewish Committee and his closest advisers, including Secretary of State Dean Acheson. His argument was simple: If the U.S. refused partition in favor of a U.N. trusteeship and neither the U.S. nor any other country would receive the refugees, the terrorism would continue and Begin would take power. Goldmann later recalled his words to Acheson: "When Jewish terrorists are killing the British will you take a stand against the British? And when the British are killing Jews, where will you be?" Acheson threw his support to the Zionists. And after a similar discussion so did Joseph Proskauer, the head of the American Jewish Committee and a lifelong anti-Zionist.[28]

But the clincher came when Jewish friends of Truman arranged a meeting between the President and Weizmann in March 1948. The old man made his case for partition, and finally won the President's commitment. Over the next month, however, the plan faltered, as the threat of war in the Middle East increased. Arab and Jewish reprisals grew savage and indiscriminate. On April 9, a combined force of the Stern Gang and Begin's Irgun killed more than two hundred Arab men, women, and children in the village of Deir Yassin, outside Jerusalem. A few days later Arabs ambushed a medical convoy on its way to Hadassah Hospital, killing seventy-nine doctors, nurses, and students. The Americans threatened to block U.S. philanthropic funds to Palestine and proposed an Arab-Jewish truce, which the Jewish Cabinet rejected.

The Jewish leaders in Palestine had decided to wait on the rest of the world no longer. In early May, Weizmann sent a letter to the White House asking the U.S. to recognize Israel when it came into existence. Truman favored recognition, though his secretary of defense, George Marshall, and undersecretary of state, Robert Lovett, did not. Truman had not forgotten his promise to Weizmann; it was also an election year, and his opponent Thomas Dewey, the popular New York governor, had already announced that he favored recognition.

On Friday, May 14, 1948, Ben-Gurion stood in the Tel Aviv Museum and declared the independence of "the Jewish state in Palestine to be called Israel." Within minutes of that declaration, Harry Tru-

man announced recognition of the infant Jewish state. Almost a half
century of lobbying by the Zionists had paid off. Against all odds
from start to finish, what had always seemed a crazy dream of a
small group of nineteenth-century romantics had become a reality. It
was an extraordinary accomplishment.

1

THE PRO-ISRAEL LOBBY
COMES TO WASHINGTON

A few months after Ben-Gurion had announced the creation of the State of Israel, an official of the United Jewish Appeal, the umbrella organization of America's Jewish philanthropies, asked the new prime minister what Israel required of the American Jewish community. Ben-Gurion answered quickly and bluntly: "What we need is Jews."[1]

Israel got very few American Jews. During its first three years, the state would absorb 650,000 immigrants, mainly European DPs and impoverished refugees from anti-Jewish movements in Yemen and Iraq. The creation of the state had moved American Jews very deeply, but not to Israel. One study reported that of the 35,000 Americans and Canadians who had immigrated to Israel during the state's first decade only 5,400 Americans stuck it out.[2] That most American Jews preferred to remain Americans would be a source of tension and animosity between their leaders and Israel's; it would also, ironically, prove a major source of each's power. The new state, as even Ben-Gurion had conceded, would need U.S. government support to survive, and by working tirelessly to assure that help, the American Jewish community would turn itself into an impressive American political phenomenon. In the process, however, Jewish leaders would fail to resolve the most important question facing them now that the question of the state was settled: What was the proper relation of Jews living outside Israel to the new state?

Traditional Zionist thinkers had never envisioned a Jewish state as the movement's only end; on the contrary, it was to be a beginning

for a renaissance of the Jewish people—a refuge for the victims of
anti-Semitism, to be sure, but also proof that Judaism had a future.
As the center of a new kind of Jewish life, Israel would provide a
focus, indeed an inspiration, for those Jews who preferred to live in
the Diaspora. As a sovereign state, Israel would assume many of the
political responsibilities that Diaspora leaders had performed—
speaking for the Jews to governments and at the United Nations, for
example—but Zionist leaders in the Diaspora assumed they would
remain partners in the movement.

It was a reasonable assumption, particularly on the part of the
Americans. The virulent anti-Semitism between the wars, Hitler's
murderous assault on the Jews, and the fight for a Jewish state during
the 1940s had brought hundreds of thousands of Jews into the movement. In 1948, American Zionists of various stripes numbered almost
one million, a fifth of the nation's Jewish population.[3] The Zionist
Organization of America was the largest and most influential Zionist
group in the world. Ben-Gurion, however, did not want partners; he
wanted to establish the primacy of Israel in Jewish history and he
needed Jews to do it. And, above all, that meant *aliyah*—Jews making "The Return" to the Land of Israel. Surrounded by political opponents and would-be prime ministers at home, Ben-Gurion viewed the
American movement as just one more source of political competition
and meddling.

He already had to defend himself against those religious Jews who
viewed Israel as a blasphemous aberration from the traditional view
that a new Zion would follow the arrival of the Messiah. In 1949, the
first organized protest of Jews against the Jewish state took place in
New York where Orthodox Jews demonstrated in the streets against
the Israeli government's denial of religious education to children in
immigrant camps. Another irritant was the anti-Zionist Jewish groups
like the American Council for Judaism, founded during the war to
denigrate Zionism as a political ideology that was only bound to
create problems for the Jews rather than solve them.

And there was the politically influential American Jewish Committee, which had accepted the state as a reality, but skeptically. The
committee's magazine, *Commentary*, was featuring cold-eyed analy-
ses of Israel's social, political, and economic policies. "What price
Israel's Normalcy?" the magazine asked in 1949, lamenting the decline of traditional Jewish culture in the new Jewish state where

young Israelis regarded themselves as "an elite—the advance guard of a people they consider to be very sick."[4] The magazine's Middle East correspondent wondered how the Israelis, with their meager economy, could be fair to the Arabs who remained in the Jewish state.[5] "Not many Israelis torment themselves with the moral and political implication of injustice to the Arabs," the correspondent wrote.

Rather than debate the American Zionists or suffer their interference, Ben-Gurion worked hard to destroy their organization. Abba Hillel Silver's authoritarian style had already created enough enemies to make the prime minister's job an easy one. Ben-Gurion encouraged a group of anti-Silverites to capture control of the ZOA's United Palestine Appeal, Israel's chief fund raiser in the U.S. (later absorbed into the United Jewish Appeal), and reconstitute it into an independent group. The UPA would now depend on non-Zionist fund raisers around the country who were more eager to raise money for Israel than challenge its leadership. Almost three decades before, Chaim Weizmann had squeezed Brandeis out of power—"There is no bridge between Washington and Pinsk"—and three years before Ben-Gurion and Silver had toppled Weizmann from head of the World Zionist movement. Now Silver's day had passed. The fiery rabbi returned to his Cleveland synagogue, and the American Zionist movement went into decline. With Ben-Gurion's blessing, the more cooperative non-Zionist moneymen reclaimed the leadership of the American Jewish community.

It was bound to happen. Israel needed three things from American Jews: their money, their political influence, and their presence in Israel. Like most of his fellow Zionists in Israel, Ben-Gurion believed that a good Jew was a Zionist and that a good Zionist moved to Israel. But the generosity of the American leaders was limited to money and politics. The prime minister pressed the issue in 1949, calling on all young American Jews to make *aliyah*. As one of his Cabinet ministers, an American Jew from Milwaukee named Golda Meir, put it, "a true, free Jewish life" was impossible outside of Israel.[6] The Americans begged to disagree.

IN August 1950, Jacob Blaustein, the wealthy oilman who was head of the American Jewish Committee, traveled to Israel to set the Israeli leaders straight about the American role in the future of Israel.

Israel's rebirth and progress, coming after the tragedy of European Jewry in the 1930s and in World War II, has done much to raise Jewish morale. Jews in America and everywhere can be more proud than ever of their Jewishness.

But we must, in a true spirit of friendliness, sound a note of caution to Israel and its leaders. Now that the birth pains are over, and even though Israel is undergoing growing pains, it must recognize that the matter of good will between its citizens and those of other countries is a two-way street: that Israel also has a responsibility in this situation—a responsibility in terms of not affecting adversely the sensibilities of Jews who are citizens of other states by what it says or does.

In this connection, you are realists and want facts and I would be less than frank if I did not point out to you that American Jews vigorously repudiate any suggestion or implication that they are in exile. American Jews—young and old alike, Zionists and non-Zionists alike—are profoundly attached to America. . . .

To American Jews, America is home. There, exist their thriving roots. . . . They further believe that, if democracy should fall in America, there would be no future for democracy anywhere in the world, and that the very existence of an independent State of Israel would be problematic. Further, they feel that a world in which it would be possible for Jews to be driven by persecution from America would not be a world safe for Israel either. . . .[7]

It was a measure of the power of the American Jewish community that one of its leaders could speak to the prime minister of Israel in this way. Recognizing how important American money and support were to the Zionist enterprise, Ben-Gurion quickly apologized for the "confusion and misunderstanding,"[8] and allowed his old enemy the non-Zionist AJC to redefine Zionism for American Jews as philanthropy toward Israel. Their generosity was huge and genuine, though often too automatic. The Americans continued to send their checks even after Ben-Gurion turned over the authority in religious, educational, and social welfare matters to the Orthodox rabbis, who did not recognize the branches of Judaism—Reform and Conservative—to which most American Jews (and their leaders) adhered. A battle between rabbis would not undermine the Americans' attachment to the Jewish state.

Finally, the issue of *aliyah*—and the disenfranchisement of the Reform and Conservative branches of Judaism in Israel—only proved how different the goals of American Jews and their cousins in Israel were. As the Zionist leaders were beginning their great social experiment in "the Promised Land," the American sons and daughters of Jewish immigrants from Poland and Russia were making the trip, as one Jewish sociologist called it, "from shtetl to suburb."[9] Synagogues and "Jewish centers" were spreading throughout the nation's new suburbs, but they had become social rather than religious establishments. Like other immigrant groups, the Jews were eager to be assimilated into the American middle class. The Americans had thrilled to the reality of the Zionist Dream—and then turned their attention to the American Dream.

Yet there remained a persistent "ambivalence." As the sociologist Charles Liebman has pointed out in his book *The Ambivalent American Jew*, American Jews wanted to be American without losing their Jewish identity.[10] Israel was the perfect solution. By supporting the Jewish state, they could affirm their Jewishness—and then go about the business of "making it" in America. The issues of civil rights, housing, religious discrimination, and anti-Semitism led the agendas of Jewish groups in the 1950s. The annual and plenary reports of the National Community Relations Advisory Council, the umbrella organization for Jewish communal groups around the country and thus a good source for how its members are thinking in any given year, do not even mention the Arab-Israeli conflict during the first half of the decade.[11]

As American Jews became more American, the Jews in Israel became more Israeli, thus widening the intellectual gap between both communities.

In Israel, young Jews were caught up in what the Israeli politician Amnon Rubinstein in his recent book *The Zionist Dream Revisited: From Herzl to Gush Emunim and Back* calls "the Sabra Myth"—that they were a new breed of Jews living outside Jewish history. Their parents had been adventurous Zionists eager to leave the life of their "miserable step-brothers in the Diaspora" behind and go to live in the ancient Land of Israel. These European and Russian Jews now living in Palestine had looked on with pride and amazement as their own children grew into the brave Jewish warriors who fought for the creation of the State of Israel and won its independence. The young Israelis did not consider themselves Jews; they were "Sabras"—desert cacti tough and thorny on the outside but sweet and soft on the inside. A stock scene in Israeli fiction in the 1950s, according to Rubinstein, is the immigrant boy, a pale weakling befriended by

Sabras, who gradually loses his pallor to assume "manly Sabra qualities," and thus true virtue. Like many of the Zionist pioneers who had
settled Palestine, Israel's first prime minister had changed his family
name of Gruen to the Hebrew Ben-Gurion, son of the lion. It was an
act of rebirth, he later explained; his childhood "in exile" no longer
counted as part of his life. As prime minister, Ben-Gurion pressed the
political and military establishments of Israel into a mass conversion
of names—Golda Myerson became Meir, Shimon Persky became
Peres.[12] In the early 1950s a small but influential group of poets,
writers, and intellectuals known as the Canaanites was not even comfortable with the label "Israelis," and argued that the ancient religion
of the Jews had been a corruption of some pure, original Hebrew
spirit.[13]

Neither the fanaticism of the Canaanites nor the Zionist chauvin-
ism of Israel's leaders left much room for those Jews who seemed to
be content with their exile in suburban America. But the Americans
would remain an essential part of Israel's future, if only out of financial and political necessity.

THE infant State of Israel desperately needed U.S. economic aid.
During Israel's first three years, the population swelled to more than
a million and was expected to triple over the next six years.[14] The
generosity of American Jews was extraordinary, but inadequate. The
U.S. had given Israel a good price on such surplus commodities as
potatoes and butter, and had arranged for a $135 million loan from
the Import-Export Bank. But Israel needed more—U.S. aid and public encouragement. American Jewish leaders believed that the Arabs
would make peace if they knew the U.S. supported a strong Israel.

Truman, however, had not been able to overcome State Department opposition to appeals from Jewish leaders to divert as much
postwar foreign aid to Israel as possible. The Israelis needed a group
of friends on Capitol Hill to propose legislation that would counteract
what the Jews perceived as the State Department's tilt toward the
Arabs. With no time to lose, Israeli leaders began searching for an
American who could create an effective lobbying operation quickly.
The perfect candidate for the job, it turned out, was already working
for them—I. L. ("Sy") Kenen, an American journalist and Zionist
who had been working for Israel's ambassador to the United Nations,
Abba Eban, as a combination press secretary and PR man.[15] During

the war, Kenen had been information director for AZEC, Abba Hillel Silver's Jewish lobby, which, after the war and the creation of Israel, had been renamed the American Zionist Council. The AZC was a tax-exempt nonprofit organization.

Abba Eban asked Kenen if he was interested in lobbying Congress for more U.S. aid to Israel. "Should I continue my registration as an agent of the Israel [sic] government?" Kenen asked. "Was it appropriate for an embassy to Lobby?"[16] Eban, who would soon be ambassador to Washington as well as to the U.N., suggested he take a "leave of absence from the Israeli government" for six months to a year to head an "*ad hoc*" American lobbying operation and return to his U.N. post for the next General Assembly.

But Louis Lipsky, the well-known American Jewish leader who was then head of the AZC, was opposed to the impropriety—and danger—of an agent of a foreign government lobbying Congress. He wanted Kenen to be the executive director of his organization. As an American lobbyist for an American organization, Kenen would not have to register as a foreign agent and would be free to lobby Congress and criticize American policies. (Kenen writes that he later learned that Lipsky and Nahum Goldmann had discussed a list of candidates to head the *ad hoc* lobbying operation that did not include one Zionist. In fact, several non-Jews were discussed, among them Truman's former political adviser Clark Clifford and Milton Eisenhower, the future President's brother.[17])

In 1951, Kenen switched from his diplomatic post to the American Zionist Council to begin an intense lobbying effort for American aid to the troubled Israeli economy. Working closely with Manhattan's Jacob Javits and Brooklyn congressman Emanuel Celler in the House and Robert Taft, Paul Douglas, and Hubert Humphrey in the Senate, Kenen managed to secure $65 million in economic assistance for Israel in 1951 and another $73 million in 1952.[18]

His aim was to establish support of Israel as a bipartisan issue, and Kenen proved his skills as a lobbyist in the summer of 1952 when pro-Israel planks appeared in both the Republican and Democratic Party platforms. Both parties commended Israel's humanitarian mission of resettling Jewish refugees and the concern of the U.S. to help bring peace to the area. The similarity in language was no accident. Kenen had helped draft both planks. He showed his version of the Republican one to Javits and Taft, who was a candidate for President. According to Kenen, Taft "approved it." The Democratic version was passed along to the Truman White House, which presented it to the platform committee.

Traditionally, a party's platforms are no more likely to be transformed into policy than are campaign promises, and the victor in 1952, Dwight D. Eisenhower, was no exception to the rule. Confirmation came when his secretary of state, John Foster Dulles, declared that the new Administration's policy in the Middle East would be one of "friendly impartiality" with the Arabs and the Israelis. Jewish leaders were convinced Eisenhower and Dulles were hostile to Israel; worse, they had no leverage with this Administration. They certainly had no David Niles at court. The national hero in the White House owed nothing to any domestic or foreign-policy interest group. A career army man, he had never been in a position to benefit from Jewish support or bear the community's enmity in Congress.

But the main problem, for Eisenhower and the Jews, was oil. A State Department analysis at the end of the war had described Saudi Arabia as "a stupendous source of strategic power and one of the greatest material prizes in world history."[19] The reconstruction of Europe depended on Arab oil, as did the future of the U.S. economy. The Administration wanted to befriend the Arab states, and Jewish leaders assumed such a move would be at Israel's expense.

There was also a new threat in the region: the Soviet Union too recognized the importance of Arab oil, and was equally eager for friends in the Middle East. Originally, Israel had planned to remain nonaligned, in an effort to take advantage of the support of the U.S., with the largest Jewish population in the world, and the Soviet Union, which had voted for the U.N. partition plan, and had supplied arms to Israel via Czechoslovakia during the War for Independence. But up against the probability of Arab hatred financed and armed by the Soviets, Israel seemed to have no choice but to abandon its intentions to play both sides of the superpower game, and seek the help of the U.S. and its politically influential Jewish community.

The American Jewish leaders were eager to help. The Israelis, however, often made the Americans' job difficult, and sometimes embarrassing. Creating a state out of refugees living in tents and shacks in hostile territory is likely to focus a government's attention on its short-term interests. And Israel's security needs did not always correspond to American interests in the region, or to Eisenhower's perception of Israeli interests.

In 1953, the White House was examining the possibility of a program to develop the Jordan River plain to benefit the surrounding nations when the U.S. learned that Israel had already begun a crash plan to build a waterfall canal alongside the Jordan River in northern Galilee, near Lebanon. The Israelis claimed it was a small project intended only to generate hydroelectric power for irrigating nearby land. Upon inspection, an official of the United Nations, which was responsible for overseeing the armistice that the U.N. had worked out between Israel and its Arab neighbors in 1949, quickly realized that the Israelis were building a canal large enough to send water through Israel's central plain to the northern Negev desert. Moreover, the project site was technically not in Israeli territory but in a demilitarized zone near the Israeli-Syrian border. The Syrians, with troops entrenched nearby since the armistice, threatened to go to war. The U.N. chief of the area advised that construction be halted. The Israelis continued. Furious, the Eisenhower Administration established a dangerous precedent for the new state: Dulles secretly put a $26 million loan to Israel on hold until Israel agreed to cooperate with the U.N. Eisenhower also threatened to cancel the tax exemption on charitable donations to the United Jewish Appeal and other Jewish organizations raising money in the U.S. to help Israel in its massive resettlement program. The Israelis continued construction.

On October 13, 1953, in the midst of the battle over water, a bomb was thrown into the home of a Jewish family in a settlement a mile from the Jordanian border. The mother and two of her six children, a baby and a four-year-old, were killed. After the funeral, angry Israeli villagers rushed across the border into the village of Kibya, in Jordan, where they killed more than fifty Arab civilians. At least that was the official explanation of Kibya.[20]

News of the raid created an international uproar. Members of Congress protested the incident, along with Israel's defiance of the U.N. request to halt work on the hydroelectric project. The State Department issued a statement calling Kibya "shocking," and formally announced that the U.S. had already suspended aid to Israel. When a group of American Jewish leaders, led by New York congressman Jacob Javits, protested that the Administration was ignoring the threats to Israel, which was only retaliating against Arab raids, Dulles replied with what has become a familiar refrain of Middle East diplomacy—that the U.S. would never be able to move the Arabs to the peace table as long as they continued to believe the U.S. was solidly and exclusively pro-Israel.

Nine months later, Israel irked the Arabs and the State Department again by transferring its Foreign Ministry from Tel Aviv to West Jerusalem, Israel's capital. Israel invited the U.S. to move its embassy there from Tel Aviv. Contending that "this would be inconsistent with the international nature of Jerusalem,"* the U.S. refused.[21]

In December 1953, in the midst of all this bad publicity, Ben-Gurion mysteriously—some said it was a "nervous breakdown," others a political ploy—retired from office and took refuge in a kibbutz in the northern Negev desert. His approved successor was Moshe Sharett, an old colleague from the Jewish Agency and Israel's first foreign minister. Sharett had the reputation of being a moderate on Arab issues. But his top advisers, notably Chief of Staff Moshe Dayan, were Ben-Gurion loyalists who would go off to the desert to confer with the aging lion.

SUCH was the state of Israel's politics and its relations with its most important benefactor, the United States. "It was a stormy year," recalled Sy Kenen three decades later in his memoirs, "and, as a result of the sharp conflict between the State Department and the Jewish community, we concluded that we must create a new organization to carry on our lobbying activity."[22]

And fast. Rumors had been circulating in Washington that the AZC was about to be investigated as retribution for its battles with the Administration over arms to the Arabs and Israel's water problems. An Israeli journalist tipped off Kenen that the State Department, as Kenen later put it, "was busily comparing my critical 1953 memoranda with those circulated by the Israeli embassy."[23]

Kenen insists he was not "parrotting Israel's views," claiming to have disagreed with the Israelis about arms. (Kenen says he was against sending U.S. arms to either the Arabs or the Israelis.) But he is protesting too much. Kenen had a job to do; if he had disagreed

---

*Jerusalem is a sacred site of the Christians, Moslems, and Jews, and the abortive 1947 partition plan envisioned an "international Jerusalem" under a trusteeship of the United Nations with free access to the city's holy places. At the time of the 1949 truce, Israel occupied most of the new section, west of the city's legendary walls, and Transjordan the Old City. On January 1, 1950, Israel moved its parliament and government ministries to Jerusalem (except for defense, foreign affairs, and police). That same day Transjordan annexed the West Bank, including the Old City; four months later King Abdullah renamed his kingdom Jordan. Current U.S. policy is that the status of Jerusalem is a matter for negotiations between the Arabs and the Israelis.

with the Israelis on too many issues, he would have been looking for a new job. Kenen was, after all, a lobbyist for a Zionist organization whose aim was to increase American economic support to Israel. The State Department thought he should register as a "foreign agent"; Kenen insisted he was an American domestic lobbyist working for an American organization, which he was. But he was also an American who had worked for the Israeli diplomatic service and was now lobbying on behalf of a foreign government. To avoid charges of impropriety—a tax-exempt organization cannot legally lobby on behalf of a foreign government—it was decided that Kenen should detach his operation from the AZC, and raise the money to finance it.

Nineteen fifty-four became the year of the pro-Israel lobby. The American Zionist Council of Public Affairs* (AZCPA) was formed with an annual budget of $50,000. In 1954, Israel needed all the lobbying help it could get to counter the growing annoyance toward the new state in the Eisenhower Administration. The opposition was bound to increase. One of the reasons the Middle East experts at State were eager to brand Kenen a "foreign agent" was that with his band of friends and influential contacts in Congress he was bound to continue to be a successful lobbyist. With Congress supporting Israel uncritically, the State Department knew that it would only get tougher to rein in the Israelis. Jewish leaders, however, believed that the Administration was leaning unnecessarily hard on Israel. But then the leaders of the American Jewish community did not always know everything that the State Department knew. Kibya was a perfect example.

American Jews had treated the attack as a "reprisal," excessive, but understandable considering the Arab threats to the well-being of Jewish settlers along the Jordanian border. In his 1981 memoir, Kenen still portrays the attack as a justifiable response of Israeli civilians to a brutal murder, which remains the Israeli government's official explanation for the Kibya raid. That Ben-Gurion got away with such an explanation, however, surprised even members of his own Cabinet, who were aware that a U.N. group visiting the scene had quickly discovered what the Israeli ministers had known from the start: Kibya was a massive *military* operation by the Israeli Army in a

---

*In 1959, Kenen's lobbying operation would be renamed the American Israel Public Affairs Committee, thus coming to terms with the reality of the largely non-Zionist nature of Jewish politics in the United States (and depriving the "Zionist conspiracy" theorists among the nation's anti-Semites of an easy victim).

demilitarized zone and thus a clear violation of the 1949 U.N. armistice between Israel and its Arab enemies.[24]

More than 250 soldiers had invaded the village firing heavy mortars and automatic weapons. The Israelis dynamited forty-one homes and one school; fifty-three civilians died. According to a report prepared by the U.N.'s armistice commission, the fighting lasted seven hours. It was also more than an isolated act of revenge. Memoirs and U.S. intelligence reports since declassified portray the raid as one of the earliest successes of a new commando unit specializing in nighttime fighting and demolition. At the time of the raid Moshe Dayan was acting chief of staff. The unit's commander was a brash, aggressive major named Ariel Sharon.

Some ministers had opposed the Kibya raid largely because they were worried that such an attack would only antagonize the Americans, who, as they knew, had already suspended U.S. aid when Israel had refused to stop the Jordan water project. They were, of course, right. Yet American Jewish leaders did not seem to know—or want to know—the full story of Kibya, or very much else that was going on in the Israeli government. Such ignorance would open them up to embarrassment time and again. But Jewish leaders continued to believe that Eisenhower and Dulles were the main problem, and decided that their groups would have to lobby the White House as effectively as Kenen was working the Congress. It was time for another pro-Israel pressure group.

LEGEND has it that Dulles himself was the prime mover of the second lobby. In fact, according to Nahum Goldmann, then the head of the World Jewish Congress, it was Henry Byroade, Dulles's assistant secretary of state, who suggested to the Zionist leader during the flaps over the Jordan River project and Kibya that it would be helpful if American Jewry could address the State Department with one voice. Byroade showed Goldmann his calendar with five different Jewish groups scheduled for appointments with him that week.[25]

Goldmann was receptive to the idea for two reasons: (1) Israel needed at least the appearance of Jewish solidarity on all fronts; and (2) Nahum Goldmann needed an American power base. Dulles certainly recognized that all these groups, Zionist, non-Zionist, right, left, and moderate, could agree on little. That every Jewish leader was eager for access to the secretary of state was axiomatic—indeed his prestige depended upon it—and Dulles was adept at exploiting splits among the Jewish leadership. Blaustein's public battle with Ben-Gurion as well as the American Jewish Committee's dogmatic non-Zionist stance were symptomatic of how easily American Jewry could turn critical of Israel, and thus undermine its case on Capitol Hill. An experienced international diplomat, Goldmann was well aware of the political advantages of forcing his fellow Jewish leaders to hold their tongues on every issue until they could come to a consensus.

Such an umbrella group of leaders, however, was likely to benefit Nahum Goldmann more than the State Department. American Zionists had considered Goldmann a carpetbagger ever since he had arrived on the scene in the early 1940s to blunt the effects of Abba Hillel Silver's hard edges on the Truman Administration. For Goldmann, heading an influential American Jewish organization would make him the most powerful Zionist outside of Israel. But there were no posts available. "Whenever it looked like Goldmann was losing power or influence, he simply created a new Jewish organization," recalls Israel Singer, a close associate and now Secretary General of the World Jewish Congress.[26] And what could be a more powerful base in the U.S. than heading an organization that represented all of organized Jewry in the United States?

Goldmann suggested to Philip Klutznick, a wealthy Chicago real-estate developer and the new president of B'nai B'rith, that they revive the American Jewish Conference, the *ad hoc*, and generally ineffective, umbrella organization of sixty-four American Jewish groups that had been put together in 1943 to consider how to cope with the problems and emergencies that would emerge for the Jews after the war. Klutznick, remembering the difficulties of getting any consensus in the "majority rule" American Jewish Conference, suggested "a loose, informal gathering of organization presidents; no budget; no administrative machinery; no staff; not even, at the start, an address; and no 'majority rule.' "[27]

The Conference of Presidents of Major American Jewish Organizations—also known as the Presidents' Conference—met for the first time in March 1954 as an informal forum to discuss how American Jewry could best help Israel in face of the Eisenhower Administration's apparent hostility. Yet their worst enemy was turning out to be Israel, which seemed intent on proving that Kibya had not been an isolated event.

Two months before, the new prime minister had called a meeting of his party's Cabinet members, and according to an entry in Sharett's diary:

> Chief of staff Moshe Dayan brought one plan after the other for "direct action." The first—what should be done to force open the blockade in the straits of Eilat. A ship flying the Israeli flag should be sent, and if the Egyptians will bomb it we should bomb the Egyptian base from the air, or conquer Ras-e-Naqueb or open our way from the south to the Gaza Strip up to the coast. There was a general uproar. I asked him: do you realize this would mean war with Egypt? He said, of course. . . .[28]

The Egyptian president, Gamal Abdel Nasser, began confiding to several U.S. and British officials, including the CIA's Kim Roosevelt, and Richard Crossman, an old Foreign Office Palestine hand who was then a member of Parliament, that he was eager for peace with Israel. Two successive U.S. ambassadors to Egypt—Henry Byroade was one of them—reported the same thing.[29] In fact, Nasser had refused military aid from the Eisenhower Administration, and informed the U.S. Embassy that Egypt would prefer economic aid. Nasser was consolidating his power, grappling with major economic problems, and trying to bring Egypt into the twentieth century with new programs in agriculture, communications, electrification, and housing, most of which were opposed by the nation's Moslem fundamentalists. The Communist Party was growing, and the Army, with a mere sixty thousand men on active duty, still depended on equipment that was outdated in 1948. Nasser was eager to improve relations with the U.S. and raise funds for the Aswan Dam project. His Army was hardly prepared for another war with Israel, and even if it were, his economy could not support it.

British and American emissaries shuttled back and forth between Egypt and Israel during 1954, and, according to one of them, an Israel-Egypt peace treaty had actually been drafted. Sharett had won the approval of the Israeli parliament to enter into the negotiations. Yet his critics considered the attempt naïve. Israel's security establishment had its own goals in mind, and peace talks with Nasser were not among them.[30]

Israeli "reprisals" across the border continued, as Sharett looked on with anger and frustration. U.S. diplomats also watched with amazement, and reported to Washington on Israel's apparent efforts to keep the border areas in turmoil and increase the appearance of threats to its own security. In a recent book that, in part, focuses on Sharett's efforts toward diplomacy (and the efforts of his political opponents to subvert him), Stephen Green has dug up, with the help of the Freedom of Information Act, a series of top secret diplomatic cables from Arab capitals and Jerusalem in which American observers criticize Israel's policy and report Israel was, as the U.S. consul general in Jerusalem phrased it, "spoiling for [a] fight." In July 1954, according to Green, Eisenhower received a National Security memo that reported "no evidence" of Arab preparations for war, and noted that the opposite seemed to be the case on the Israeli side. The memo continued: ". . . the Israeli Government, concerned at the failure of its efforts to secure peace on the basis of the status quo, appears to be following a deliberate policy of reprisals based on the theory that matters will have to be made worse before they become better."[31]

That is what the State Department and the White House knew in 1954 about events in Israel and along its borders, and made it clear to Israel that they knew. The raids only increased the tension between the U.S. and Israel. It was a predictable result, but there were forces in the Israeli government with a curious taste for folly.

In October, the Egyptians announced they had rounded up a ring of Israeli spies and saboteurs who had been involved in a series of bombings and arson attempts against Egyptian, British, and American targets, including the U.S. Information Agency offices in Cairo and Alexandria, which were damaged by fire bombs. The Egyptians charged that Israeli intelligence was behind it all with the aim to poison relations between the U.S. and Egypt, in line for some military aid from the Eisenhower Administration. The Sharett government denied any involvement, and denounced the Egyptian claim as a fabrication.

The Egyptians held a public trial of the eleven suspects. With members of the international diplomatic corps and Western human rights organizations in attendance, eight of the defendants were convicted, and two of them—Egyptian Jews—were sentenced to death. (One had committed suicide in prison.) On January 31, the two convicts were hanged.

A month later, Israeli soldiers raided the Egyptian town of Gaza, killing thirty-six Egyptian soldiers and two civilians. Again, there was an international uproar, and much grumbling about the Israelis from the State Department.

On March 5, 1955, with sixteen supporting Jewish organizations in attendance, the Presidents' Conference convened for two days at the Shoreham Hotel in Washington for its first public session with representatives of the State Department present. Absent, however, was the American Jewish Committee, a much resented blow to Goldmann and Klutznick's efforts to prove to the White House that American Jews could not be split on the issue of Israel. But the AJC was simply ideologically opposed to any one group speaking for American Jews, particularly a group initiated by the Zionist politician Nahum Goldmann, a man of style and learning who kept the instincts of a Chicago ward heeler in reserve.

It was a historic moment for American Jewry. Yet the participants turned up at the Shoreham in a gloomy mood. At a time when American Jewish leaders were making an all-out effort to convince the Administration that it owed Israel more than, as Dulles had put it, "impartial friendship," the Israelis, once again, embarrassed the Americans. "I hope this conference does not launch into an elaborate discussion of the Gaza incident," Goldmann beseeched his fellow leaders.[32] Gaza was not debated, but the meeting was not, according to participants, "an unqualified success because of the Gaza story."[33]

Gaza was a difficult matter for American Jewish leaders, particularly the Zionists. Sympathetic to Israel's serious security problems, the Americans were nevertheless very uncomfortable about putting their own reputations on the line on Israel's behalf only to pick up the paper and read about Kibya and Gaza. As one Zionist leader warned at the time, an incident like Gaza

... seriously undermines the world Zionist movement and may even shatter it completely. What can Zionist leaders say when they are confronted with facts about which they have been kept in total ignorance. The impression is created that they are sworn defenders of Israel no matter what the case may be.[34]

No matter how much American Jewish leaders recognized they ought to be more than "sworn defenders" of all Israeli actions that was what they were on their way to becoming. Israel was telling American Jewish leaders what they wanted them to hear—indeed what the Americans wanted to hear. And no American Jewish leader would have wanted to hear that Gaza, like Kibya, was part of a grand plan that had been hatched a few years before by Ben-Gurion and his lieutenants to push the Arabs into a war they could never win.

On March 5 and 6, 1955—while the Conference of Presidents of Major American Jewish Organizations was still meeting at the Shoreham Hotel in Washington—Sharett was scribbling in his diary about Israeli terrorism of "the worst type." A group of army reservists avenged the murder of an Israeli couple, later confessing to army authorities that they had rounded up five Bedouin boys, interrogated them about the murders, and knifed each of them to death. Publicly, the Army had denied any involvement. On the basis of what he knew and suspected, Sharett concluded: "This may be taken as decisive proof that we have decided to pass on to a general bloody offensive on all fronts: yesterday Gaza, today something on the Jordanian border, tomorrow the Syrian DMZ; and so on. In the Cabinet meeting tomorrow, I will demand that the killers be put on trial as criminals."

A few days later, Sharett mused about the "talent" and "spiritual grace" of the young Sabras set up against their capacity "for calculated, cold-blooded murder, by knifing the bodies of young defenseless Bedouin," and asked himself, "Which of these two biblical souls will win over the other in this People?"

It was not the sort of question that American Jewish leaders were asking at the Shoreham Hotel. Given what the State Department was hearing from the Middle East, the speechifying at the Shoreham about the dangers confronting, as Klutznick put it, "an isolated Israel, a democracy surrounded by belligerent and bellicose governments" must have set the men from State's teeth deep into their lips. According to their information, the prime minister of Israel seemed incapable of containing the bellicosity of his own generals.

American Jewish leaders were definitely being kept in the dark. They were, it turns out, in very eminent company. Members of the Sharett government were keeping Sharett in the dark. The young Israeli government was already severely split, with the Foreign and Defense ministries going in different, and thus dangerous, directions. The Americans seemed unaware of the policy of war that was going on inside the Israeli Cabinet.

It is startling how few American Jews even know who Sharett was, though he was a true Founding Father of Israel, its first foreign minister and second prime minister. His reputation has even suffered in Israel where he is remembered as a weak, ineffectual politician, a

Jewish Chamberlain whose tendency toward appeasing the Arabs was, thankfully, overwhelmed by Ben-Gurion.

Of all of Israel's top leaders, Sharett seems to have been the most sympathetic to the Arabs of Palestine. Unlike Ben-Gurion, who seemed eager to overpower the Arabs into accepting the reality of the Zionist state, Sharett tried to defuse their animosity toward the new nation in their midst with diplomacy. Born in the Ukraine, Sharett (né Shertok) emigrated to Palestine with his family in 1906 at the age of twelve and settled in an Arab village near Nablus where he lived and studied Arabic until moving to Tel Aviv two years later. Educated at the London School of Economics, Sharett was a founding member of Mapai (Party of the Workers of the Land of Israel) and editor of Labor Zionism's newspaper, *Davar*. Intellectually, he was akin to Weizmann, yet, personally, he was drawn to Ben-Gurion, in no way his intellectual peer.

For a quarter of a century Sharett was Ben-Gurion's collaborator and rival. How deep that rivalry ran only became known in 1978 when Sharett's family published his diaries, in Hebrew, in Israel, despite the opposition of the Begin government. So far, the only analysis in English of the former prime minister's personal commentary of events in Israel—twenty-four-hundred pages and eight volumes' worth—is the brief study by Livia Rokach called *Israel's Sacred Terrorism*.[35]

Sharett's *Diary* is a blockbuster, belying most of the conventional wisdom about the Arab threat to Israel's security during those early years. Throughout the document, a prime minister of Israel reveals that his own government and that of his predecessor and successor Ben-Gurion were so confident of Israel's military preeminence in the region that they were eager to provoke Arab states into military confrontations that the Arabs were sure to lose. Their main strategy was to mount border "reprisals" against Arab military and civilian targets.

Sharett preferred diplomacy to baiting the Arabs. He had addressed the Cabinet and condemned the Kibya raid, which he had opposed, for having "exposed us in front of the whole world as a gang of blood-suckers, capable of mass massacres regardless, it seems, of whether their actions may lead to war. . . ."[36] The next day Ben-Gurion harangued the Cabinet for two hours about the "army's preparations for the second round," as Sharett described it, and "presented detailed figures on the growth of the military force of the Arab countries which [he said] will reach its peak in 1956. . . ."[37]

Sharett confided to his diary:

> As I listened . . . I was thinking . . . that we should proceed against the danger
> with nonmilitary means: propose daring and concrete solutions for the Refu-
> gee problem through payment of compensations, improve our relations with
> the powers, search ceaselessly for an understanding with Egypt.[38]

But as Sharett tried to negotiate with Egypt, his opponents were
trying to provoke Egypt into a fight, unbeknownst to the prime minister. The spy ring was proof of secret Israeli efforts to sabotage
Egypt's relations with the U.S. and Britain—a fact that Sharett
learned only after he had publicly denied Egypt's claims of Israeli
espionage and attacked the trial. In the course of his own 1955 investigation of the Egyptian claims, Sharett learned that either his own
minister of defense, Pinchas Lavon, and/or the head of military intelligence, Colonel Benjamin Gibli, and perhaps even Chief of Staff
Moshe Dayan had authorized the ring of saboteurs and spies. Israel's
prime minister had known nothing about any of this, nor had he been
informed of the plan to raid Gaza.[39] Ben-Gurion replaced Lavon, who
was switched mysteriously into a top job in another ministry all the
while looking for the evidence to exonerate himself.

It took five years for the Lavon Affair, as it became known in
Israel, to turn into the biggest political scandal in the short history of
the Jewish state, a shady moment that still mars the career of Shimon
Peres, who as director general of the Defense Ministry had been
implicated in the scandal. A special commission eventually exoner-
ated Lavon and recommended prosecuting Dayan and Gibli for basically framing Lavon. But due to the unofficial nature of the first
investigation, the years that had passed, and, doubtless, the threat the
scandal might have for Israel's reputation abroad, no action was
taken.

SHARETT and his allies did win a few victories in the Cabinet for
moderation, but, in the end, Ben-Gurion's belligerence defeated his
successor's efforts toward diplomacy. The election results of July
1955, which left his party with five fewer seats, were interpreted as a
public blow to Sharett's dovish policies. Ben-Gurion attacked Sharett
for worrying too much about "what the Gentiles will say" as opposed
to his own concern for the security of Israel and the education of its

youth. Sharett's days were numbered; he remained head of a nominal government until November when Ben-Gurion put together a new coalition and took up the prime minister's job once again.

ON October 29, 1956, in collusion with the British and the French, the Israelis dropped paratroopers into the Sinai, and quickly dominated most of it, along with the Gaza Strip and Sharm es-Sheikh, the latter the gateway to the Strait of Tiran, which Nasser had closed to Israeli shipping. It was a masterful military operation with Moshe Dayan in the director's chair. Two allies and one close friend had invaded Egypt, and the Eisenhower Administration was not even warned. Neither were American Jewish leaders, who, once again, had to suffer the ire of Dulles and Eisenhower while defending Israeli policies that had surprised them even more than the Administration, which at least had received intelligence reports about a military buildup in the region.

The American Jewish leaderhsip was not pleased, and several even warned the Israeli government of the folly of antagonizing the Eisenhower Administration and the American Jewish community, which had only a few weeks before been assured by its own leaders (who had been assured by Ben-Gurion) that Israel would not start a war. It turned out to be nothing more than an emotional catharsis—and further proof to American policy makers that, in the relationship between the Jews of Israel and the United States, the Americans had been assigned the role of silent partner, and had accepted it.

As the invasion was taking place, Philip Klutznick was speaking at a dinner. Asked about rumors that the Israelis were invading Egypt, he said they were not. He had conferred with a minister at the Israeli Embassy in Washington that morning. To this day, Klutznick resents the fact that the Israelis left the Jewish leadership open to intense embarrassment, not to mention loss of credibility in Washington and before their own Jewish constituency.

Abba Eban, in his autobiography, recalls that "among American Jews the confusion was great." He received a call from Abba Hillel Silver, who criticized the Israeli attack as "an error in judgment." Eban asked American Zionist leaders for "full solidarity with Israel," and dispatched a deputy to get a similar show of support from the Presidents' Conference. Eban writes: "From his report I gathered that he had a difficult hour. For the first time in our memory there was reluctance to justify Israel's action without reserve.... Some suggested that Jewish reservations about Israel's step be openly published."

The Israelis had, once again, made America's Jewish leaders look silly, and, for the sake of Israel, they seemed willing to continue in that state. "In the end," Eban reports, "more normal counsels prevailed, and the Jewish leaders rose with an expression of solidarity for Israel and an appeal to the United States to strengthen Israel's security and Middle Eastern peace."[40] The Presidents' Conference and the American Jewish Committee appealed publicly to the President "for a fresh appraisal of the conflict," pointing out Nasser's ties to the Soviets and calling for the U.S. to seek settlement through direct negotiations between Israel and Egypt.

Dulles, however, wanted Jewish support for the Administration's efforts to force the Israelis to withdraw, and he went looking for his own Jewish "leaders." Within twenty-four hours after the invasion, the White House had enlisted the aid of Rabbi Silver to send a message to Ben-Gurion. According to Abba Eban, Eisenhower sent word through his chief of staff, Sherman Adams, that in his public broadcast on the Suez Crisis he wanted to include "a statement of deep appreciation and of friendship toward Israel."[41] All Ben-Gurion had to do was pull back to the previous boundary. Eisenhower also reminded the prime minister that regardless of how he viewed his ties to Britain and France, "the fact is that Israel's power and future are in fact bound up with the United States." Silver informed Eban, who told him to telephone Ben-Gurion directly.

Eban met with Blaustein, who, he recalls, "did not criticize" Israel.[42] He then went to Wall Street to talk to Thomas Dewey, who told him the White House was worried that the Israelis were in the Sinai to stay, and that the Russians would intervene. Ben-Gurion sent this message: for withdrawal he wanted peace, the end of Arab terrorist attacks against Israel, the abolition of the economic boycott against Israel, the opening of the Canal, and no alliances against Israel. The prime minister also said he hoped that Israel's military action would not disrupt the friendship between the U.S. and his country.

By the end of February 1957, Dulles was still looking for supporters and requested a meeting with a small group of carefully selected Jewish leaders which included Klutznick, Blaustein, and Barney Balaban, the latter president of Paramount Pictures and an

Eisenhower supporter. Klutznick recalls sitting down in Dulles's office, looking around the table, and noting, to his horror, that "there was not a Zionist in the room." Worse, in the eyes of his fellow Jewish leaders, the possibility of such an *ad hoc* group was precisely what the Presidents' Conference had been designed to prevent. Though Klutznick was the chairman of the Conference, he had been secretly invited to this meeting as head of the B'nai B'rith, and he hadn't even alerted the Conference of the meeting. "I sat there wondering what I would tell the others after the meeting," he recalled almost thirty years later. But the group refused to qualify their support of Israel, and Klutznick was able to tell the Conference that the secretary of state was unable to divide Jewish leaders. At least those in that room.[43]

In fact, the leadership was already divided, more by the embarrassment the Israelis had caused them than by the secretary of state. Suez put American Jewish leaders on the hot seat. The President feared a confrontation with the Soviets; he wanted the Israelis out of the Sinai or there would be an economic boycott of Israel and the United Jewish Appeal would lose its tax-exempt status. These moves would torpedo Israel's already wounded economy. But organized Jewry was not powerful enough to win any concessions for the Israelis. Ben-Gurion was asking for too much.

The Israelis quit the Sinai by the middle of March. The UJA tax exemption was still in the balance, but Kenen appealed to the Senate Democratic Majority Leader Lyndon Johnson, who spent some of his own chips with Eisenhower and saved it. Johnson proved a good friend of Israel in Congress. As Dulles was threatening Israel with sanctions, LBJ was on the phone to Abba Eban expressing his indignation over the Republican Administration's tactics of threatening to punish the Israelis when it had not threatened the Russians for their brutal invasion of Hungary. "They're not going to get a goddam thing here [from Congress] until they [treat you fairly]," Johnson told Eban.[44]

Yet Kibya, Gaza, and Suez could not damage Israel's reputation among the American people. Ben-Gurion, it seemed, could, literally, do no wrong. Americans knew what the Jews had suffered at the hands of Hitler; they were impressed by their fight for independence in Palestine and by what they heard about Israel's pioneers "making the desert bloom." Most Americans, of course, knew virtually nothing about Zionism, and less about events in Israel.

In 1958, that changed with the publication of what *The New York Times* called "a passionate summary of the inhuman treatment of the Jewish people in Europe, of the exodus in the nineteenth and twentieth centuries to Palestine and the triumphant founding of the new Israel."[45] Leon Uris's *Exodus* became an instant best seller, and the primary source of knowledge about the Jews and Israel that most Americans had. It was hardly an unbiased picture; as the *Times* reviewer noted, "the Arabs come off badly in this book." The heroes were fighting Jews, including the Irgun, which, though criticized for its terrorism, took on, according to the *Times*, "quite a hint of glory."

Exodus was great public relations for Israel, priceless, in fact. And when Otto Preminger's movie of the book came out two years later starring Paul Newman as a Sabra hero—a member of what one character in the book calls "a race of Jewish Tarzans"—Israel's reputation seemed secure in the U.S. Suddenly, Jews were glamorous. When the moment came in the film for "Ha-Tikvah," the national anthem of Israel, to be played, people danced in the aisles of movie theaters. Since publication, *Exodus* has sold more than twenty million copies. The Israel of most Americans, including Jews, is still the *Exodus* version.

2

"TURNING ON THE SPIGOT": LOBBYING JFK AND LBJ

AFTER two terms of Eisenhower's, at best, indifference, to the Jewish state, American Jewish leaders were in need of a friend in the White House. In 1958, one potential candidate for the Presidency looked particularly promising—the young senator from Massachusetts, John F. Kennedy. The Jewish leaders were Democrats and liberals, and here was a man who looked like he shared their beliefs, at home and abroad. Eminent Jews in Massachusetts, including the Zionist Dewey Stone, had helped Kennedy beat Henry Cabot Lodge for a Senate seat in 1952.

But there were problems. Senator Kennedy's record on Israel was vague, certainly not as staunchly supportive as Hubert Humphrey's. And unlike Lyndon Johnson, Kennedy did not rush to Israel's defense during the Suez affair. He was also a Catholic. Many Jews associated American Catholics with right-wing, pro-McCarthy, and anti-Semitic causes. Worse, there was the touchy issue of the candidate's father, Joseph P. Kennedy, who, as ambassador to Great Britain in the late 1930s, had been a supporter of Neville Chamberlain's policy of appeasing the Nazis. His son, however, turned out to be a better diplomat than his father.

From the moment he considered making a bid for the Presidency, Kennedy was eager to win over the Jewish vote. Philip Klutznick recalled a private meeting with JFK in 1958 when he put the young politician on the spot about his attitudes toward Israel, which had been, Klutznick noted, "rather cloudy." His answer, according to Klutznick, "was cloudy," and indicated a concern about the Arab refugee problem and the risks of war in the region. Klutznick's response was not cloudy. "Look, Senator," he said, "if you plan to run for the presidency and that is what you're going to say, count me out and count a lot of other people out, too."[1] Kennedy asked Klutznick what Jews might want him to say. Klutznick advised Kennedy that Eisenhower on Suez was unsatisfactory, while Truman in 1948 was on the mark.

Kennedy got the message. Delivering a speech before a Jewish organization marking the tenth anniversary of the founding of Israel in 1958, Kennedy gave a pro-Israel speech in which he attacked the Arab contention that peace would arrive in a Middle East with no Jewish state. Kennedy declared: "Quite apart from the values and hopes which the state of Israel enshrines—and the past injury which it redeems—it twists reality to suggest that it is the democratic tendency of Israel which has injected discord and dissension into the Near East."[2] Afterward he sent the speech to Klutznick with a note: "What do you think of this now?"

After his nomination at the 1960 Democratic Convention, Kennedy agreed to meet with a large group of Jewish leaders in New York at the Hotel Pierre apartment of Abraham Feinberg, a Kennedy supporter and wealthy banker. The participants, who included Dewey Stone and Klutznick, were asked to have questions prepared. There was a straightforward and candid exchange during which Kennedy dealt with a wide range of domestic issues, and denied his father's alleged anti-Semitism.[3] When the issue of Israel came up, so did Kennedy's guard.[4] He talked of the need of the Israelis and Nasser to negotiate for peace, pointed out that the U.S. had to find a way of living with Arab nationalism, discussed the possibility of Israel accepting some Arab refugees and resettling the rest in Arab countries, and assured everyone in the room that should Israel be attacked, the U.S. would rush to her aid.

It was not as much as his audience would have liked, but it was enough. Though the meeting was not a fund raiser, the group pledged $500,000 to Kennedy's campaign coffers. Klutznick was aboard as an adviser. For good measure, Kennedy turned some of his fabled charisma on the Jews. At a Zionist Organization of America convention during the campaign, he delivered another well-informed speech on the Middle East and also used the opportunity to puncture the charge he was too young to be President. The forty-three-year-old candidate pointed out that Herzl was only thirty-seven when he proclaimed the "inevitability" of the Zionist state, and then added, "The

Jewish people, ever since David slew Goliath, have never considered youth as a barrier to leadership."[5]

It did not hurt Kennedy's quest for Jewish support that he was the target of some nasty anti-Catholic bigotry among Protestant leaders. The American Nazi Party helped too by throwing its support to Richard Nixon—"Nazis for Nixon, Kikes for Kennedy" was one of its slogans. Another of its placards read, "FDR and JFK mean JEW deal."[6]

In the famous close finish in November 1960, 80 percent of American Jews voted for Kennedy. They had made clear what earned Jewish allegiance at the ballot box: progressive causes at home and support for Israel abroad. American politicians may have their special causes and high-minded concerns, but their prime concern is getting elected.

The results of the 1960 presidential election only confirmed to other politicians how stupid it was to ignore the political power of the Jews. That power basically has three sources, all well known, though cautiously discussed. The first is a political weapon of last resort, which may be the most powerful, and most abused by the hardliners. Jews can brand—and thus ignore—their or Israel's critics by labeling them "anti-Israel," "pro-Arab," or worse, "anti-Semitic" (or if the dissenter happens to be a Jew, "self-hating Jew"). No politician wants to be called an "anti-Semite," particularly a politician who is a genuine anti-Semite.

American Jews are also politically influential because, quite simply, they vote. For all the lip service to the great democracy that is America, few Americans actually take advantage of their right to vote: in fact, nearly half the electorate *never* votes. While America's six million Jews make up only 3 percent of the population, they have increased their power at the polls by showing up to vote—90 percent of them. Congressional and state elections are often won by fewer than 5 or 10 percentage points. Traditionally, Jews have lived in large urban areas where their votes can sometimes swing the election to one presidential candidate or another. This was the case in the Kennedy-Nixon battle.*

*The significance of Jewish votes in presidential campaigns, however, seems to be overrated. According to a study by M. S. El Azhary—*Political Cohesion of American Jews in American Politics* (Lanham, Md.: University Press of America, 1980)—after 1960 Jewish voters did not play a crucial role as President-makers until Jimmy Carter beat Gerald Ford in 1976. In 1984, Ronald Reagan was re-elected in a landslide that included only a third of the Jewish vote.

The third source of its political power is that the Jewish community gives money to political campaigns. The importance of money in American electioneering is almost as old as the Republic. In the late 1790s, when Federalist banks were refusing loans to Democrats eager to buy property and thus the right to vote, Aaron Burr set up an anti-Federalist state bank to lend them the money.[7] A century later, Mark Hanna, the notorious Ohio businessman who headed the Republican Party during the 1896 presidential campaign, raised most of candidate McKinley's $7 million from major corporations throughout the country eager to preserve protective tariffs threatening the prices of their products. In his book *Jews and American Politics,* Stephen Isaacs reports that it was the Jewish banker Abraham Feinberg, who was "the first Jewish fund raiser for national politics."[8] Feinberg raised money for Harry Truman and was a major backer of John Kennedy.

The most important donations to a political campaign are the earliest ones, the "seed" money, particularly for the unknown candidate. Unlikely to base their contributions on friendship or helping out sentimental favorites, corporate donors tend to wait to see who has the best chance to win. American Jews, however, have been known to be generous to any candidate who they believe will support their interests. Should a dark horse win, all the better; he will probably be more beholden to those who supported him in the beginning of his campaign when the money was most needed. "You can't imagine how appreciative a politician is for that early money," says one experienced Democratic fund raiser.[9]

Giving away money holds a long and honored place in Judaism. In the Middle ages, some countries required Jews to support their poor. Giving became a duty, and then a point of pride and prestige. In Russia, every home in the Pale of Settlement had a small box—a *pushke*—where the family would put a penny or two for families even worse off than they. Jewish philanthropy thrived in the United States as national and local organizations proliferated to help poor Jewish immigrants and defend the community from anti-Semitism. The charity of American and European Jews was crucial to the first Zionist settlements in Palestine.

Businessmen, not rabbis or intellectuals, dominated the American Jewish community. Any Jew with social ambitions had to prove his generosity. Psychologically, the move from contributing to the welfare of fellow Jews to donating money to the campaigns of politicians who might secure that welfare was an easy one. In any city that merited the description, Jews had established "federations" of Jewish charities to coordinate giving. The federations' most skillful fund raisers quickly became the leaders of the Jewish community—and the most reliable donors and fund raisers for political candidates.

THE Jews supported John F. Kennedy, and he was most appreciative. At the end of his first meeting with Ben-Gurion at the Waldorf Astoria in New York in the spring of 1961, President Kennedy turned to the Israeli leader and said, "I know I was elected because of the votes of American Jews. I owe them my election. Tell me, is there something that I can do for the Jewish people?" Ben-Gurion, according to his biographer Michel Bar-Zohar, was nonplussed by this "astonishing frankness," and evaded the question. "You must do what is best for the free world," he told the young President. To his own advisers, "the old man," as they called him, privately denigrated Kennedy's *quid pro quo* approach. Ben-Gurion's take on JFK: "What a politician!"[10] Kennedy, however, with his prep-school good manners and Boston pol's instinct for rolling out the pork barrel for friends, was simply expressing his own gratitude for the obvious.

For American Jewish leaders, Kennedy's victory was reward enough. They had regained the kind of political influence that they had enjoyed under Truman. There was a personal relationship between the President and several Jewish eminences. Feinberg remained an adviser, and the President appointed Klutznick as Adlai Stevenson's deputy at the U.N. Kennedy also named one of his campaign aides, a Washington lawyer named Myer ("Mike") Feldman, to be his assistant for domestic relations, a job that was (and remains) the White House's link to the American Jewish community. In the face of Eisenhower's and Dulles's perceived hostility to Israel, Kenen had worked hard to establish strong support for Israel on Capitol Hill. With several Jews "at court," the White House too was covered.

Or so it seemed to Jewish leaders. Ben-Gurion had his doubts. At their meeting in 1961, Kennedy had asked the Israeli prime minister what he was planning to do about the Arab "refugees" who either had fled from Palestine during the Arab-Israeli war in 1948–1949 or had been expelled. Ben-Gurion tried to change the subject, but Kennedy kept raising it.

Once in the White House, a U.S. President soon recognizes that the quickest way to make his mark in the world, and history, is in the making of foreign policy. Since the 1950s, a primary target of this ambition has been the Arab-Israeli conflict. Kennedy too thought he could contribute to peace in the Middle East. It seemed simple enough: all that had to be done was persuade Israel to compensate or repatriate some of the Arabs, which would thus encourage the Arab states to resettle the rest. Kennedy knew the Israelis would resist and that their supporters in the U.S. would back them up. But his own Jewish support at the polls led him to believe that American Jews had no place to go but the Democratic Party. If he moved quickly, he would be able to withstand Jewish criticism of any efforts to befriend the Arabs.

The President was wrong. His strategy, as embodied in the Johnson Plan,* which called for the choice for Arab refugees to return to their homes in what was now Israel or be resettled in other parts of Israel or other Arab countries or elsewhere in the world and be compensated by Israel, was doomed from the outset. Before it was formally announced, the Israelis had already informed the American Jewish Committee that they were against Kennedy's Arab initiative. The Presidents' Conference too was working behind the scenes to block any effort to force Israel to repatriate Arab refugees. "During the next 18 months, American Jewish leaders worked together with Israeli officials to prevent American adoption of a plan for the refugees contrary to Israeli interests," writes Etta Zablocki Bick in her analysis of U.S.-Israeli relations between 1956 and 1968.[11]

The Johnson Plan was finally made public in the fall of 1962. The Ben-Gurion government rejected yielding any control over the number of Arabs allowed across Israel's border. No sovereign nation should be forced to accept anyone, Israel argued; worse, the Israelis argued, the plan put Israel at the mercy of Arab leaders who could easily encourage large numbers of refugees to choose to settle in Israel, and thus, the Israelis feared, create a potential fifth column plotting to destroy Israel from within. Ben-Gurion made his own views plain in a letter to his ambassador in the U.S. that he expected to be circulated among American Jewish leaders: "Israel will regard

---

*Named after Joseph Johnson, head of the Carnegie Endowment for International Peace, who had been commissioned to prepare the report.

this plan as a more serious danger to her existence than all the threats of the Arab dictators and kings, than all the Arab armies, than all of Nasser's missiles and his Soviet MiGs . . . Israel will fight against this implementation down to the last man."[12]

No American Jewish leader was about to ignore the force of that opinion. Kennedy had hoped, in vain, to buy Ben-Gurion's cooperation by loaning Israel the $23 million it needed to buy the HAWK (Homing All the Way) guided-missile system to defend against Egyptian bombers. Congressional elections were coming up, and threats of checkbooks closing around the nation to Democratic candidates were in the air. The Arabs too denounced the Johnson Plan as a pro-Israel ploy to cancel out the Palestinian issue. The President was a smart enough politician to know when to cut the line. The Johnson Plan vanished.

It is a classic example of a President miscalculating how hard an Israeli government—and the American Jewish community—will fight any measure that it perceives to be against Israel's interests— regardless of how much the White House insists it is in American interests. But who determines Israel's interests? Only its leaders? Israel had been established by the World Zionist Organization for Jews everywhere, and Jews in the Diaspora believed that they still had a role to play in shaping the Jewish state. Some American Zionists were concerned that Ben-Gurion and the non-Zionist American Jewish leaders who dominated Jewish life in the United States had already pushed them to the sidelines. In his book *The Eternal Dissent,* David Polish, an American Reform rabbi and ardent Zionist, argued that American Jews would have to justify not making *aliyah* by proving that the Diaspora had a role in helping shape the new Jewish state.[13] The book stirred up a debate over American Jewish– Israeli relations among Jewish leaders and intellectuals. There was even some sympathy at the top levels of the Zionist movement for a stronger Diaspora role in the new nation's future. But the notion of a true "partnership" between the Jews of Israel and those living outside the state had one inveterate enemy, Ben-Gurion, who still insisted that anyone who wanted to affect Israeli policy would have to move to Israel. American Jewish leaders decided to leave Israeli policy up to the Israelis.

•   •   •

SHORTLY after John F. Kennedy's assassination in November 1963, President Lyndon Johnson told an Israeli diplomat, "You have lost a great friend. But you have found a better one." LBJ made good on his promise. He was not only a better friend; Johnson became the best friend the Jewish state has ever had in the White House.[14]

LBJ seemed to be a genuine fan of the Israelis. He enjoyed pointing out to Jewish audiences "my Christian faith sprang from yours."[15] Johnson also noted the similarities between the Jewish pioneers building a home in the desert and his own family's hardscrabble life farming along the Pedernales in the Hill Country of Texas.

The Democrat from Texas was no expert in foreign policy. For Johnson, politics was a personal affair; it was about friends and connections. And some of the Johnsons' oldest and best friends were Jews and loyal supporters of Israel. The treasurer of his first successful campaign for the Senate was James Novy, a member of an old Texas, Jewish family who was a frequent guest at the White House.[16] Another old friend and adviser was the skilled Washington lawyer Abe Fortas, whom Johnson would name to the Supreme Court. His appointee to the United Nations was Supreme Court Justice Arthur Goldberg. Johnson's national security adviser Walt Rostow, Rostow's older brother, Eugene, the number-three man at the State Department, and the historian John Roche, LBJ's "intellectual-in-residence," were avid supporters of Israel. Abe Feinberg was a close associate; so was Arthur Krim, the head of United Artists and a major fund raiser for the Democratic Party. Krim's wife, Mathilde, a Ph.D. in genetics and a former cancer researcher at Israel's Weizmann Institute, was a convert to Judaism who had been married to an Irgun fighter; during the first Arab war, she too had worked with the Irgun, and later moved to the U.S. after her marriage to Krim.[17] The Krims were frequent guests at the White House and the LBJ Ranch. So was Ephraim ("Eppy") Evron, a top minister at the Israeli Embassy and the closest thing to a good ol' boy American-style politician the Israelis had.

One might even go so far as to say that LBJ had learned all he knew about the Middle East from the Israelis (or had to know, from the Israeli perspective). In his autobiography, Abba Eban recalls first meeting Johnson when he was Senate majority leader in 1952.

In those early days I had felt that he came hesitantly to our concerns. His mind and heart were then turned inward toward the forces which shaped

American society. . . . Accompanied by a friend from Houston, Jim Novy, who had first introduced us, Lyndon B. Johnson had come to my Washington residence in 1952 in an effort to find out everything essential about Israel in the briefest possible time.[18]

There is no evidence that the Senate majority leader paid any visits to the Saudi or the Egyptian ambassadors' homes. Shortly after LBJ entered the White House, he became the first U.S. President to receive officially the prime minister of Israel at the White House, and, according to Eban, LBJ "established with Prime Minister Eshkol the kind of intimate confidence that had never before existed between heads of American and Israeli governments. We no longer had to use the back door for access to the center of American policy."

In fact, Eban, as ambassador to the U.S., had emerged as the real leader of the American Jewish community. Jewish leaders now rarely met with Administration officials without first being briefed by the embassy. One former Israeli diplomat recalled for an interviewer a meeting between the ambassador and the Presidents' Conference in the mid-sixties.

But what did the briefing consist of? The Arabs are strong; there is a military build-up. Israel is weak; we are not getting arms. The Jews reacted with great sympathy. "Oy vey! We will try to help you!" But what did it really mean? Could they speak intelligently to anyone in the State Department about the need to sell Israel arms? They did not begin to understand arms sales. So we talked to them in simple terms and they felt very important. . . . [19]

Indeed, whenever an American Jew met with a government official without speaking first to the embassy, he was quickly informed afterward that the embassy had been aware of the meeting. Several leaders interviewed for this book confessed that it was frustrating never to be able to discuss matters without Israeli interference; yet, at the same time, they conceded their admiration for an Israeli intelligence network that so quickly knew who was meeting whom. One former head of the Presidents' Conference, William Wexler, frankly told the Israeli scholar Etta Zablocki Bick that he had met with the Israeli ambassador almost every week during his two-year stint; he had also traveled to Israel to discuss tactics for Jewish support in the U.S. with the prime minister of Israel and aides "six to nine times a year." Said Wexler: "The American Jewish community has been used and should have been used, and it should continue to be used in a positive sense of the word. Nobody is going off on their own and doing things without proper instructions. The only place where those instructions could really originate was in Israel."[20]

Thus Israel "used" the American Jewish community as a kind of large public-relations agency that would put together pro-Israel demonstrations, prepare releases, or generate telegrams to the U.N., the White House, or congressmen. When one prominent American Jewish leader expressed his reservations to a deputy minister to the Israeli Consul in New York about the propriety and the risks of this system, particularly the regular briefings—the State Department surely knew that the Jewish leaders were toeing the Israeli line—the Israeli diplomat said, "Of course, they know. But we want them to know we know they know. We want the Americans to know that we can turn on the spigot whenever we want."[21]

But was that what the Jewish community in America had come to—defender of Israel, a spigot to be turned on and off by the Israeli Embassy? What about their life as Jews? No one questioned their success as Americans. By the mid-sixties, American Jews had arrived. The nation's success had depended upon its immigrants, and the Jews were the most successful immigrants of all. In 1965, the annual income of almost half of all Jewish families was between $7,500 and $15,000; only 25 percent of all American families had been as successful. The percentage of Jews in white-collar jobs was three times the national average, and Jews were succeeding impressively in the nation's best colleges, universities, and professional schools.[22] In their speechifying, politicians made much of the noble "Judeo-Christian tradition" in American life. Anti-Semitism seemed a relic of a less socially mature past: in a national poll in 1962, only 1 percent of those surveyed said they viewed Jews as a threat to America.

But some began to address their failure as Jews. Intermarriage was running at the disconcerting rate of 30 percent. Synagogues had spread throughout the nation, but their role now seemed more social than spiritual or theological. By 1966, the debate arose, once again, about the possibility of a rich Jewish life in the Diaspora. Some even wondered whether the emotional commitment of American Jews to Israel was subverting the future of the American Jewish community itself; too much of the community's energy—and money—was being diverted to Israel while American Jewry's own institutions, particularly those aimed at Jewish education, were poverty-stricken. In *Zion Reconsidered,* published that year, Jakob Petuchowski criticized Israel's dominance of American Jewry, contending that it threatened its dignity and very existence. Petuchowski raised doubts about the future of a community that was directed by Israel, and that ignored the political consequences of philanthropy to Israel—tax-deductible gifts that most Jews knew went into Israel's budget and were used as the Israelis saw fit.[23]

No matter how prophetic those opinions would turn out to be, few listened. Indeed, the Israelis persisted in their condescension to American Jewry and their efforts to delegitimize the Reform and Conservative movements, which dominated the community, all the while depending on their financial and political support. The belief that a good Jew was a Zionist, and all Zionists belonged in Israel, remained an axiom among Israel's leadership. While a few Jewish leaders, notably Nahum Goldmann, continued to argue that Jews in the Diaspora should not be afraid to criticize Israeli policy, the Israelis insisted that it was their country, a democratically run one at that, and if American Jews wanted a say they could make *aliyah.*

Yet the fact that the question of how the Diaspora should relate to Israel had arisen, that some Jews were uncomfortable with being a rubber stamp for Israel, was significant. This kind of reassessment marked a maturity in American Jews as Americans and as Jews.

Events in the Middle East, however, soon made such soul-searching seem irrelevant. U.S. efforts to stabilize the region since the Suez Crisis, and to roll back Soviet influence among Arab countries, particularly Nasser's Egypt, stumbled against the Egyptian leader's increasing bellicosity. As Arab hostility toward Israel increased—the Palestine Liberation Organization (PLO) had been founded in 1964—and Soviet support of pan-Arab dreams intensified, U.S. and Israeli interests seemed more in line, and the young nation began to look more and more like a strategic plus for U.S. policy in the Middle East. Israel celebrated its nineteenth anniversary on May 14, 1967, facing the threat of war; that same day Nasser suddenly put Egyptian forces in a state of "maximum alert," and began marching his troops into the Sinai. Within a week, Nasser had packed off the U.N. Emergency Force from Egyptian soil and Gaza

and closed the Gulf of Aqaba and the Strait of Tiran to Israeli shipping—in spite of a U.S. commitment against such a blockade.

The State Department drafted a statesmanlike speech for Johnson
that was quickly leaked to the Israeli Embassy. Jewish leaders were
soon on the phone to the White House. Their source, however, had
not learned that the President had turned the speech over to his pro-
Israeli aide John Roche, who then provided Johnson with a script that
strongly denounced the blockade as "illegal" and "potentially disastrous to the cause of peace."[24] Roche recalled that: "Jewish pressure
groups in this country were lined up all the way from Washington to
California." According to Roche, LBJ had some "malicious" fun
reading the State Department document over the phone to Jewish
leaders. Walt Rostow told Roche not to worry; the President was
"just getting a little therapy for all this pressure they put on."[25]

Johnson tried to calm the Israelis and win political support for the
opening of the Strait. But on June 5, 1967, Israeli planes bombarded
Egyptian airfields, and thus took the offensive against the might of
the entire Arab world. American Jews were stunned. They saw before them another Holocaust in the making. And before Israel could
even ask for their help, they went into high gear. Arthur Hertzberg
later described that mobilization in *Commentary*.

> In general, the immediate reaction to the crisis was far more intense and
> widespread than anyone could have foreseen. Many Jews would never have
> believed that grave danger to Israel could dominate their thoughts and emo-
> tions to the exclusion of all else; many were surprised by the depth of their
> anger to those of their friends who carried on as usual, untouched by fear for
> Israeli survival and the instinctive involvement they themselves felt.[26]

Suddenly, for American Jewry, Israel had become the most important thing, perhaps not in their life, but certainly in their Jewishness.
At the time of the Six-Day War, pollsters, Hertzberg noted, "found
that 99 percent of all the Jews in America undeviatingly supported
the Israeli position." As Jewish pundits were soon saying, American
Jews had all become "Zionized."

The generosity of American Jews was incredible. Over the first
three weeks of the emergency, the community raised more than $100
million, most of it cash. One UJA luncheon in New York generated
$15 million in as many minutes. At the time, Hertzberg and others

saw this all-out support for Israel as a reaffirmation of their Jewishness. In a sense it was. But it had nothing to do with Judaism as a religion. Long ambivalent about their Jewishness and the ease with which they had become the Americans they so wanted to be, America's Jews sought to anchor the identity that, emotionally and psychologically, they seemed to require. They found their solution in Israel.

As Jewish pundits soon began saying, Israel had become "the religion of American Jews." Like other ethnic Americans, the Jews now had an "old country" they could be proud of, perhaps even retire to, certainly visit. The threat of the annihilation of the Jewish state in 1967 was perceived as a threat to the existence of Jews everywhere. No Jew could permit another Holocaust. After the war, as the Israeli political theorist Shlomo Avineri has written, "it is a fact that being Jewish today means, in one way or another, feeling some link with Israel."[27]

Ironically, there was no real threat to the existence of Israel in 1967, as the Israeli's swift destruction of the armies of Syria and Egypt had proved. Historians have discovered that neither the Israeli military nor the CIA was ever worried that the Arabs would annihilate Israel. The only question in intelligence circles at the time was whether the war—the "turkey shoot," as Walt Rostow called it[28]— would be over in six days or seven. Ben-Gurion later admitted that he never thought Nasser wanted war;[29] in an interview with an Israeli newspaper in 1977, Yitzhak Rabin, who was chief of staff during the war, confessed that he too had believed that "Nasser wanted to achieve gains without having to go to war."[30] But as the armies of Syria, Jordan, and Iraq joined Egypt in late May, the Israeli public feared the worst. They clamored for the leadership of Moshe Dayan, and the new Defense Minister mounted his brilliant attack—and forever changed Israel's standing in the world.

BUT the Eshkol government had not forgotten the humiliation that had quickly followed the triumph of the 1956 Sinai campaign when the U.S. forced Israel to withdraw from captured territory. The prime minister moved quickly to turn Israel's greatest military triumph into a political victory too. On June 19, Eshkol's National Unity Government, which included, for the first time in Israeli history, Begin's

Herut Party, adopted a peace resolution, which was communicated to the U.S.: Israel was willing to withdraw to the international border with Egypt in exchange for freedom in the Strait of Tiran and the Suez Canal and provided the Sinai could be demilitarized. If the Golan Heights was also demilitarized, Israel was willing also to withdraw to the international border with Syria. The resolution was silent on the West Bank, Gaza Strip, and Palestinian refugees, assuring the Americans that "these issues" would be considered separately.

Preferably not at all, if Begin could have his way. For Begin and his followers, the West Bank—they used the Biblical names Judea and Samaria—was originally a gift to the Jews by God himself, and thus not captured but "liberated" by the Six-Day War. No Israeli government with Begin's Herut in it would be in a position to concede any part of *Eretz Israel*. Nevertheless, the Labor side of the Unity Government talked of the Israeli-occupied territories as a perfect "bargaining chip" to offer the Arabs in return for peace and security. The Eshkol resolution was passed along to the Americans, but was never made public. The peace process was in limbo. There was Begin's opposition, but, more significantly, the Israelis were waiting for the Arabs to make their move, and the Arabs refused to budge.

Instead of peace, the Arabs gave Israel the famous "three noes" formulated at a summit in Khartoum in August 1967: "no peace, no recognition, no negotiation." To encourage movement on both sides, the United Nations passed in November Resolution 242, which remains the basis for negotiating peace in the Middle East. There was something for both sides: for the Arabs, 242 called for Israeli withdrawal from "territories occupied in the recent conflict" and just solution for the refugee problem; for the Israelis, it called for the end of belligerency and the right for every state to "live in peace within secure and recognized boundaries" and affirmed freedom of navigation through international waterways.[31]

The Arab states were willing to go along with 242, though the Palestinians rejected it because the resolution did not acknowledge them as more than a "refugee" problem. They were no less a nationality than the Jews, and like the Jews they wanted "self-determination" in the form of their own state. The Israelis too accepted 242. Yet the language was vague enough for both sides to interpret the resolution as they saw fit. The Arabs interpreted 242 to

mean that Israel had to withdraw totally from the area it had captured, without negotiations. The U.S. argued that "secure and recognized boundaries" implied negotiations to determine what those
might be. The result was a stalemate at the U.N. But the Israelis
seemed content with the status quo—so long, that is, as they could
maintain their military superiority.

That would take American money, from the government and the
Jewish community, and U.S. arms. Soon after the war, the Russians
began helping the Arabs rebuild their armies. The French were keeping an Israeli order of fifty Mirage fighter planes on hold. President
Charles de Gaulle remained upset by what he thought had been an
unwarranted attack on the Arabs, and he wanted Israel to withdraw
immediately from Arab territory. The U.S., which had sold Israel
two squadrons of Skyhawk bombers for delivery at the end of 1967,
also had put an embargo on arms to the area for 135 days. When the
time period was up in December, Johnson lifted the ban and sent the
jets.

That same month, Israel's request for fifty F-4 Phantom jet fighters
hit the headlines. Eager to de-escalate tensions in the region and
check an arms race, the State Department opposed the Phantom sale.
Besides, the argument went, any dangers to Israeli security were dis-
pelled by its massive defeat of the Arab armies the previous summer.
The Pentagon agreed, and so, for a time, did LBJ.

At the urging of the Israeli Embassy, the American Jewish community begged to disagree. Israel's most influential friend in the U.S.
was treated as if he were an enemy. "LBJ told me at the ranch that
never in all his years of political life did he have such political pressure—Jewish groups and Congressional pressures," recalled Lucius
Battle, a former U.S. ambassador to Egypt who was, at the time,
assistant secretary of state for Near Eastern and South Asian affairs.
"He said, 'You have to give me more reason not to do it.'" Battle
reiterated the State Department's position that it was not in U.S.
interests to escalate the arms race in the region.[32]

But 1968 was an election year. AIPAC went to work on Congress
and the Democratic and Republican parties. Jewish organizations
mounted a PR campaign to win over the press. They encouraged
non-Jewish organizations, notably the AFL-CIO, Americans for
Democratic Action, and the American Legion, to endorse the sale. In
March, AIPAC issued a policy statement calling for the U.S. to sell

arms to Israel to bolster its security. The lobby delivered both houses of Congress: in the summer the House and the Senate passed a sense of Congress resolution calling on LBJ to go forward on the Phantom deal. The platforms of both political parties endorsed the sale of Phantoms to Israel. Presidential candidates Hubert Humphrey and Richard Nixon both supported the sale in speeches to Jewish groups.

Johnson stood firm. For once in his long political career LBJ was actually in a position to resist political pressure. He had surprised the nation in March of 1968 with a moving television speech announcing he would not run for re-election, another victim of U.S. involvement in Vietnam. Throughout his Presidency, the Israelis had been loyal to him; unlike Nasser, they had never attacked him. Unlike many American allies, Israel had never criticized U.S. policy in Vietnam. American Jews, however, had. Johnson viewed Israel much the same way he viewed Vietnam—a small country menaced by external aggression, and he was genuinely befuddled by the intense opposition to his policies among prominent Jews active in the antiwar movement. Near the end of 1968, he complained to Abba Eban about the dangers of the kind of American isolationism that would allow Israel to "go down the drain," and added, "A bunch of rabbis came here one day in 1967 to tell me that I ought not to send a single screwdriver to Vietnam, but on the other hand, should push all our aircraft carriers through the Strait of Tiran to help Israel."[33]

The President, like his predecessors and successors, proved how little he knew about the deep emotional relationship between American Jewry and Israel. Prominent Jews had well-considered arguments against LBJ's policies in Vietnam, but they were unwilling to listen to any arguments for not sending Phantoms to Israel. LBJ's close friends Feinberg and Krim spent hours trying to convince the President that sending the Phantoms was in the interests of Israel and the U.S.[34]

At the hastily arranged summit meeting between LBJ and the Soviet leader Aleksei Kosygin in Glassboro, New Jersey, in June 1967, the Russian leader had seemed obsessed by, as Johnson himself later put it, "Arabs and Israelis."[35] When Kosygin had asked why the U.S. was so supportive of Israel while the friendship of the Arab states was clearly in U.S. interests, Johnson had given his famous answer: "Because it's right." On the matter of the Phantoms, Johnson seems to have yielded to personal pressure and his own abiding respect for

the Israelis. The President announced the final agreement for the
Phantom deal in December 1968, after the election; it was, in a
sense, his going-away present to Israel. Feinberg boasted to an interviewer, "When the Phantoms were delivered to Israel, I was the only
American at the airfield."[36]

3

PEACE IN THE MIDDLE EAST: THE YEARS OF INDECISION

THE Six-Day War had changed the American Jewish community forever. A great military victory, the war was an even greater public-relations triumph for Israel in the U.S. Moshe Dayan, Israel's defense minister, became the most famous man with an eye patch in the U.S. since the Hathaway Shirt man. (Comedians joked on television that the Israeli general should be hired to make short work of the Vietnam War.) Donations from the American Jewish community poured into the UJA at record levels. U.S. economic aid to Israel jumped from á $15 million loan in 1967 to $75 million the following year, mainly to help Israel out of a financial crunch caused by the costs of war. The war had also achieved what no Zionist leader ever could have achieved, no matter how charismatic or persuasive; it had turned millions of American Jews into "Zionists," albeit distant members of the faith but total supporters of Israel nonetheless. And if any American politician thought U.S. support for Israel had grown excessive, he now had six million American Jews to answer to.

In Israel too exhilaration spread throughout the nation. There was a sense of power and invulnerability. The occupation of the West Bank convinced religious nationalists in Israel that the Jews would regain the Biblical Land of Israel. Critics called the Israeli elation "arrogance" and "religious fantasy." But among Israeli moderates, there was talk of peace. Now that Israel occupied Arab territory in the Sinai, the West Bank, the Golan Heights, and the Gaza Strip, surely the Arabs would come to the peace table.

And there was soon a change of players all around. Richard Nixon succeeded Johnson in 1969; later the same year, Eshkol died, and Golda Meir succeeded him as prime minister. Thanks to American Jewish donations and U.S. aid, she inherited a booming economy. There was also a sense of security in Israel, and what seemed a successful occupation policy engineered by Moshe Dayan. Yet no one seemed quite sure how to transform talk of peace into action. As the journalist and historian Jon Kimche has written, "When therefore the Israeli Government—and especially Mrs. Meir and her Foreign Minister, Abba Eban—spoke of Israel's desire for peace, they were giving voice to a hope and not proposing a policy."[1]

American Jews, more committed to Israel than ever before, were not about to nudge the Meir government any closer to the peace table either. No one in Israel, in fact, understood the psychological needs of the American Jewish community better than the prime minister, herself a former member of the Milwaukee Jewish community. Golda Meir would encourage the Americans' sudden emotional attachment to Zionism, embrace the biggest donors to the funds pouring dollars into Israel, and, at the same time, ignore American Jewish leaders' reservations about Israel's genuine interest in making peace with her Arab neighbors.

U.N. 242 just sat there. Dayan, still defense minister, proposed, at the urging of the Americans, an Israeli pullback from the Suez Canal, and was hammered by his prime minister and the rest of the Cabinet. Any suggestion that Israel withdraw from any part of the occupied territory was interpreted as naïve, and a clear and present danger to Israeli security. But U.S. Presidents were notorious for their eagerness at the beginning of their term in office to try to settle the Arab-Israeli conflict. In his first press conference the President called the Middle East a "powder keg" and expressed his concern about the danger of a U.S.-Soviet confrontation in the area should another war break out. The State Department initiated a series of talks with the British, French, and Russians at the U.N. through the spring and summer of 1969. Israel and its American supporters saw an imposed peace in the making.

Golda Meir returned to the United States in the fall of 1969 as prime minister of Israel. She and Nixon quickly formed a mutual admiration society. The President compared Meir to the Biblical leader Deborah and praised Israel's success at making "the land bloom." According to one report, Nixon's press secretary, Ron Ziegler, was humming the theme from the movie *Exodus* in the wings as the two leaders met.[2] Even Henry Kissinger, the national security adviser, was amazed by the rapport between the two leaders. Meir hailed Nixon as "an old friend of the Jewish people," which Kissinger in his memoirs noted with candor "was startling news to those of us more familiar with Nixon's ambivalences on that score."[3] Nixon intimates knew the President had his prejudices, and Jews numbered among them (as the rest of the world would discover reading the Watergate transcripts).

Nixon led the Israelis to believe that he was not committed to the State Department moves and was eager to set up direct contact between him and the Meir government through Kissinger and the Israeli ambassador, Yitzhak Rabin, the chief of staff during the Six-Day War.[4] The absence of Secretary of State William Rogers at the meeting reinforced the Israelis' perception of Nixon's support for Israel.

After such a cordial meeting in Washington in September, the prime minister was surprised when Secretary Rogers, in the course of a routine speech in December, announced what would be the basis of the Rogers Plan. The proposal was not much more than a gloss on 242, proposing withdrawal from most of the occupied territories, the right of Arab refugees to choose between repatriation and resettlement, and Jordanian and Israeli participation in the civic and religious life of the Old City of Jerusalem. Israel rejected the Rogers Plan, charging that it left nothing to negotiate, and, as Meir bluntly phrased it, "We didn't survive three wars in order to commit suicide . . ."[5]

American Jewish leaders followed the prime minister. The Israeli journalist and historian Simha Flapan recalls a meeting at the American Jewish Committee offices in New York shortly after Rogers's announcement during which his host excused himself to "arrange an urgent matter." Returning, he announced, according to Flapan, "The Israeli government has asked me to help arrange a demonstration protesting the Rogers Plan." Then he turned to his Israeli guest and said, "Now, Mr. Flapan, explain to us the Rogers Plan and why the Israeli government is against it." Flapan was flabbergasted. "They made it clear that they felt obliged to support the decision of a democratically elected government in Israel," Flapan recalls. "I pointed out that this particular democratically elected government in Israel was a 'National Unity' government which might collapse at any moment, change the government and force American Jews to change their line overnight [i.e., support the Rogers Plan]. They said it would be embarrassing, but they would do it." Flapan added with a shrug: "This was the American Jewish Committee—at the time the most independent Jewish organization in the U.S."[6]

Golda Meir did not encourage independence among her American Jewish supporters. At the end of 1969, the prime minister sent a telegram to Richard Nixon publicly praising his defense of "small peoples" everywhere. Like Johnson, Nixon was annoyed by the opposition of the Jewish community to his policies in Vietnam. Meir assured him of Israel's support, and a few Jewish leaders took offense.

At a meeting of the board of the World Zionist Organization in Jerusalem on New Year's Eve day 1969, Arthur Hertzberg newly appointed to "the Executive," attacked the prime minister's telegram as not only "wrong" but "counterproductive in the U.S." for Israel's image, particularly among the Jewish college students who were leaders of the antiwar movement. Making it an act of Zionism to defend the war risked turning those kids against Israel, Hertzberg argued, with some support from two other American members of the Executive. Word got back to the prime minister, who was scheduled to address the meeting the same evening. When she arrived, she asked what had been said, and the chairman offered Hertzberg the floor. Hertzberg recalls receiving a note from a colleague saying, "You've been invited to the dance, let's see if you accept the invitation." The note itself, not to mention the tension in the room, indicated how welcome dissent was during the Meir regime. After repeating his earlier remarks, Hertzberg ended his speech with: "Madame Prime Minister, if you expect to put me as a Zionist between your version of Zionism and my children, you will lose."[7]

Meir angrily debated Hertzberg's charge that she had aligned herself with U.S. policy in Vietnam, and soon after the meeting, she sent the Executive a formal letter protesting that Hertzberg had attributed "untruths" to her. Hertzberg wanted to reply, but the chairman asked him to refrain.

ON January 25 and 26, 1970, fourteen hundred Jewish leaders from thirty-one states descended on Washington to protest the Rogers Plan. AIPAC arranged appointments for them with 250 members of Congress.[8]

One reason the Americans were being asked to oppose the Rogers Plan was that Israel was trying to buy some time to come up with a peace plan of its own, or at least a consensus on what peace ought to look like. Keeping the heat on Washington was also likely to block further promises from Nixon to the Arabs. According to the British journalist Jon Kimche, well known for his contacts inside the Israeli government,

> Privately, a number of the most vocal ministers admitted that the Rogers proposals were not really as negative as the Israel Government had made them out to be, but they were particularly sensitive about outsiders making suggestions since the Government itself had neither a plan, a map or a consensus of opinion among its members on what Israel wanted as the price of peace and what they were prepared to concede.[9]

The government's foreign-policy apparatus was, in fact, mired in intrigue. Abba Eban, who had sewed up LBJ's unwavering support and whose brilliant defense of Israel in the U.N. during the Six-Day War made him the best-known and most popular Israeli among Americans of all religions, was being carefully squeezed out of the dealings between Israel and the Nixon White House. Ambassador Rabin had Kissinger's ear, and he was no fan of Eban's.[10]

One sympathizes with Meir's confusion in the face of Nixon's Middle East policies. She could not be expected to understand the power struggle going on between Nixon's national security adviser and secretary of state. Yet, the President did support the Rogers Plan, to a point. The Israelis decided to sit tight until that point was reached.

Meir was not only opposed to dealing with the Arabs, she believed any rapprochement along the lines of U.N. 242 or the Rogers Plan risked the destruction of Israel. Hostilities had continued. Egyptian troops were firing on Israelis along the canal, and the Meir government initiated the first of a series of "deep penetration" raids into Egypt on January 7, 1970. "The Rogers Plan," noted Rabin in his memoirs, "was in its death throes."[11] The closed Suez Canal, essential to Egyptian shipping and trade, and the Israeli troops alongside it were also constant reminders to the Egyptians of their impotence. Nasser went to Moscow for Soviet support, and got it, mainly by threatening to resign in favor of a pro-American president in Egypt.[12] The Israelis were worried about the consequences of increased Russian support for Egypt, which included MiG-23 fighter planes and SAM-3 missiles. On July 30, Israeli fighter planes blew four Soviet

MiGs out of the sky, about nineteen miles west of the Canal. The planes were piloted by Russians.

It was precisely that kind of craziness that Rogers wanted to avoid with a plan that called for parties in the area "to stop shooting and start talking." With the threat of increasing Russian involvement and American pressure, the Israelis accepted a cease-fire and the Rogers version of 242. The scene was once again set for peace—and once again peace was averted.

In August, Begin pulled his party out of the governing coalition, enraged over the acceptance of 242. He took his case into the streets with dire warnings about another Holocaust or Masada: giving up any part of the Occupied Territories was, he argued, a sure route to mass suicide. It was a curious turn of events. As Begin knew very well, Eshkol had accepted 242, and so, by implication, had Begin, a member of Eshkol's Unity Government.

With the possibility of the Russians across the Canal, displeasure at home, and pressure from the U.S., Meir had plenty to worry about. Then, in September 1970, the Syrians saved the day by invading Jordan. Suddenly, the Americans were forced to depend on the Israelis to keep the region from blowing up. Israeli troops moved to the Jordan River, and the Syrians retreated. Nixon was impressed. The U.S. released a shipment of forty-five more Phantoms and eighty Skyhawk bombers to Israel, which Rogers had put on hold in March in hopes of winning Soviet support for limiting the arms race between Egypt and Israel. There had been a flurry of diplomatic activity between the U.S., the Russians, and the Egyptians. Nahum Goldmann, still head of the World Jewish Congress, had received an invitation from Nasser to go to Cairo in the fall to discuss peace. The Meir government told him to stay home, the time was not right. Nasser died on September 8, 1970.

Prime Minister Meir was sitting tight. The War of Attrition was over; Israel had proved it was a "strategic asset" to the U.S. along the Jordanian border. And anyone who demanded an Israeli peace plan was simply reminded of the "three noes" of Khartoum.

And then the Israelis got another surprise: on February 4, 1971, Nasser's successor, Anwar Sadat, proclaimed in a speech to the Egyptian parliament the advent of "The Year of Decision," and proposed his own "peace initiative." According to his memoir, Sadat informed his parliament that

... if Israel withdrew her forces in Sinai to the [Sinai] Passes, I would be willing to reopen the Suez Canal; to have my forces cross to the East Bank ... to make a solemn official declaration of a cease-fire; to restore diplomatic relations with the United States; and to sign a peace agreement with Israel through the efforts ... of the United Nations.[13]

It was an extraordinary move on Sadat's part—one that has virtually been ignored by most American Jews. The Egyptian leader opened the door to peace, and the Israelis ignored his invitation, with almost tragic consequences.

Confirmation of the Sadat initiative was sent to the United Nations, and the U.N. dispatched Gunnar Jarring, the Secretary General's representative on Middle East matters whose efforts to bring both sides together since the end of the Six-Day War had been unsuccessful. This time too he got nowhere. Kissinger encouraged the Israelis to deal with Sadat. He got nowhere. The Israeli journalist Amos Elon later wrote in the Israeli daily *Ha'aretz* that Sadat's proposal threw the government of Golda Meir into "panic."[14] Israel, it seems, was no more prepared to deal with the "Sadat Plan" than the Rogers Plan.

The Meir government really didn't have a foreign policy. It certainly did not have a foreign minister with any power to make one. In addition to Rabin's efforts in Washington, Abba Eban was also competing with Moshe Dayan, who believed that foreign policy was the prerogative of the minister of defense. Eban was barely functional, and grumbling about resigning. In the spring of 1971, he drafted a response to Sadat that in effect committed Israel to 242, and thus some form of withdrawal as outlined in a previous communication with Jarring.[15] Eban's superiors added an amendment to his draft proposing withdrawal that ruled out withdrawal: "Israel," declared the addition, "will not withdraw to the pre-June 5, 1967, lines."

That was the end of Sadat's peace plan, and a serious obstacle to any future plan designed along the lines of 242, which required some kind of withdrawal from the Occupied Territories. The Egyptian leader had laid everything on the line—including recognition of Israel. In Jerusalem, Golda Meir called his speech "very nice."[16] A week later in an interview with *Newsweek* Sadat discussed his desire for "coexistence" with Israel.[17] The Egyptian president had come a long way, and the Israelis answered, in effect, that any treaty acceptable to them would retain for Israel a large chunk of Egyptian territory. Even supporters of Israel in the Nixon Administration now questioned the Meir government's interest in peace.

Sadat took the lame Israeli response as an insult. The Meir government soon applied another neat slap in Sadat's face. In 1972, the Knesset declared "that the historic right of the Jewish people to the Land of Israel was beyond challenge," and publicized plans to settle the Occupied Territories.[18] Begin and his Herut Party may have quit the government, but he would not disagree with the Laborites on the right of Jews to *Eretz Israel*. On the issue of settlements, the two sides were not really that far apart. As proof, Moshe Dayan would later authorize a Jewish settlement in Yamit, in formerly Egyptian territory. The settlers would be followers of Begin.

The domestic pressure on Sadat was intense. An official Jewish settlement on Egyptian soil would threaten his own political future. His own generals were demanding a forceful reply. A coup against Sadat was the last thing the Americans wanted. In May 1971, he had jailed the leading pro-Soviet figures in Egypt, and the next year sent his Russian advisers packing. The Nixon Administration was in a position to have the two most powerful nations in the Middle East as its own clients. But the Israelis had rejected Kissinger's pleas to deal with Sadat, and the Nixon Administration had little leverage. Israel had proved its value as a "strategic asset" in helping to scare the Syrians out of Jordan. More significantly, 1972 was a presidential election year and the worst possible time to apply pressure to Israel.

The American Jewish community was certainly in no mood to criticize Israel. On the contrary, their ambivalence toward Israel—and the resentment of Israelis toward the Americans who failed to make *aliyah*—had quickly turned into a mad love affair. Between 1967 and 1973, more than thirty thousand American Jews moved to Israel.[19] There was such a pride about Israel, and being Jewish, no one seemed willing to point to any defects in Israeli policy, at least publicly. Private disagreements, like Hertzberg's contretemps with Israel's pro-Vietnam policy, were also rare; few Jewish leaders were willing to risk the favor of the Israeli government, and thus their status as Jewish leaders. Total support of Israel had become a requirement of leadership in local Jewish communities throughout America. An American Jewish "leader" could be married to a gentile, he could be a stranger to the synagogue, but if he became a public critic of Israel, he would soon become a former Jewish leader.

It was much easier and safer to criticize American policy than Israeli policy. After the furor over the Rogers Plan, American Jewish leaders seemed to have little to do. In fact, the traditional ties between American leaders and the Israeli government were weaker than they had ever been. Ambassador Rabin did not need any American help to get access to the White House. In fact, Rabin had always disliked the traditional method of communicating with American policy makers through American Jewish leaders. "I too honored this mode of operation, though I patiently and cautiously tried to change it without offending the sensibilities of the Jewish community's leadership," Rabin writes in his memoir. "I believed that the Israeli embassy should assume the principal role of handling Israel's affairs at all political levels and that it was entitled to avail itself of the help of Jews and non-Jews alike, as it saw fit."[20] He adds, "It goes without saying that the Jewish leaders in the United States were never under my control. They are not subject to the will of the Israeli government . . ."

That's diplomatic nonsense. On one hand, Rabin insists that Jewish leaders were not in his pocket; on the other hand, he contends that he prefers Israel to use American Jewish help, "as it saw fit." Recognizing that their very status as Jewish leaders rested on Israel's good will, the leaders of the American Jewish community seldom saw fit to criticize Israeli policy, even in private. Organizing demonstrations against a Rogers Plan was less risky.

Indeed, members of Congress might have wondered what had happened to American Jewish pressure on the Hill, except for an issue unrelated to the Arab-Israeli conflict, which put American Jewish leaders back into the headlines, and into the Washington game, much to the displeasure of Henry Kissinger and Richard Nixon. In the early 1970s, with Israel apparently strong and secure in the Middle East, Jews around the world turned their concern, and the political activism that usually accompanies it, to anti-Jewish crackdowns in the Soviet Union. In 1972, American Jews decided to use the political clout generally reserved for Arab-Israeli issues to persuade the U.S. government to pressure the Soviets to lay off the Jews eager to emigrate.

In September, Senator Henry Jackson, speaking before the National Conference on Soviet Jewry, proposed linking U.S. trade benefits to emigration rights from the U.S.S.R. His idea received the overwhelming approval of 120 Jewish leaders. When Jackson introduced it as an amendment to the East-West trade bill on the Senate floor, he already had seventy-five cosponsors.[21] Nixon and Kissinger were opposed, concerned that it would harm their efforts toward dé-tente. Ohio congressman Charles Vanik introduced a similar bill in the House with 131 sponsors. Working closely with Vanik aide Mark Talisman, AIPAC rushed to the support of the measure and was able to boost the list of cosponsors in the House to 190. Throughout 1973, AIPAC's lobbying efforts were aimed at getting Jackson-Vanik passed in spite of strong opposition from the Administration.[22]

It was the worst possible time for Nixon to be faced with anti-So-viet demonstrations in the U.S. The Administration was eager to ease the tensions building in U.S.-Soviet relations. When Golda Meir ar-rived in Washington again in March 1973, Nixon and Kissinger warned her that American Jewish pressure would destroy détente, and, ultimately, Jewish emigration from Russia. According to Rabin, Nixon told the prime minister that the Senate's strategy (and the Jew-ish community's) was "self-defeating." "The Kremlin simply could not accept dictates from the American Congress," the President ex-plained. Meir tried to finesse the issue, but Nixon, according to Rabin, persisted. Rabin recalls Nixon's argument: "The problem is that the members of Congress say that they are guided by the Jewish organizations here. The future of détente . . . is liable to be foiled by the Congress. Personally, I can get better results for you." Kissinger, according to Rabin, was "brutally direct" in his warning: "Don't let the Jewish leadership here put pressure on the Congress." Both the prime minister and her ambassador made it clear that they could not overrule the American Jewish leadership on, in Rabin's words, "a cardinal issue." Adds Rabin: "Nor could I possibly take any step that would be interpreted as stabbing Senator Jackson in the back."[23]

That, of course, was the sticking point, and not the well-established practice of giving marching orders to American Jewish leaders. Henry Jackson was, in Rabin's own words, "among my most—and Israel's most—cherished friends in the Senate." He was also, at the time, a potential presidential candidate. Jackson's critics in the Senate, particularly chairman of the Senate Foreign Relations Committee Senator William Fulbright, who agreed with Nixon and Kissinger that détente was crucial, charged that Jackson was willing to sacrifice détente for his own political ambitions. A Presbyterian from the state of Washington, which has an insignificant Jewish pop-ulation, Jackson had initiated the strategy to help Soviet Jews on his own, and neither the Israelis nor American Jewish leaders wanted to abandon him.

For the White House, it was time for some quiet diplomacy. Nixon had been depending on a trio of American Jews for advice: Detroit multimillionaire Max Fisher, a Nixon supporter and Republican fund raiser; Jacob Stein, another Nixon loyalist and head of the Conference of Presidents of Major American Jewish Organizations; and Arthur Hertzberg. Fisher, a former head of the Council of Jewish Federations and Welfare Funds, chairman of the United Jewish Appeal, member of the Executive Committee of the American Jewish Committee, a major donor to the Republican Party, the new head of the Jewish Agency in the U.S., and Nixon's closest Jewish adviser, was convinced that if the Russians were pushed too hard, they would cut back on the number of Jews allowed to emigrate. Nixon told them privately that Brezhnev had promised to allow 38,500 Jews a year to emigrate to Israel provided Congress did not pass the amendment. Fisher, Stein, and Hertzberg tried to prevail upon other Jewish leaders to abandon their crusade for Jackson-Vanik.

The trio's pleas were rejected. "Not pushing for Jackson-Vanik was vetoed inside the Jewish Establishment," Hertzberg recalls. "The view was, 'Jackson has helped us a lot in the past, and he has a shot at being President.' I suspect that all around the country Jews were measuring themselves for ambassadorships in the Jackson Administration."[24]

Meantime, of course, there was Watergate, and Nixon believed détente was crucial to his survival. As he saw it, the American Jewish community was standing between him and détente; worse, a major foreign-policy defeat—a failed antidote to Watergate—might signal the end of his political career. It is not the most convincing argument in the world, but then by the fall of 1973, no one in the besieged Nixon White House was thinking very clearly.

ALMOST six years had passed since the fear for Israel's future and then the quick shift to delirium over its smashing success against the Arabs during the Six-Day War. Amidst celebrations of the twenty-fifth anniversary of the creation of the Jewish state, American Jewish intellectuals resurrected their concerns about the one-sided partnership between Israel and the American Jewish community. The American Jewish teacher, writer, and editor Leonard Fein wrote in 1973 that "a growing number of Jews in America are becoming somewhat restive, are beginning to search for a new and more mature understanding of Israel. And the time for such reassessment, painful though it must be, may be said to have arrived."[25]

Incredibly, efforts of American Jews to reassess their ties to Israel were short-circuited once again, for the same reason that they had been six years before: war in the Middle East. Between 1971 and 1973, Sadat had examined his alternatives, and decided that the only route to peace was war. Israeli and American diplomats as well as historians who have examined the period now believe that Sadat had decided that perhaps the only way to strip Israel of its arrogance and contentment with the *status quo* was to attack it. At best, Sadat figured he might recapture some Egyptian territory; at worse, the superpowers would step in, call a cease-fire, and drag Israel to the negotiating table.[26]

On October 6, 1973—the day of the most solemn religious holiday in the Jewish calendar, Yom Kippur—Egyptian forces smashed through the Bar Lev Line, crossed the Suez Canal, invaded the Sinai. Within three days, the Egyptians had demolished one hundred tanks and fifty planes, and killed hundreds of Israeli soldiers. During the next five days, Israel tottered on oblivion. The Russians threatened to intervene. The U.S. alerted its troops abroad to the possibility of war with the Russians—DEFCON III.

With American help and brilliant countertactics, Israel managed to turn the Egyptian attack into an Israeli victory. Psychologically, though, Israel had lost a major battle. The Six-Day War had produced exhilaration; Yom Kippur had brought trauma. The self-image of invincibility that they had cultivated since the Six-Day War now in doubt, Israelis slouched into a state of depression. Could their nation have been so powerful just six years before and so weak now that they had narrowly averted destruction? Their Arab enemies had obviously grown stronger than Israel had believed possible. The Yom Kippur War also demolished the reputation of Golda Meir—and that of Moshe Dayan, who had ambitions to be prime minister. Dayan was blamed for not alerting the Israelis to the growing strength of the Arab armies.

The American Jewish community was shocked. Yet it also had been too caught up in the delirium that followed the Six-Day War and in its newfound devotion to Zionism to consider Sadat's alternatives.

Israeli and American leaders seemed content with the *status quo* in the Middle East without considering the real constant of the politics of that region, namely, that the *status quo* changes regularly. They failed to recognize that Israel's near miss was perhaps due to Meir's inability to confront first the Rogers Plan and then Sadat's peace initiative in 1971. The Israeli government had been no more prepared for war, it turned out, than for peace. Nor had American Jews been prepared to criticize the Israelis for not pressing for peace. Meir, years later, admitted to an interviewer that a more rigorous debate between Israel and its critics in the Diaspora might have shaken her government out of its almost fatal arrogance.[27] However, in Israeli politics such an affection for Diaspora critics is more likely to emerge out of office than in.

AMERICAN Jews were in no mood to turn into critics of Israel in 1974, as the Meir government, blamed for the near defeat in October, struggled toward re-election at the end of 1973, losing seats to the Likud coalition headed by Begin's Herut and a group of other right-wing parties. In January 1974, Kissinger, who had replaced Rogers in the fall as secretary of state, and Dayan began negotiations with Sadat to disengage troops from the Canal area and re-create a U.N. buffer zone. Israelis perceived the move, known as First Sinai, as a victory for Sadat (and Kissinger) and additional proof that the Meir government was not fit to lead, and took to the streets to demonstrate against any disengagement. The Labor coalition could not stand the strain, and on April 10, 1974, the prime minister announced her resignation. Dayan soon followed. The new leader of Labor was Yitzhak Rabin, who, as a former chief of staff and ambassador to Washington, seemed a natural choice to supervise Israel's two crucial tasks: military readiness and U.S. relations. Whether Rabin was up to defending Labor's dominance of Israeli politics against the Likud's growing popularity remained to be seen.

For Israel's lobbyist on Capitol Hill, however, 1974 was a very good year, and a revolutionary one. AIPAC's founding director, Sy Kenen, was stepping down, U.S. aid to Israel was leaping up, and Congress would assure that Jewish donors to political campaigns would become more influential than ever.

AIPAC was Sy Kenen. Businessmen and leaders of Jewish groups sat on the board, but Kenen ran the show. "It was a mom-and-pop shop," says a source familiar with the evolution of the lobby. "Its success rested on Kenen's personality and relationships with a handful of influential members of Congress."[28] There were Brooklyn's Emanuel Celler and Speaker Carl Albert from Oklahoma in the House, and Pennsylvania's Hugh Scott as well as Jacob Javits, Hubert Humphrey, and Henry Jackson in the Senate. (When the issue of funds to help resettle Soviet Jews had come up in 1972, Albert told Kenen, "I'll lobby it through Congress.")

Outside Washington, Kenen was hardly known to most Jews. In fact, few Jews had even heard of AIPAC. When one of Kenen's lieutenants asked an audience of three hundred Jews in Memphis in 1974 how many had any idea what AIPAC was about, two raised their hands. Sy Kenen had no ambitions to become a "Jewish leader": he viewed himself more as a journalist and propagandist than as a lobbyist. He thought his job belonged out of the limelight, and he certainly did not enjoy fund raising. The *Near East Report,* AIPAC's newsletter, was Kenen's primary passion. In 1974, according to a source close to Kenen, AIPAC's operating budget didn't exceed $20,000—half went to publish the *Near East Report,* the other half financed the lobbying operation. Kenen often lent penurious staffers money out of his own pocket. The AIPAC offices at 14th and G Streets, on Capitol Hill, were dingy and cluttered.

Kenen, however, was pressing Congress for record amounts of U.S. aid for Israel—$2.2 billion for fiscal 1974—to help Israel rearm after the Yom Kippur War and prop up its sagging economy. (In 1972, total U.S. aid to Israel had been only $404 million.) Along with representatives of the American Jewish Committee and the Anti-Defamation League of B'nai B'rith, Kenen also created a "Truth Squad" to counter the growth of pro-Arab propaganda and an infant "Arab lobby" in the form of the National Association of Arab Americans established two years before as an unabashed imitation of AIPAC.[29] AIPAC worked overtime to counter charges that support for Israel had led to the oil shortages of the past year, and kept an eye on efforts in the Middle East to establish Yasser Arafat's Palestine Liberation Organization (PLO) as the "legitimate representative" of the Arabs who had fled Palestine or continued to live in the terrorities occupied by Israel since the 1967 war. Terrorism against Israel was also on the upswing, providing a strong argument for increased military aid to bolster Israel's security.

Kenen could not have chosen a better time to retire. Public support for Israel among Americans of all religions was high; so was pro-Israel feeling in Congress. But after Vietnam and Watergate, the House and Senate began to change; there were younger and more activist politicians inclined to buck their own leadership. Kenen's pals were either retiring or dying. No longer would a few strong arms be able to keep everyone in the pro-Israel line. And with U.S. aid becoming Israel's military and social lifeline, there was no variable more important in the U.S.-Israeli relationship than Congress—AIPAC's traditional turf.

"It was a new ballgame," recalls Morris Amitay, who succeeded Kenen in December 1974. "After the Yom Kippur War, Israel required billions. I wanted to make AIPAC an effective modern lobby." As one of his deputies put it, "The organization had to change. AIPAC had to move into the twentieth century."[30] Amitay was a Harvard lawyer with an M.A. and State Department experience who had also worked on the Hill as an aide to Connecticut senator Abraham Ribicoff. He was a deft enough politician to convince Jewish fund raisers that $250 million pledged to the United Jewish Appeal was impressive but insignificant compared to the billions that Israel would need to survive. The prime source of that money would have to be the U.S. Treasury.

Amitay also recognized that AIPAC would have to extend its network and concentrate on influencing—and educating—scores of young congressmen and an increasing number of senators ignorant of Middle East history and diplomacy. Many had opposed the war in Vietnam, and were now concerned that the U.S. might get dragged into another regional dispute in the Middle East.

Morris Amitay was a hard-charging activist who was as expert at ruffling feathers on Capitol Hill as Kenen was at smoothing them. Unlike the diplomatic and chummy Kenen, who tried to look at a problem from a senator's point of view—"Always feel empathy for the pressures on members of Congress," he used to advise his staff—Amitay, according to one friend, "is not only aggressive but he also looks aggressive. His style is biting, and his demeanor could never be called soft-spoken."[31] Empathy was not part of the internal machinery of the new AIPAC boss, and the egomaniacal denizens of Capitol Hill did not appreciate the head of a lobby threatening to shut off Jewish campaign funds if they didn't vote AIPAC's way.

In the past, Kenen's group had little control over that category of campaign donations known as "Jewish money." Politicians, particularly Democrats, had depended on the generosity of a small group of wealthy American Jews. John Kennedy's career had benefited from Dewey Stone, Phil Klutznick, and Abe Feinberg, who, along with Arthur Krim, also raised money for Lyndon Johnson.

Wall Street investment banking firms founded by Jewish families in the nineteenth century—Kuhn, Loeb; Lazard Freres; Goldman Sachs; Lehman Brothers—were generous to the Democratic Party. In 1964, various Lehmans gave a total of $37,000 to Democratic candidates; Andre Meyer, the head of Lazard Freres, anted up $35,000 of his own money. In 1968, John L. Loeb, his family, and partners in the firm of Carl M. Loeb, Rhoades deposited $90,500 into the Democratic coffers, while Loeb loaned another $100,000 of his own money. A few members of the New York banking crowd wrote big checks for Republicans. Kuhn, Loeb's John Schiff donated $24,500 to the GOP in 1968.[32]

Businessmen the bankers financed, like New York's Lawrence Wein, a multimillionaire real-estate developer and philanthropist, and the Tisch brothers, Laurence and Preston Robert, who own the Loews Corporation, were prime players in Democratic Party politics. On the West Coast, Jews who had made millions in the movie business also were good for huge donations. In 1968, Lew Wasserman, chairman of the entertainment and television production giant MCA and a leading member of Hollywood's "Jewish Mafia" (as the big donors were known in Democratic Party circles), was on record giving Hubert Humphrey at least $254,000. According to Stephen Isaacs's *Jews and American Politics,* of the twenty-one people who loaned more than $100,000 to Hubert Humphrey's presidential campaign in 1968, fifteen of them were Jewish, with Wasserman in the lead. The California businessman Eugene Wyman, who was active in local Jewish philanthropic activities, raised millions for Humphrey, and was known as the best miner of political gold in California at the time of his early death in 1973.[33] Max Fisher was a generous supporter of Richard Nixon. The word in political circles was that Jews were responsible for more than 30 percent and perhaps as much as 50 percent of the Democratic Party's campaign funds.

The political significance of Jewish money is a subject about which only a few politicians will even stutter an opinion. American Jews too used to maintain an intense silence on the issue—until this power source was threatened by a new campaign financing law passed in 1974, the result of the Watergate scandal. Richard Nixon's campaign organization—the Committee to Re-elect the President (CREEP)—had raised almost $17 million, an impressive figure by any measure. But even more impressive—and scandalous—was that the money had come from only 124 contributors who had given more than $50,000 each. More than 10 percent of that total—$1.7 million — had come from donors who were later rewarded with ambassadorships. Congress's remedy was the Campaign Financing Act of 1974. The new law allowed individuals to contribute $1,000 to a candidate for Congress in a primary, a runoff, and a general election—or a total of $3,000 for each American eager to help bankroll a politician. That seemed to be the end of the "fat cats."

Jewish groups had opposed the reform, and a leader of one of them, for the record, has stated why. Speaking at a symposium sponsored by *Commentary* magazine, Rita Hauser, a New York attorney who is a major force at the American Jewish Committee, frankly declared that the new campaign financing laws had "eliminated the strongest weapon the Jewish community exercised in influencing the selection of nominees in both political parties."[34] Namely, money.

Attorney Hauser was quite mistaken. She had totally underestimated the advantages of a growing phenomenon—the "political action committee," generally defined as any committee sponsored by a corporation or labor organization, trade association, or any other group of people that receives contributions or makes expenditures related to federal elections that total more than $1,000 during a calendar year. Invented by organized labor in the 1940s to offset the huge amounts of cash donated to candidates by rich Americans hostile to labor unions, the political action committee—or PAC—was a perfectly legal way to sidestep the restrictions of the 1974 campaign financing law.*

Jewish fund raisers soon realized that they could not have created a better power tool for the American Jewish community than PAC. According to the 1974 law, although one was limited to $1,000 per candidate, one could give up to $5,000 a year to a PAC and $20,000 to a political party, and a spouse and children may each donate the same amounts. No individual can donate more than $25,000 to all national candidates running in an election year. While the law restrained CREEP-ish individual donations of $50,000 from individ-

---

*The emergence of the PAC has made AIPAC's name misleading, but the group—the American Israel Public Affairs Committee—is not a political action committee. It is against the law for a lobby to solicit campaign contributions.

uals, it did not keep PACs from doling out huge amounts to favored candidates. Each PAC was limited to $15,000 a candidate, but multiply that by several committees, or scores of committees, devoted to the same issue, and the total amounts can easily outdistance the donations of the fat cats of old.

Creating political action committees turned out to be a snap for the American Jewish community, which already had in place the most impressive grass-roots fund-raising apparatus in history. (Hyperbole is hard to reach when discussing the expertise that American Jews have developed for getting fellow Jews to dig deep until it hurts, and then asking them to write another check.) The move from the fund-raising offices of the United Jewish Appeal or Jewish National Fund or Israel Bond Drives or local Federations of Jewish Philanthropies to setting up a pro-Israel political action committee was a baby step. American Jews had actually gained a stronger weapon for influencing policy. Indeed, the spread of PACs would put that weapon in the hands of more people than ever before as American Jews seemed to become interested more in pressing Congress for increased support to Israel than in making sure the Israeli government was moving toward peace in the Middle East.

Jewish leaders were quick to criticize anyone who dared criticize Israeli policy, most notably the Jewish secretary of state Henry Kissinger, who had decided to settle for less than the kind of comprehensive peace plan envisioned by U.N. 242 and the Rogers Plan and seek peace "step by step" in a series of negotiations with Egypt and Syria into the spring. His relations with the Jewish community had been cool since the end of the Yom Kippur War; many suspected that he had delayed sending U.S. arms to Israel. So in the fall, after Nixon's resignation, when Kissinger returned to his "shuttle diplomacy" with the support of President Gerald Ford, Jewish leaders and Rabin seemed more eager to battle the U.S. secretary of state than to make peace in the Middle East.

IN 1975, Kissinger was attacked regularly in the Hebrew press in Israel, and it would not be long before *Commentary* magazine, whose editor, Norman Podhoretz, had emerged as an avid Zionist only after the Six-Day War, attacked Kissinger for plotting to abandon Israel.[35] Kissinger, however, seemed willing to take some heat from his fellow Jews if progress could be made toward peace. But Israel's own inflexibility could drive him wild. He managed to keep his frustration with the Israelis under wraps for the most part, but on one occasion he let the Israeli leadership know what he thought of their "policies." It was March 22, 1975, at a time when his shuttle diplomacy looked as if it had failed, mainly because neither the Israelis nor the Egyptians were willing to make major concessions: the Israelis did not want to give up strategic passes and oil fields, and Egypt would not budge unless they did. Kissinger had just visited Masada, the famous mountain fortress where in the first century nearly a thousand Jewish "rebels" besieged by the Romans committed mass suicide rather than surrender. That sabbath, after sunset, Kissinger vented his frustration on Rabin and a group of his top Cabinet ministers.

According to transcripts of one of two meetings that evening reported by Edward R. F. Sheehan in his book *The Arabs, Israelis, and Kissinger,* the secretary of state denounced the Israeli attitude toward concessions to the Arabs as "a real tragedy" that undermined U.S. efforts to deflect international pressure to force Israel to pull back to the 1967 borders. Kissinger could not understand why Israel would not concede "a trivial" ten kilometers of territory to avoid being forced to give up all the Occupied Territories. "It's tragic," the secretary of state said, "to see people dooming themselves to a course of unbelievable peril."[36] According to one of his entourage in an interview a decade later, "Kissinger had a way of crawling out of his role as Secretary of State and becoming Professor Henry Kissinger, adviser to Israel—the person who painted the big picture, analyzed things for them, not in any inappropriate way, but sharing with Israeli leaders his reflections on things. He had just been to Masada so suicide was on his mind."[37]

But the Israelis were more focused on the narrower picture of their self-interest, then and there. Disturbed by the increased influence of the Arab world due to its wealth and oil, Israel's leaders were worried that Kissinger and Ford might be too weak to stand up to Arab threats to use the "oil weapon" against Israel's friends. For the moment, Israel preferred to stand strong, no matter the long-term consequences. Kissinger returned to Washington still steaming, and passed his bitterness toward the Israelis, like a cold, to his President. In his own biography, Ford reports that he was "mad as hell" at the Israelis, and was convinced that the Egyptians had "bent over backward," while the Israeli government was unwilling to yield anything to get anything in return.[38] At Kissinger's urging, Ford decided to lean on

Israel in an effort to break what they perceived as its intransigence. In a speech on the Middle East in March 1975, Gerald Ford called for a "reassessment" of U.S. policy.

The Jewish leadership flipped. "Reassessment" was interpreted as abandonment. And if anyone doubted the possibility that the "special relationship" between Israel and the U.S. would no longer be so special, Ford conspicuously delayed delivery of weapons to Israel, including the F-15 fighter plane; the Administration also suspended negotiations for pending financial and military aid to Israel. Kissinger then met with former government officials and Middle East experts known to be critical of Israeli policy or suspected of being pro-Arab; he instructed the State Department and the Pentagon to explore future alternatives to the traditionally close relations between the U.S. and Israel.[39] (All a Jewish leader had to do was close his eyes and he could see the shades of Eisenhower and Dulles.)

A consensus emerged—and it was precisely what the Israelis and their supporters in the U.S. had resisted since the Six-Day War. The Kissinger/Ford new route to peace in the Middle East looked very much like U.N. 242 and the Rogers Plan: it was time, most experts agreed, to adopt a peace plan based on withdrawal to the pre-1967 borders, provided Israel's security could be guaranteed. The key to this new-old approach would be something very new indeed: a speech by the President of the United States spelling out America's basic interests in the Middle East, which required Israeli withdrawal.

Gerald Ford never got to make his great speech on the Middle East. The President and his secretary of state seemed to have miscalculated the power of the Presidency—and the strength of the pro-Israel lobby. Henry Kissinger had just tossed a bomb into the American Jewish community, and it quickly, and expertly, heaved it back.

AIPAC shifted into high gear on Capitol Hill. Within three weeks, after considerable wrangling and wheedling in the halls of Congress, there arrived in the White House mail a letter dated May 21, 1975, and signed by seventy-six U.S. senators confirming their support for Israel, and suggesting that the White House see fit to do the same. The language was tough, the tone almost bullying. The senators suggested a "reassessment" quite contrary to what Ford and Kissinger had in mind. The letter made it quite clear that the senators saw Israel as a crucial check to Soviet influence in the region, and that "withholding military equipment from Israel would be dangerous." The letter's key paragraph warned the President that

> within the next several weeks, the Congress expects to receive your foreign aid requests for fiscal year 1976. We trust that your recommendations will be responsive to Israel's urgent military and economic needs. We urge you to make it clear, as we do, that the United States acting in its own national interests stands firmly with Israel in the search for peace in future negotiations, and that this premise is the basis of the current reassessment of U.S. policy in the Middle East.[40]

What Henry Kissinger said or did when he received this letter bomb is not known. But the "letter of 76," as it was called, definitely exploded his efforts to reassess U.S. policy. Kissinger's advisers agreed that a presidential speech was now politically out of the question. The Administration returned to pursuing peace in the Middle East step by step.

It was an impressive bit of lobbying. The "letter of 76" featured the predictable names, the loyal "friends of Israel"—Senators Jackson and Mondale and Case and Stone. But George McGovern signed it too, even though he quickly got back on the record supporting Israeli withdrawal from the territories and negotiations with Yasser Arafat. Daniel Inouye, a senator from Hawaii, liked boasting about how impervious he was to Jewish pressure since Jews were as rare in Hawaii, as an aide once boasted to some reporters, "as snowflakes." He signed the letter. "It's easier to sign one letter than answer five thousand," said Inouye, alluding to the mail he would receive from non-Hawaiians on an issue related to Israel. Iowa's John Culver had told a fellow senator that he wouldn't sign because it would tie the Administration's hands and encourage Israeli inflexibility. Culver's name was on the letter. He later admitted to a colleague, "The pressure was too great. I caved."[41]

There was plenty of grumbling in the Senate cloakroom after the letter became public. Many of those who signed weren't happy with their behavior. A colleague heard Senator Edward Kennedy say, "You know, we get picked off one by one. They really beat us over the head with this goddamned letter. . . . Why don't we all try to get together, and the next time any issue like that comes up again talk to each other first before any of this singular picking-off stuff."[42] Still bothered five years later, Senator Charles Mathias publicly admitted in an article in *Foreign Affairs* about "Ethnic Groups and Foreign Policy" that due to lobbying pressure, "Seventy-six of us promptly affixed our signatures although no hearings had been held, no debate conducted, nor had the Administration been invited to present its views."[43] Mathias added that "as a result of the activities of the [pro-Israel] lobby, congressional conviction has been measurably reinforced by the knowledge that political sanctions will be applied to any who failed to deliver."

Kissinger and Ford, however, may have made a gross tactical error. In their anger, they made it appear that the U.S. was about to lean on Israel, which was bound to force the American Jewish leadership to pull together to give their own appearance of solidarity with Israel. In truth, since the shock of the Yom Kippur War, there was a growing dissatisfaction among American Jewish leaders about Israel's willingness to pursue peace, which the Administration might have tapped on its behalf. Some were concerned that Israel no longer really wanted to trade even some of the territories occupied in the 1967 war for peace; indeed, the Labor government had already authorized a few Jewish settlements in the formerly Arab lands, confirming Arab fears that Israel never intended to withdraw and forcing American Jews to wonder whether Israel would ever face up to its Palestinian problem. There were Israelis too who were worried about the increasing militance and intransigence of their government. Some well-known politicians and military figures had become the focus of a growing peace movement in Israel. The American dissidents identified with these Israeli "doves."

As the Administration was making its stand, there was evidence of a "reassessment" of sorts taking place among American Jews. The moving force was a small group of American Jewish intellectuals and rabbis who worked on college campuses, and young activists from the civil rights and antiwar movements, who called themselves Breira—the Hebrew word for "alternative" or "choice."[44] The choice Breira offered American Jews was to ally themselves with the forces of peace and moderation in Israel. Founded in 1973 as a Project of Concern in Israel-Diaspora Relations, by mid-decade the group had grown to between seven hundred and one thousand members committed to an alternative—a *Zionist* alternative—for supporting Israel while coming to terms with the need for Israel to face up to its Arab problem.

During 1975, Breira prepared and distributed the group's manifesto:

> Our immediate and overriding concern is peace in the Middle East. Our concern grows out of our love and respect for the people and the land of Israel as well as our understanding that the continuity of Jewish life in the Diaspora is inextricably linked to the existence of Israel.
>
> We are not innocent bystanders. If we share the anxieties about Israel's policies, we have the responsibility to say so. If we detect mistakes which might have catastrophic consequences, we must not ignore or swallow our concern. . . .

There followed a paraphrase from Isaiah 62:1: "For the sake of Zion, we shall not be silent."[45]

Israeli doves bestowed their blessing on the group, and in the spring of 1975, Breira sponsored a speaking tour of the U.S. by one of Israel's most prominent, and controversial, proponents of negotiating with the Arabs, the retired general Mattityahu Peled. The tour, however, only confirmed that most American Jews were still unwilling to criticize Israel openly, and resented any efforts to do so, even by an Israeli general. Upon his return home, Peled wrote in a magazine article that he had found American Jews uneasy with dissenting from Israeli policies and thus "more Israeli than the Israelis."[46] Peled complained further that the Jewish community was "supporting the most intransigent views in Israel on the Arab-Israeli conflict, in belief that this is expected of it, and oblivious of the fact that Israel is not monolithic politically and the hard line taken by the Israeli government is seriously challenged within Israel."[47]

Efforts to stifle, or ignore, the kind of dissent that Breira and he were espousing, Peled charged, did "tremendous damage" to Israel in the U.S. by only reinforcing the image of Israel as "a society of conservative chauvinists of whom nothing can be expected except intransigence and a desire for war." Clear proof of Peled's charge that American Jews preferred to be "more Israeli than the Israelis" and hostile to any U.S. criticism of the current policies of the Rabin government came in AIPAC's attack on the Ford-Kissinger "reassessment," which was a manifestation within the U.S. government of the same concerns Israeli doves had about their government's policies.

Nevertheless, there remained pockets of support among Establishment Jewish groups for taking a closer look at Israeli policies. In June, the Central Conference of American Rabbis, the official representative American Reform movement on rabbinical matters, adopted a resolution on "Freedom of Speech" that noted "with interest and favor" the debate in Israel about peace. Applauding "the openness that is present in Israel," the rabbis called upon American Jews to recognize this "diversity," and urged similar open debate in the U.S. "No subject, including options for a solution to a Palestinian problem, should be ignored," the group declared.[48]

Such "openness" was not to be; in fact, quite the opposite tactic was already in the works, and the main victim was Breira. Breira's sin was to say what many Jews were thinking. Between 1973 and 1976, the group, with the help of its own well-edited magazine, *Interchange,* successfully stirred up some home-grown dissent from Israeli policies. Breira soon won the attention of *The New York Times* and the Washington *Post,* the latter running a story in April 1976 headlined "American Jews Beginning to Go Public in Criticism of Israel." But as Breira tried to draw American Jews into its dissenting, other loyal, center Zionist groups attacked it for being on the radical fringe, anti-Israel, and, worse, a dangerous cell of PLO supporters.

According to Paul Foer, whose undergraduate thesis, "The Attack on Breira," gives a detailed account of the issues and events surrounding the controversy, a Hadassah newsletter branded Breira as "cheerleaders for defeatism," and suggested the group was allied to the neo-facist U.S. Labor Party, headed by Lyndon LaRouche, not known for his affection for Jews. An editorial in a West Coast Jewish weekly attacked the group as "a creation of . . . a coterie of left-wing revolutionaries." Sy Kenen, still editing AIPAC's *Near East Report,* charged that Breira had "undermined U.S. support for Israel."

Over the next few months Breira was pilloried and smeared by American Jewish and Zionist groups around the country. The Greater Washington Jewish Community Council refused Breira membership, and passed a resolution deploring its existence.[49] The Zionist Organization of America weighed in with its own nasty attack on Breira in September 1976 in the form of an article in the *American Zionist* headlined, "Why Our Doves Are Pigeons." Any Jewish "dove" who supported Palestinian rights, the article charged, was really "an unhealthy dangerous pigeon." The ZOA struck out against Breira a few months later with another article describing the group as the "Jewish spokesman of the PLO and the mythical Palestinians." The ZOA tried to get one Breira member, a rabbi, removed from his job at the national offices of the Hillel Foundation. B'nai B'rith initiated an investigation into Breira in an effort to come up with an official position toward the dissidents. Breira leaders were summoned to the Israeli consulates in Philadelphia and Boston. To prove their loyalty to Israel, they went, and were told that criticism of Israeli policy amounted to an attack against the state.[50]

"We were immediately put on the defensive and never had any time to discuss the real issues," recalls Arthur Samuelson, the editor of *Interchange* and now an editor at Summit Books.[51] Breira insisted it was a loyal Zionist group. Many of its members were young American Jews who, like Samuelson, had lived in Israel, knew Hebrew, and followed events in the Holy Land much closer than most of the American Jewish Establishmentarians who were now questioning their motives. Breira had attracted many young Jewish liberals and a few well-known rabbis who held positions in Jewish life, like Rabbi Balfour Brickner, a top official in the Reform rabbinate (now a rabbi at the Stephen Wise Free Synagogue in New York City), and Joachim Prinz, a legendary Zionist figure who had been a rabbi in Berlin during Hitler's rise and had served as head of the Presidents' Conference. Unlike the leaders of other American Jews, they were prepared to echo in public the position of the Israeli doves that there was no route to peace in the Middle East without taking seriously the cause of Palestinian self-determination.

One of the few major Jewish leaders to defend Breira's right to dissent was Rabbi Alexander Schindler, the president of the Union of American Hebrew Congregations, the official representative of the Reform movement on nonrabbinical matters, who compared the attacks on Breira to "a witch hunt."[52] Schindler's backhanded support for dissent was significant because he had been recently selected for a two-year stint as head of the Presidents' Conference, and seemed bent on remaking the Conference into an American Jewish voice loyal to but independent of Israel—"to create a dialogue of equals," as the American Jewish leader put it in an interview with the Israeli dovish magazine *New Outlook* in early 1976.

The Presidents' Conference and its members have been instruments of official governmental Israeli policy. It was seen as our task to receive directions from government circles and to do our best no matter what to affect the Jewish community. For a whole host of reasons, I think it is not acceptable. American Jewry is in no mood to be used by anyone. If their help is needed, then they would like to be involved in the decision-making process.[53]

It was ironic that Schindler's own reassessment of the partnership between American Jews and Israel was published in Israel at the same time AIPAC was whipping up opposition to the Ford "reassessment" of U.S.-Israeli relations. No less ironic was that Schindler seemed to be supporting the very kind of debate among American Jews that Breira was calling for, and Breira was about to be clobbered by American Jewish groups quite happy to do Israel's bidding —the very habit that Schindler was eager to kick. No matter how hard Schindler might try to change the relationship between the two largest Jewish communities in the world, Jerusalem preferred an *unequal* partnership with American Jews.

IN the middle of 1976, Rabin summoned three Israeli academics for what one of them described seven years later as "an incredible meeting."[54] The professors were all American-born and had some experience working for or closely with U.S. Jewish organizations. Rabin quickly stated the purpose of the meeting: his government was worried about growing public criticism among American Jews of Israeli policies. No one expected Diaspora Jews to agree with everything Israel did, but in the past, criticism had been "in house." Jewish leaders made their views known to Israel's ambassador or even to the prime minister. There was no need, the argument went, to let non-Jews, particularly American policy makers, know that American Jews were not solidly behind everything Israel did. Jewish leaders did not support bitter criticisms on the op-ed page of *The New York Times*. Rabin was talking about Breira.

"Anyone who knew Breira knew that it was certainly no threat to the security of Israel," said one of the men who met with Rabin. "Yet the Prime Minister of Israel was so worried that he called us in and asked us to tell him what to do. We were quite amazed because we knew that Rabin's adviser on Arab affairs had just quit because he could never get a meeting with him, and here we were taking up two hours of the Prime Minister of Israel's time discussing this small group of American Jewish dissenters. Rabin was in a panic. It was symptomatic about the worry over dissent." Recalling the meeting, this same Israeli professor said he was "overwhelmed by [Rabin's] ignorance of the American Jewish community and the assumption that he knew everything about it."

The word soon went out from Jerusalem to bury Breira. From his days as ambassador in Washington, Rabin had never been comfortable with any American Jewish role in shaping Israeli policy. He and Golda Meir had worked directly with their friends in the White House, not through American Jewish leaders or lobbyists. Rabin would now show what happened to American Jews who disagreed. (The same Rabin, incidentally, who had once told Nixon and Kissinger he had no control over American Jews when they had warned the Israelis that Jewish support for the Jackson-Vanik amendment would undercut détente.)

At the time the Breira people were not sure who was behind it all. "It felt like an orchestrated campaign," says Samuelson. "We heard rumors that the Israelis were behind it, but we could never be sure." The best clue was a slick pamphlet called "Breira: Counsel for Judaism" that members of the Jewish community began receiving at the end of 1976 and January 1977. The author was an American sociologist named Rael Jean Isaac, whose sympathies for the ultra-right-wing religious nationalists in Israel, including the Gush Emunim, were not as well known in 1977, as they are now. Her sponsor, the Americans for a Safe Israel, was equally obscure, though the group has since emerged as an increasingly vocal segment of the pro-Israel lobby, far-right division. With shaky facts and a shakier argument, Isaac attacked—some say slandered—Breira, *ad nauseam,* as a front group for anti-Zionists and the PLO. "If Jews want to organize on behalf of [Yasser Arafat's] Fatah, that is their privilege," Isaac declared. "But let them call it 'Jews for Fatah' and not Breira."

Breira held its first annual meeting in February 1977. It was also its last. As the furor against the group grew, as the bogus attacks on its loyalties accelerated, Breira itself had become the issue, not dissent in the Diaspora, the peace movement in Israel, the Palestinians on the West Bank, or peace in the Middle East. Internal ideological battles between Breira's far left and center also threw its future in doubt. Attacked by the Jewish Establishment, branded as "anti-Israel" from synagogue pulpits around the country, Breira's money and membership dried up, and so did Breira. Its leaders went their separate ways; those, like Samuelson, eager to stay active in Jewish life could not find jobs. "There may have been an organized conspiracy to destroy us, but it really didn't matter," says Samuelson. "American Jews didn't have to be manipulated. All someone has to do is whistle a tune, and everyone else improvises. Showing our dirty laundry in public, giving aid and comfort to Israel's enemies, is not allowed in American Jewish life. Various organizations competed for the pleasure of destroying us to please the Israelis."

Why did even those who shared most, if not all, of Breira's criticism of what was happening in Israel not support the group, or, worse, cooperate with the ZOA and the Rabin government to destroy it? "When Arthur Hertzberg went to Israel, he was a dove," recalls Samuelson with considerable bitterness. "When he returned to the United States, he was a hawk." Why?

"It was not an idea whose time had come," says Hertzberg of Breira. "So long as Labor was in power, I believed at that time there still could be a coalition. That for the right price Labor would settle. I believed at the time that one could be more effective inside the government. The Israeli government wanted to prove to the kids that you couldn't be in opposition and survive."[55] Now the most vocal and omnipresent dissident in American Jewish life, Hertzberg thinks back on the Breira battle with some pain, and regret. "I was wrong," he admits.

Breira was the victim of overzealous Zionism, at best, and, at worst, McCarthyite tactics. Its demise, however, was simply more proof that even when American Jews were uneasy about Israeli policy, they were still unwilling to criticize Israel publicly—and more than willing to hammer anyone who did, as AIPAC's "letter of 76" has proved beyond any doubt. The death of Breira was also proof of a revolution in American Jewish politics from which AIPAC was emerging as the most powerful leader in the community on any issue relating to Israel. By attacking Breira, Jewish leaders had turned over much of their power to AIPAC, Israel's most loyal agent in the U.S. and a proved enemy of dissent from Israeli policies, among Jews as well as gentiles. Time, in fact, had run out for the American Jewish leadership, at least the majority of leaders, who, like Hertzberg, had always aligned themselves with Israel's Labor Party. No American Jewish leader seemed to be paying close enough attention to the social and political changes taking place in Israel.

The Labor Party and its dominance of Israeli life was moribund. Dissent, ironically, was about to win out in Israel, but it was not the critical voices of the doves that were to be heard. It was the voice of the most vocal and persistent dissident politician in Israeli politics since the creation of the state—the man who had battled Ben-Gurion's vision before day one, who had demonstrated in the streets against German reparations, who had opposed U.N. 242, who had

quit Golda Meir's government over the Rogers Plan, who would galvanize the voters of the Jewish state, and who would stir up more
doubts about the future of Israel among American Jewish leaders:
Menachem Begin.

4

JIMMY CARTER'S "JEWISH PROBLEM"

THROUGHOUT his long, and remarkable, campaign for the Presidency in 1975 and 1976, Jimmy Carter stressed his commitment to preserving the "integrity" of Israel. In a major campaign speech in mid-June 1976, the Sunday-school teacher from Plains, Georgia, stood in a synagogue in Elizabeth, New Jersey, wearing a blue-velvet yarmulke, and told his Jewish audience, "I worship the same God you do; we [Baptists] study the same Bible you do." And then moving on to the point of it all, Carter declared to a happy, applauding crowd that "the survival of Israel is not a political issue. It is a moral imperative."[1]

During the campaign, Carter publicly raised what by then had become familiar buzz words of Middle East diplomacy: the "special relationship" between the U.S. and Israel, both democracies; the need for "direct negotiations" between the Arabs and the Israelis; the importance of U.N. Resolution 242. "The heart of the matter," declared candidate Carter, was that "peace in the Middle East depends more than anything else on a basic change of attitudes." That meant Arab recognition and diplomatic relations with Israel, a peace treaty, open frontiers, and an end to the Arab economic boycott on Israel.[2]

The time had passed for "the small steps" that had worked so well for Henry Kissinger. Most experts (including Henry Kissinger) seemed to agree that no matter who won the election, it was time for the U.S. to make a major move toward peace in the Middle East.

Jews were skeptical of Jimmy Carter, a Southern Baptist with no experience in Washington or with the American Jewish community, which, in the beginning of the campaign, was lined up behind Senator Henry Jackson. No matter how good the candidate's intentions seemed toward Israel, no prominent American Jewish leader could boast that Jimmy Carter was his friend. When the New York businessman Howard Samuels invited 150 Jewish notables from the Northeast to meet the candidate, only 40 showed up. "They totally misunderstand the man, and are scared to death of him," the embarrassed Samuels told a reporter.[3] Carter worked hard during the 1976 primary season to change that, and had considerable success as his candidacy became increasingly stronger. Members of the Jewish Establishment, such as Edward Sanders, a Los Angeles attorney who was president of AIPAC, and Paul Zuckerman, president of the United Jewish Appeal, joined his campaign staff in Atlanta. In the final weeks of the campaign, the executive director of AIPAC, Morris Amitay, made it so clear whom the pro-Israel lobby was backing that a Ford aide joked, "If Ford should win, Morris Amitay will have twenty-four hours to get out of town." Sy Kenen himself, in retirement, voiced some concern about AIPAC's partisan stance.[4] Ford, of course, didn't win, but he did manage to win more than 30 percent of the Jewish vote.

A week before his inauguration, Carter noted that "there is a fine opportunity for dramatic improvements" in the Middle East.[5] Three years after the Yom Kippur War, Arab leaders were showing moderation, Israel's Labor government was showing flexibility, and both sides seemed willing to go to Geneva for peace talks. The time for peace had never seemed better—or more necessary, since, as Vice President Walter Mondale later noted in a speech the following summer, "conflict there carries the threat of a global confrontation and runs the risk of nuclear war."[6]

Ten days after his inauguration, the new President was already holding meetings on the Middle East with his secretary of state, Cyrus Vance; his national security adviser, Zbigniew Brzezinski; and his old friend from Georgia Andrew Young, whom the President had named his representative to the U.N. There were two more meetings in February, the second after Vance's trip to the Middle East. "It was agreed the peace initiative in the Middle East was of the highest importance," writes Brzezinski in his 1983 memoir of his stint as Carter's national security adviser.[7]

•   •   •

CARTER, Vance, and Brzezinski all seemed to agree that it was crucial to move as fast as possible, that very quickly domestic political concerns—the 1978 congressional elections and the 1980 presidential go-around—would get in the way. Brzezinski emphasized that "there would be no breakthrough to peace without U.S. persuasion of Israel," because, his argument went, "no Israeli politician could take the responsibility for advocating a genuine compromise unless he could make also the added argument that otherwise U.S.–Israeli relations would suffer."[8] Carter had to move in his first year or else risk the financial support and general irritation of the American Jewish community. Brzezinski contends that this tactic had the support of Carter's political advisers, "though in the later phases of the Presidency both [Hamilton] Jordan and Mondale swung around and urged Carter to avoid any actions which might irritate the American Jewish community."

From the start, Jewish leaders had been worried about Brzezinski. In an article in *Foreign Policy*, Brzezinski had written that the psychological and political realities in the Middle East pointed to abandoning Kissinger's "step-by-step" approach to peace in favor of a negotiated comprehensive settlement with the U.S. and the Soviet Union as brokers. To American Jews, that looked like imposing peace on Israel rather than permitting the Israelis to negotiate it directly. Brzezinski's article also criticized the "inherently rigid" political situation in Israel, which was unable to face up to "trading the occupied territories for Arab acceptance of partition of the old Palestine mandate territory between Israel and what probably would be a PLO-dominated state of Palestine on the West Bank and Gaza Strip."[9] To American Jews, that sounded like a Palestinian state sitting right down the road from the Israeli Knesset.

Exhibit Number Two was Brzezinski's role (and that of NSC aide William Quandt, an academic specialist in Middle East affairs) in preparing the controversial Brookings Report issued in December 1975.[10] The study also proposed territorial withdrawal and Palestinian "self-determination." It was additional evidence for suspecting that Brzezinski would be pulling the Administration in the direction of the Arabs. Few critics, however, noted that two prominent American Jewish leaders—Rita Hauser of the American Jewish Committee and the omnipresent Philip Klutznick—had also signed the Brookings peace proposal.

Knowing where Brzezinski stood, American Jews were not sure

what to expect of Jimmy Carter—so they did what came naturally and expected the worst.

During his first year in office, Jimmy Carter pursued, according to one Carter Middle East specialist, "an ambitious Middle East policy without the usual preoccupation with domestic political considerations."[11] In fact, Carter seemed *too* involved with the Middle East. It seemed to those around him as partly "a religious preoccupation" and partly an eagerness to score big early in his Administration. "Our scenario wouldn't have been quite the same," recalls the aide. "But we saw the Middle East as a major priority and we were happy that the President did too." Vance writes in his book about his tenure as Carter's secretary of state: "I was very much aware that the Israelis were acutely nervous about our newborn activism and I did not want us to appear to be rushing things."[12]

The literature and oral tradition of the Carter years is filled with theories about Carter being the dupe of Brzezinski and Vance.[13] In fact, Vance and Brzezinski seem to have been more conscious of the political consequences of rushing peace than Carter, who seemed to believe that if he could withstand the heat from the American Jewish community, it would eventually disappear, and peace would take its place. Instead, Carter got burned.

In an interview, Vance recalled how impressed he was with Carter's willingness at the outset "to risk being a one-term President, if it meant bringing peace to the Middle East."[14] Yet, well aware of the political implications of the kind of comprehensive settlement he had in mind, Vance saw no reason to press their luck and move ahead any faster than necessary. Brzezinski seemed to agree. They intended to begin with the least controversial points and move toward the stickier ones. Thus Vance and Brzezinski were eager to push security, border questions, and the nature of the peace. "Then we would raise the questions needed to solve that trilogy. The Palestinian issue was clearly the most sensitive, and we wanted to stay away from that one for the time being," says a Middle East expert familiar with the policy decisions of the Carter Administration.

ON March 16, 1977, Jimmy Carter disrupted that plan. In a speech to a town meeting in Clinton, Massachusetts, the President declared that dealing with the Palestinian problem was "a requirement of peace." Carter continued:

The Palestinians claim up 'til this moment that Israel has no right to be there, that the land belongs to the Palestinians, and they've never given up their publicly professed commitment to destroy Israel. That has to be overcome. There has to be a homeland provided for the Palestinian refugees who have suffered for many, many years.[15]

That final sentence was like putting a match to a stick of dynamite and throwing it into the American Jewish community. Nevertheless, the President picked up some influential supporters. The Washington *Post*, *The Christian Science Monitor*, and *The New York Times* all reacted favorably to the Clinton statement. A *Times* editorial called his remarks a "wise policy," an outline that held the prospect of "real peace, real withdrawal and a real solution to the problem of the Palestinians."[16] The Clinton statement, however, had caught everyone by surprise—including Carter's own advisers. "The problem was that the remark was *his*; 'Palestinian homeland' was Carter's own usage," recalls a former Middle East specialist in the Carter Administration. "Jimmy Carter was not yet sensitive to the code words of the Arab-Israeli debate. He just threw the phrase out—it was not even part of his prepared remarks—and it evoked the first negative response to his policy." Brzezinski, in his memoir, refers to the Clinton gaffe as "spontaneous and unexpected," and recalls telling the Israeli ambassador "that in my judgment the word 'homeland' had no special political connotation."[17]

The Administration's policy was not that there ought to be an independent Palestinian state but that there had to be some sort of Palestinian "entity," preferably linked with Jordan, which was already populated by a Palestinian majority. The actual nature, boundaries, and political status of this kind of "homeland" were matters for negotiations. But two things were clear: (1) to get this option, the Palestinians (and thus their designated representative, the PLO) would have to abandon terrorism and recognize Israel; and (2) for a negotiated peace to endure, the Palestinians would have to have a role in those negotiations.

Israel agreed with the first point and was fiercely opposed to the second.

Carter does not even mention the Clinton episode in his memoirs. "The whole thing made Mondale very nervous," recalls a Carter foreign-policy adviser. "But we decided to write it off as a stumble. It was basically consistent with our views anyway, and we figured it might shake people up and change the approach to the problem. But what it did was set off alarms in the Jewish community."[18]

The alarms, in fact, were already ringing. The Clinton remark was the second time in nine days that Carter's lack of Washington experience and disregard of the code words of Middle East diplomacy had landed him in boiling water. On March 7, he had received Israeli prime minister Yitzhak Rabin, a meeting Carter later described as an "unpleasant surprise."[19] In the opinions of both Brzezinski and Vance, the Carter-Rabin talks, in Brzezinski's phrase, "did not go well."[20] Carter was annoyed at what he saw as Rabin's "reticence" and inflexibility regarding negotiations with the Arabs, particularly the Palestinians. Vance, according to Brzezinski, had told him he thought the Israelis were "stonewalling" it.[21]

The Israeli prime minister also did not help warm up the meeting much by refusing the President's invitation during a private meeting to look in on his sleeping daughter, Amy. Rabin had listened to the President, and immediately sized him up as a supporter of the dreaded Brookings Report, and, perhaps more dangerous, as a neophyte in Middle East diplomacy. Rabin also met with American Jewish leaders, and sent the word out that the President wanted total withdrawal from the Occupied Territories. Vance denied that the policy was flat-out withdrawal. Again, confusion emerged because Carter had decided, as he puts it in his memoirs, "to plow some new ground" on the issue of Israel's borders, and then proceeded to plow into dangerous territory. The President suggested the possibility of establishing "two different borders for Israel—one marking the limits of national sovereignty and the other, farther out, forming a defense perimeter, with Israeli or international forces in between to guard Israel against attack."[22]

The American Jewish community, like Rabin, read that as withdrawal. Jimmy Carter already had a domestic political problem on his hands—and even after the Clinton hubbub, he still didn't get the message.

Rabin returned to Israel concerned that "Israel would probably have to pay heavily until the new American government acquired expertise and political maturity."[23] The Israeli leader, however, had his own domestic political problems to contend with; elections in Israel were imminent, and any softening of his government's position toward the PLO and a Palestinian state would hurt him at the polls. Rabin insisted that an independent Palestinian state between Israel and Jordan was out of the question, though, he added, "We have no objection to Palestinians being included in [a] Jordanian delegation" at any Geneva talks. Rabin also said that his government "would be prepared to share control over the West Bank with Jordan, placing the Jordanians in charge of the Arab civil administration and Israel in charge of security matters."[24]

The Carter people failed to notice that Rabin was opening a door to genuine negotiations, with Palestinian participation. Had he grabbed Rabin's offer—instead of seeming to press for an independent Palestinian state—Carter might have pushed the peace process forward immediately, and shielded himself from further criticism from American Jews who were worried that he wanted to give up too much to the Arabs (though they too had not seemed to notice how much Rabin was willing to concede).

Instead, by mid-June, Israel's friends on Capitol Hill, with the help of AIPAC, circulated a list of twenty-one grievances against the Carter Administration, including a demand for the dismissal of a few of Carter's Middle East experts. Letters poured into the White House, criticizing the Administration's "pro-Arab" policies. A board member of the Zionist Organization of America candidly told *Time* magazine, "People thought they had seen a Jewish lobby operate before. They haven't seen anything yet."[25] That unveiled threat soon became a reality.

The attitude of American Jewish leaders had turned from suspicion to outright hostility. In the history of the pro-Israeli lobby, no one had seen anything like what Jewish leaders had in store for Jimmy Carter, the man whom nearly 70 percent of Jewish voters backed in 1976. "If Carter had said in October what he has been saying this spring, he would not be in the White House," a New York rabbi told *Time*.[26] Carter's political operatives took no action, other than reassuring Jewish leaders. Jewish leaders, however, remained convinced that they smelled a double cross. Carter couldn't seem to do anything that might satisfy the American Jewish community.

"THEN," Carter writes in his memoirs, "on April 4, 1977, a shining light burst on the Middle East scene for me. I had my first meetings with President Anwar Sadat of Egypt, a man who would change history and whom I would come to admire more than any other leader."[27] Sadat proved flexible where Rabin wouldn't budge. He discussed an end to the trade boycott on Israel, and he was willing to discuss diplomatic recognition of Israel and "some minimal deviation from the 1967 borders . . . provided the Palestinian issue is resolved."

Sadat was betting everything on Carter's being able to lead the way to peace, which would then allow him to work single-mindedly at solving the political, economic, and social problems that were ripping Egypt apart. When he came to Washington in April 1977 to find out how serious Carter really was, the Egyptian leader, according to Vance, "wanted to be absolutely confident that Carter was committed to carrying through despite the domestic political problems he would have to face."[28] Carter and Vance assured Sadat that the American President was up to those pressures.

At the time, it was not an unreasonable hope. The Rabin government seemed willing to sit down and deal with the Arabs, including the Palestinians. There was good reason to believe that the Israelis would work with Carter, and thus keep American Jewish leaders and Israel's friends in Congress in line.

Those assumptions vanished a month later when Menachem Begin was elected prime minister of Israel. Labor blamed Carter's policy shifts for its defeat. "If Israel was unable to rely upon the United States as a friend and ally," Rabin offered in explanation of his defeat, "then she would have to entrust her fate to a 'tough' and 'uncompromising' leadership to protect her vital interests."[29] To the Israeli electorate, those qualities described none other than Menachem Begin. Rabin, however, disingenuously avoids any mention of the series of political scandals charging Labor officials with corruption that hurt the party at the polls. He also fails to mention that he had to withdraw his name from the race because of a scandal over allegations that he and his wife had kept secret bank accounts in the United States.

Carter later wrote about the news of Begin's election: "Israeli citizens, the American Jewish community, and I were shocked. None of us knew what to expect."[30] Actually, the Israelis had a pretty good idea, having lived with Begin for almost thirty years. The President also got a hint of what to expect from Begin when he reviewed a videotape of the Israeli leader discussing his policies during the campaign. Carter confided to his diary that it had been "frightening to watch his adamant position on issues that must be resolved if a Middle Eastern peace settlement is going to be realized."[31]

In Begin's opinion the West Bank had always belonged to Israel, and had been "liberated" in the Six-Day War of 1967. Carter, of course, recognized that this remark "seemed to throw United Nations Resolution 242, for which Israel had voted, out the window." He reported in his 1982 memoir, *Keeping Faith*, "I could not believe what I was hearing."

A little reading in Zionist history would have helped. Begin's views hadn't changed since he had been a young Revisionist Zionist leader in Poland before World War II. As most Israelis knew (and a few Americans), the symbol of Begin's Irgun—the forerunner of his Herut Party, which dominated the Likud coalition that had pushed Begin into the prime minister's office—was a hand grasping a rifle in the foreground, and in the background was a map of the territory on both sides of the Jordan River (including what is now King Hussein's Jordan). The slogan across it: "Only Thus." Begin had since abandoned his claim on Jordan, but never his quest to make the West Bank and Gaza—he insisted on using the Biblical names "Judea and Samaria"—part of modern Israel. As for 242, Begin's distaste for its implications was precisely what had provoked his departure from Golda Meir's National Unity Government in 1970.

Begin also asserted, as Rabin had warned, that there was absolutely no way that the Israelis would consider PLO participation at a Geneva peace conference, even as members of a Jordanian delegation. Carter quickly recognized that if Begin was serious, then "there was no prospect of further progress in the Middle East." But he had heard Begin was "an honest and courageous man."

That he was. But those qualities were not likely to turn Begin into an American politician with a taste for compromise. Quite the opposite, in fact; they would only confirm his almost missionary zeal to convert the world to his vision of Israel. Carter himself had entered office with a reputation as a religious man who sought to restore "principles" to the realpolitik of U.S. foreign policy. "He had a set of values that I found attractive," wrote Cyrus Vance after his first taste of Carter's foreign-policy objectives in 1976. "His thinking reflected a principled approach to foreign affairs, which I believed essential for the reestablishment of a broad base of domestic support for a more comprehensive foreign policy."[32]

Begin also had a set of "principles" that he had been carrying throughout his adult life as a Jewish warrior and politician. The collision between the Baptist moralist and the Jewish ideologue would fracture the very domestic support that Vance had hoped for, not to mention the comprehensive peace he and Carter held so dear. In the next few months, U.S. policy makers and American Jews would discover that they had a lot to learn about this extraordinary Israeli politician.

FROM the creation of the Jewish state until 1977, when most American Jews looked at Israeli politics, they saw David Ben-Gurion, the patriarch of the new Israel, or Golda Meir, its matriarch (and an American Jewish mother too); American Jews pointed with pride at Abba Eban, the Cambridge-educated Israeli diplomat whose charm and eloquence had represented Israel brilliantly at the U.N. (A record of Eban's emotionally charged speech to the U.N. during the Six-Day War sold out in New York like a Beatle's LP.) And there was Moshe Dayan, the dashing archeologist-general, the hero of the Six-Day War (and the goat of the next one, though few American Jews remembered that even four years later).

Menachem Begin had no place in the American version of Israel. He was a menacing shadow in Labor's history of Israel, a history that few American Jews knew very well, if at all. Begin's warrior days—and no Israeli, no matter how much they disliked his politics, could deny Begin's courage and patriotism—had ended with the creation of the state. To most Americans the fighting Israeli came of age in the 1967 war, in which Begin had played no military or political role. Begin was the representative of a branch of Zionism that had lost every single political battle it had entered in Israel. Isolated from Israeli politics, most American Jews and their leaders had forgotten about the Jewish terrorist leader who had engineered the bombing of the King David Hotel in 1946 and the massacre at Deir Yassin in 1948.

Nahum Goldmann had convinced Dean Acheson and other members of the Truman Cabinet that the best argument for supporting a Zionist state in Palestine was that it would block the political rise of Begin. Now, in 1977, few American Jews remembered the battle between Begin and Ben-Gurion during the war for Israel's independence, that Begin had called Ben-Gurion a "lunatic dictator," and Ben-Gurion had branded him a "fascist." Fewer still remembered the notorious "*Altalena* affair" in 1948 when Ben-Gurion ordered an arms ship that Begin was on blown up, and—just five weeks after the creation of the state of Israel—civil war broke out in Israel for a few days, with Jews shooting at other Jews. Nor were there many who remembered Einstein and Hannah Arendt's letter to *The New York Times* denouncing Begin's "Fascist" and "Nazi" tactics when the Irgun leader visited the U.S. in late 1948.[33]

Ben-Gurion's famous recipe for staying in power was "Coalition —without Herut or the Communists!" The majority of the Israeli electorate seemed to agree. For most of his political career, Begin sat in the Knesset like Catiline in the Roman Senate, surrounded by his loyal disciples, scorned by the rest of the members, and patiently awaiting the day when the Herut would lead Israel according to the New Zionism of their idol, Vladimir Ze'ev Jabotinsky.

And now, incredibly, almost three decades after the founding of the Jewish state, Begin was leading it.

"I was convinced that Begin would be able to move from one end of the political spectrum to the middle," says Rabbi Alexander Schindler.[34]

At the time Begin came to power, Schindler was chairman of the Conference of Presidents of Major American Jewish Organizations. "I felt the office would pull him to the center, like Nixon," Schindler recalled in an interview seven years later. It was generous of Schindler to think so since he himself was a self-proclaimed "liberal" on the American political scene and a "dove" regarding Israel's policies toward the Occupied Territories and the Palestinians. Begin's Revisionism and the strong support he received from the Israeli right, not to mention the influential presence of the hardline, Orthodox religious and nationalist parties in his Likud coalition, were in conflict with Schindler's own political and religious positions as well as his vision of Israel. At the time Schindler was (and continues to be) the head of the Union of American Hebrew Congregations, which represents the nation's Reform congregations. The Reform rabbis have been unsuccessful in their attempt to break the Orthodox half-nelson on Israeli domestic policy since the 1950s.

Schindler had publicly warned that the Presidents' Conference, under his chairmanship, would not be the trained seal the Israelis had grown accustomed to. But that was when Rabin was still in power. Begin's surprise election had provoked an unusual amount of public criticism. American editorial writers and doomsayers among the columnists talked of an "extremist" coming to power, the end of Israel.

The New York Times was concerned that politics in Israel were dangerously "out of sync." *Time* earned Begin's animosity by advising its readers that "Begin rhymes with Fagin." The new prime minister demanded—and got—an apology from CBS News, which had called him an "ex-terrorist." (Even so the American criticism was mild compared to comments in Britain where many had not forgotten that when their nation still ruled Palestine there was a price of 10,000 pounds on Begin's head for the Irgun's murderous attacks on British soldiers. "Israel's founding father reaps the rewards of terrorism," a columnist in *The Times* of London wrote. "Terrorism does pay. Arafat should be encouraged."[35])

Begin was hurt by the criticism abroad, but by no means incapacitated by it. After all, history had finally caught up to him, and events in Israel were on his side. Anyone in the American Jewish community or the American press who had been paying attention to Israeli politics for the past five years would have seen Begin's rise coming. In the 1973 election, the Labor Alignment, led by Prime Minister Golda Meir, had lost five members in the Knesset, while the Likud, mainly a coalition of Herut and the not so liberal Liberal Party, led by Begin, had picked up seven seats. Labor's plurality was slim, and shaky. Examining the period leading up to the 1977 election, the sociologist Dan V. Segre writes: "What is surprising is not the fact that the socialists were replaced after thirty years of rule: it is the fact that they remained in power so long in spite of the great demographic and cultural changes in the Israeli society."[36]

According to Segre, labor had outlasted its welcome; the rapid economic growth after the 1967 war, fueled largely by foreign money, had created a new middle class that wanted to be rid of the economic and social intervention of the government. Following the trend around the world, young Israelis were turning to the ballot box to register their protest against their parents; even intellectuals, according to Segre, were bridling against the ideological conformity of the dominant socialist brand of Zionism, which appeared to have lost its moral force. Oriental Jews—"Sephardim"—were in open revolt against the Ashkenazim, the European Jews who had founded the state. Envisioned as a classless society of Jews in search of normality, Israel was now in the midst of class warfare.

The changes taking place in Israeli society were profound. The Israel that American Jews knew and worshiped from afar—the Israel of the pioneers, the *kibbutzim*, the *Exodus* version—was vanishing.

And so was Labor's power as its mistakes and problems piled up: the debacle of the Yom Kippur War, economic troubles produced by wildcat strikes, the loss of the religious parties in Rabin's coalition, and a series of political and financial scandals involving major figures in the Labor Party, including Prime Minister Rabin.

Israel was suffering from a classic case of "crisis of leadership"—and the only leader from the generation of Founding Fathers who seemed untouched by the scandals and political ineptitude of Labor was the man who had been largely shunned by Labor since the beginning of the state, Menachem Begin.

Begin became a father figure who represented change—Segre calls it a "new regime"—while maintaining a connection to the great history of the state. He deftly aligned himself to the dreams of the Oriental Jews, and exploited their bitterness toward the dominant Labor Party, which he of course shared, though for different reasons. Begin's once unfashionable Zionism was now at the head of a political and social trend in Israel.

All of this went little noticed in U.S. political circles. Most American Jewish leaders were closely tied to the Labor Party. Few of them had ever met Begin, and fewer seemed aware of (or willing to take seriously) his vision of Israel.

Schindler recognized that the public attack on Begin might jeopardize U.S. support for Israel. As Schindler explains it: "It's impossible to say, 'Begin's terrible, but we want you [the American government] to support the State of Israel anyway.'"

Begin's election raised the problem of dissent anew. The new prime minister's vision of a "Greater Israel" made most American Jewish leaders uneasy. While Labor's efforts to settle the West Bank had been masked in defense strategy, Begin forced American Jews to consider the "demographic problem" that was already a major concern among Israeli doves: if Israel annexed the territories, as Begin's party desired, then the Arabs, as Israeli citizens, could vote to transfer Israel into a binational secular state; if those Arabs were not allowed to be citizens, Israel could no longer be considered much of a democracy. Begin's policies were stirring up the old charges of Israeli "colonialism," while the second-class status of Palestinians living in the Occupied Territories raised the specter of Israel as a Middle East version of South Africa. But, as Schindler asked, could one attack Begin without encouraging the "pro-Arab" Carterites to abandon Israel?

Shortly after the election, the American Jewish Committee's Middle East expert, George Gruen, published an article on "Solidarity and Dissent in Israel-Diaspora Relations" in which he outlined the arguments for and against criticizing Israeli policies. Gruen left no doubt that anyone claiming to be committed to the future of Israel must be "intimately involved" in its domestic, social, and political life, "even in examining the strategic concepts underlying the Israeli and American defense budgets."[37] Though there are Israeli doves who wonder why their government ought to be trusted solely with such important matters, no American Jewish leader had ever called for an independent examination of Israeli security needs. Gruen's position was extraordinary, and largely ignored. Jewish leaders continued to believe that criticism of Israel would only feed the Administration's pro-Arab sympathies; instead of publicly differing with Begin's policies, they began to circle the wagons to defend against Jimmy Carter's policies.

SCHINDLER soon found himself in the not-so-pleasant situation of sitting in the office of the man Begin had beaten, Shimon Peres, watching Peres on Israeli television denounce Begin's appointment of Moshe Dayan as foreign minister. It was there in Peres's office that Schindler made the decision to signal the end of American Jewry's affair with the Labor Party (at least while it was not running Israel), which he immediately conveyed to the press staked outside.

"We understand that American Jews are outraged at the Dayan appointment," said one reporter. "No, that's not true," Schindler answered, explaining that Dayan was bound to go over well in the U.S.: he was a familiar face, while Begin was a strange one; Dayan, in spite of his decline in popularity in Israel after the Yom Kippur War—bereaved mothers were to stone Begin's apartment in Tel Aviv after the Dayan announcement[38]—was still admired by American Jewish leaders, particularly for his efforts to understand the Arab world; above all, Schindler noted, he was recognized as a pragmatist and not an ideologue. In short, American Jews were comfortable with Dayan because he was part of the Israel they believed they understood; the new foreign minister—unlike the new prime minister—was more like them.

Moments after Shimon Peres, the man most American Jewish leaders had supported for prime minister of Israel, had attacked

Begin's appointment, the most important American Jewish leader endorsed it. In Israel, that was front-page stuff. "Right then I discovered what the press could do," Schindler recalls. And he was to use
the press, in Israel and the U.S., to his—and Begin's—advantage
many more times over the next few years.

Schindler finally met Begin for the first time in the hospital where
the Israeli leader was recuperating from a heart attack suffered in the
beginning of the campaign. "On a personal level we had an extraordinary rapport," says Schindler. Begin's own aides confirm that. According to one, "Schindler was a European, very smart, and a good
politician." Schindler was immediately struck by Begin's "sense of
responsibility to the Jewish people as a whole," as opposed to Rabin,
who, in Schindler's opinion, was "more Israeli than Jew" and "hostile to the American Jewish community."

"Begin was civilized and warm," recalls Schindler, echoing many
who have met Begin and who expect a hard-boiled ex-terrorist and
find a courtly lawyer who speaks a literate and sonorous Hebrew.
Schindler visited Begin's famous tiny apartment on Rosenbaum
Street in Tel Aviv, and was impressed by "the modest way he lived."
Begin's simple life-style and commitment to the future of the Jews
were no small qualities, as Schindler is quick to note: "The last year
of Labor's power was scandalous, filled with venality, and stealing."

When Schindler returned home, he reported to Vance and Carter
that Begin would be a man willing to pursue peace in the Middle
East. "I was convinced of that," Schindler recalled. "Schindler's support was a big break for us," explains one member of the Likud who
was close to Begin at the time. "He was important because he was
head of Reform, liberal Jewry in the U.S. He could have dumped on
Begin and caused a real problem. Instead, he decided to really play
the game with Israel."[39] Dan Meridor, a Likud member of the Knesset who was Begin's spokesman when he was in office, described
Schindler's endorsement of Begin as "very brave, very important—a
historic move."[40] Others, in Israel and the U.S., viewed the alliance
between the "dovish" Reform rabbi and Begin as "a total sellout" and
a disaster."[41] "Just when American Jews should have been more critical of what was going on in Israel," says one Israeli intellectual active in the religious peace movement, "a major American Jewish
leader—a self-proclaimed 'dove'—throws his support to Begin. It
was positively whorish."[42]

Criticizing Jimmy Carter was a lot easier. In one week in June, more than 90 percent of the one thousand letters flowing into the White House concerning the Middle East were critical of Carter's position. Carter finally activated his ranking Jewish aides—Stuart Eisenstat, Robert Lipshutz, and Mark Siegel, the new White House liaison to the American Jewish community—to assuage Jewish fears about Administration policy in the Middle East. Vice President Mondale, who had close ties to American Jewry, was dispatched to San Francisco where he delivered a carefully worded speech reiterating U.S. support for Israel.

IN his first few months in office, Begin ignored the American Jewish Establishment. When Israeli politicans in the Labor Alignment looked to American Jewry, they saw political backers and dollar signs. "When Begin looked at American Jewry, he saw something quite different," explains a former Begin aide. "He had never been invited to speak in the United States to the UJA. He had never addressed a Bonds Rally. Begin was very sensitive to his lack of mainline support in the United States."[43] The prime minister knew most American Jewish leaders saw his election as an aberration and him personally as a usurper. "Begin had developed a habit of contempt for the American Jewish leadership," says the aide. "He knew they were still talking secretly to Labor, and he did not take them seriously."

He dispatched Shmuel Katz, a Herut associate and the former propaganda chief for the Irgun, and another Herut deputy, Eliahu Ben-Elissar, to work on the American press and politicians. Katz, who used to visit the U.S. to encourage Jewish leaders to criticize Labor policies, asked for American Jewish support. Begin had expected that his own network of loyal Herutniks in the U.S. would be able to take over the job of marshaling the support of American Jewry and the politicians for his government, but he realized that the American Herut had been on the sidelines of American Jewish political power for too long, with few contacts in Washington or even among the Jewish Establishment. And there was the *simpático* Schindler at the head of organized Jewry with his access to the Carter White House. "Begin was impressed by Schindler's abilities to make things happen," recalls one former Begin aide.

Schindler was not alone in thinking the office would make a statesman out of the ideologue Begin. Ezer Weizman, the Israeli air force

general and war hero who had engineered Begin's absentee campaign
while the candidate was in the hospital, also believed, as he later
wrote in his memoir of the events leading up to Camp David, "that
the office would change him." Both Schindler and Weizman, however, would eventually discover that Begin would always remain
Begin. As Weizman put it in his memoir, "Begin is far stronger than
the forces of reality."[44]

Longtime Begin watchers in the Israeli press were warning as
much from the beginning. Simha Flapan, writing in the English-lan-
guage journal *New Outlook*, derided the notion that Begin would
somehow turn into Nixon, the die-hard anti-Communist who went to
China, or de Gaulle, who came to power to keep Algeria and then
gave it independence. "Not all the extremists of yesterday become
moderates, and not all patriots understand what is good for their
country," Flapan pointed out, and added his own take on Begin's
flexibility: "Those for whom extremism was not only a means to
achieve power, but an expression of faith, remained extremists.
Begin looks less than likely in the role of de Gaulle."[45] As another
journalist put it, half admiringly, in the Jerusalem *Post*, "His is a
terrifying credibility."[46]

The first American Jewish leader to have this confirmed was
Arthur Hertzberg, then a member of the executive committee of the
World Zionist Organization and vice president of the World Jewish
Congress, who was in Jerusalem in early July 1977 on congress business, and also was carrying a message from the Carter Administration to Begin, who was scheduled to visit Washington later in the
month.[47] Rabbi Hertzberg had known Begin for years, and on his
regular trips to Israel, the American Jewish leader would occasionally
lunch with the leader of Israel's right-wing Herut Party in the Knesset
cafeteria. Politically, they could not have been further apart: Hertzberg was a self-proclaimed "dove" on the Israeli political scene who
had already quarreled with the Labor Government about the future of
the West Bank. But like Begin, the American rabbi was a Polish Jew,
and the pair enjoyed trading jokes and gossiping in Yiddish about
Israeli and American political personalities.

Begin invited the American rabbi for coffee, and after some small
talk, Hertzberg got to the point: "I have been instructed to tell you
that if you come to the United States to talk about the West Bank and
Israeli security, the Administration will be enormously forthcoming,"
Hertzberg reported. "But if you are going to Washington to sell your

ideology about Israel's God-given right to Judea and Samaria, they see lots of trouble with you, and you with them." Begin was visibly upset by what he was hearing, and didn't let the rabbi finish. "Of course, I would go to discuss security," he said.

"Good," said Hertzberg, "because my impression from those in Washington is that if you want to discuss security, their experts will sit down with your experts and work things out as to how Israel can be secure of the West Bank."

At that point, Hertzberg recalled, "Begin went up in smoke." The angry prime minister informed the American messenger: "I'll never allow Israel's security to be decided by others. This is not only a security matter, it is also a political matter."

Hertzberg agreed, and countered: "But as a political matter that means that Israel might have to give up some territory. It cuts both ways. Israel does not have to occupy the West Bank. We can buy peace other ways—a bridge here, some land there."

This was definitely not what Begin wanted to hear. After all, the principle that was central to Begin's brand of Revisionist Zionism was that all of Palestine belonged rightfully to the Jewish state. Begin intended to make the West Bank the property of the Jews again by annexing the West Bank.

"The real issue," the prime minister informed Hertzberg, "is that I was elected prime minister of Israel because the people accepted my ideological view. I must respect that, and I will in Washington. I must say, *Dr.* Hertzberg [for the first time in the conversation, Begin slipped into the formal mode], that I regard it as my task among the Jewish people to reverse twenty-nine years of Jewish history. The Jews have been victims of bad Zionist education by the Labor Party. I exist to reverse that bad education."

The "new Begin" sounded very much like the old Begin, and Hertzberg reported his findings to his friends in the Carter Administration. Yet the Carterites knew virtually nothing about Begin, new or old. To help prepare for the prime minister's visit, members of the National Security Staff had asked the Israeli Embassy for some written material about Begin. The embassy sent over copies of the recently published *Terror out of Zion*, an admiring portrait of Begin's days as leader of the Irgun, which had little to do with what the Israeli Establishment thought of their new prime minister in 1977.[48] They seemed to have already forgotten Rabin's warning that Begin would not be as forthcoming, and similarly, had waved a hand at

Hertzberg's report that the new prime minister was unwilling to budge on the issue of the West Bank. Surely, Begin would come around to their version of Israel's future. And then they met the real Menachem Begin.

THE Americans sat there in the Cabinet Room of the White House staring at maps of the Middle East. Colored in red were the Arab countries; Israel was blue. Standing before the maps, pointer in hand, was Shmuel Katz, the foreign-press adviser to the prime minister of Israel. Katz was on hand to give a geography and history lesson colored not in blue or red but in the ideology of the Revisionist Zionism of Jabotinsky and his loyal disciple Menachem Begin. One member of the audience, who has devoted his adult life to studying the Middle East, had the feeling he was in "a class for four-year-olds."[49] Among the rest of the class were the President of the United States, Jimmy Carter, his secretary of state, Cyrus Vance, Carter's national security adviser, Zbigniew Brzezinski, along with members of their respective staffs, most of them professional or academic specialists on the Middle East.

It was the first day of Begin's first meeting with Jimmy Carter. Israel's new prime minister had taken the floor during the morning meeting, and the afternoon session he had turned over to Katz, whose task was to explain that Israel's "Palestinian problem" had a simple solution resting in what he considered the obvious difference between "Palestinian Arabs" and "Palestinian Jews" and their respective rights to be in the Land of Israel. Katz's main argument was that most of the Arabs in Palestine had actually arrived only within the last hundred years. "Proof" that the Arabs were relatively new immigrants to Palestine was that they abandoned their property so quickly in the 1948 war. Farmers deeply rooted in the land, the Katz argument went, would not have left. Therefore, Katz concluded, the only Arabs with a right to live in the Land of Israel were those who remained there in spite of the war."[50]

"The thrust of the presentation was that the Arabs in the so called 'Land of Israel' should go live in those red Arab countries and leave poor little blue Israel alone in peace," recalled one of the Middle East experts in the audience. When Begin's foreign minister, Moshe Dayan, read the report of Katz's remarks cabled back to Jerusalem, he recalls in his memoir *Breakthrough*, "I did not even try to guess what the Americans must have thought when they heard them."[51]

The fact was the Americans were not quite sure what to make of the Katz performance, or of Begin. Jimmy Carter may have known his Bible, but his knowledge of the history of modern Israel was thin, and his own Middle East experts seemed to be no better informed about the subtleties and conflicts in Zionism. What had embarrassed Dayan—Katz's unvarnished right-wing Zionism—had struck the Americans as boorish condescension. "We were relieved that Begin himself hadn't delivered the lecture," recalls a member of the audience.

The Carter people wanted to talk peace, ignoring the role that ideology would inevitably play in any peace talks. For these American pragmatists, everything was negotiable. For the Israeli ideologue across the table, certain things would never be negotiable. "It was a naïve American approach," an Administration Middle East expert admitted seven years later. "It was very ahistorical."

After extensive meetings with Arab heads of state, Carter believed confronting the Palestinian problem was the only thing that would get the Arabs to the negotiating table. The Israelis had to be willing to give up territory to get peace. Besides, that had been U.S. policy since after the Six-Day War, and "territorial compromise," as Carter and Begin well knew, had been official Israeli policy.

But it had never been Menachem Begin's policy; in fact, he had opposed every U.N., American, Arab, and Israeli plan that suggested yielding territory. Begin brought many things to the table, but flexibility was not one of them, particularly where the future of the West Bank and Gaza was concerned. The new prime minister insisted the area always be referred to as Judea and Samaria, as if it were already part of Israel proper, and, to make it so, had already announced a major plan to allow Jews to settle on the West Bank. At their meeting, Carter warned the prime minister not to go through with those settlements.

When embassy officials later asked Begin what he was going to do about the settlements in view of Carter's obviously intense opposition, Begin waved it off and, according to his biographer Eric Silver, "replied that he would build the settlements as planned. The Americans, he predicted, would turn cold for six months, then they would revert to normal."[52]

• • •

BEGIN returned to Israel after his Washington trip beaming publicly about the "deep personal friendship" established between him and Jimmy Carter (one more example of how differently Begin and Carter viewed the world). American Jewry had given him a rousing reception comparable to their public affection for Golda Meir. A master of the lectern, Begin, like Ben-Gurion and Golda Meir (and unlike the steely Rabin), was legendary for being able to push all the right emotional buttons with a speech. His favorite rhetorical flourish was raising the specter of the Holocaust and the Arab threat of another one.

But unlike his predecessors, Begin was careful to ask American Jews "to stand together" with Israel; he never rang the alarms of *aliyah* and learning Hebrew. Begin's promise of a more entrepreneurial-based economy with less government control was music to the ears of American Jewish businessmen who had always been uncomfortable with (and reluctant to invest in) Labor's socialist aspirations. Not insignificant too was the fact that Begin was a religious man. Unlike Ben-Gurion and Golda Meir, he was respectful to rabbis, and the clergy made up a significant part of the American Jewish leadership. As Eric Silver writes, "Begin was the first Prime Minister who identified himself as a Jew rather than as an Israeli."[53]

Back in Jerusalem, Begin echoed the famous words of Julius Caesar, conqueror of Gaul, *"Veni, vidi, vici...."* (I came, I saw, I conquered.) It was typical Begin hyperbole, but both American Jews and the Israelis were relieved by Begin's new image of international statesman. Claiming he was ready to go to Geneva, Begin seemed ready to deal with the Arabs; he stressed Israel's support of the free world (the socialist Laborites were always uneasy about attacking the Russians), and he boldly did what no other Israeli prime minister had ever done: he stressed how important Israel was to the U.S. To prove it, he had offered to share intelligence with the U.S. and deliver any Soviet secrets Israeli spies picked up. To American Jews, this was no "terrorist fanatic" speaking. And to those Israelis who had lived for three decades with Begin's bombast, his successful trip to the States exceeded their expectations.

But there was that nagging issue of the settlements. As if to remind Carter that he would go his own way, Begin authorized three existing settlements shortly after his return to Israel. Carter and Vance were enraged and condemned the settlements as "illegal" and a serious "obstacle to peace."[54] Even Schindler was uneasy about the settlement issue. While the Jewish politician in him was willing to support Begin's government, the dove in him saw Begin's efforts to annex the West Bank as a roadblock to peace as well as a threat to support for Begin among American Jews. Schindler claims that from the first time they met, he leveled with Begin about the reservations of American Jewry to his policies regarding the territories, the Palestinians, and Begin's interpretation of U.N. Resolution 242, often to the prime minister's dismay.[55] Other American Jews warned Israeli leaders that Begin's hardline policies would wash neither with the Administration nor the Jewish community.

While disagreeing with Begin privately on this fundamental issue, Schindler was nevertheless committed to building a solid front of support for the government of Israel among Jews in the U.S. At the time, he was sticking to the view, as the 1977 annual report of the Presidents' Conference flatly stated it, "Dissent ought not and should not be made public because . . . the result is to give aid and comfort to the enemy and to weaken that Jewish unity which is essential for the security of Israel."[56]

Yet the settlement issue was not about to go away. Carter complained about the Begin policy to Moshe Dayan during his first visit to the U.S. as Begin's foreign minister in September. He and Vance also told Dayan that they were about to announce a joint statement with the Soviet Union in which the superpowers were committing themselves to a comprehensive settlement including all parties—and that meant the Palestinians. "Dayan refrained from reacting—perhaps deliberately," Brzezinski recalls in his memoir.[57]

Dayan knew that such a move did not require his dissent. When the White House announced the U.S.–U.S.S.R. "joint communiqué on October 1, there was a ruckus in Congress and the American Jewish community. The President's critics on Capitol Hill were mystified as to why the Administration wanted to bestow on the Soviet Union a prominent role in the Middle East when Sadat had sent the Russians packing five years before. The Jews were upset about what seemed an expanded role for the Palestinians in the peace process. In one fell swoop, Carter had managed to incite all the people who were worried about Israel plus those who were upset about the return of the Russians to Middle East diplomacy. Four thousand telegrams a day from outraged Jews and anti-Soviet Americans poured into the White House after the announcement. Carter had not even warned his liaison to the Jewish community, Mark Siegel, about the joint communiqué and Siegel had to scramble to explain to angry Jewish leaders what it all meant.

Carter and Vance were mystified by the Jewish reaction, since the agreement with the Russians hadn't committed the U.S. to anything new; moreover, Vance pointed out to Dayan in a tense meeting a few days after the announcement, the Russians had actually softened their demands; there was no mention of an independent Palestinian state. Dayan said the rub was the phrase "legitimate rights of the Palestinian people"; Vance explained that was also a compromise. And what was wrong with the rights of the Palestinians anyway? "Totally unacceptable to the Israeli government," replied Dayan.[58] The foreign minister, according to witnesses, played it tough; he simply threatened to turn on the spigot of Jewish criticism. The Americans were well aware that he was scheduled to go on a fund-raising tour of the American Jewish community. As Dayan frankly stated it in his own memoir, "There was no doubt that in my speeches I would criticize the American position on peace in the Middle East."[59] The White House decided it could live without more Jewish pressure; Dayan departed with a compromise that gave Israel more control over which Palestinians could be present at a Geneva peace conference on the Middle East.

Carter needed peace between himself and American Jewry. The day after the deal with Dayan was hammered out, October 6, the President called a meeting of Jewish congressmen in the White House, and told them, "I'd rather commit political suicide than hurt Israel."[60]

In the eyes of many Jews, Carter had been slashing his wrists since about March. The President seemed to be spending as much time fending off angry Jewish leaders as contemplating his strategy for peace at Geneva. Though it might have seemed impossible at the time, in the weeks to come, the heat on the White House from American Jewish leaders would be rising several more degrees.

IN November, Nahum Goldmann traveled to Washington to meet the President. Vance, Brzezinski, and Mark Siegel were also present as the eighty-two-year-old Zionist leader and former head of the World Jewish Congress offered his own experienced and very candid opinion on how the Carter Administration might best pursue its peace efforts in the Middle East. Goldmann urged them to "break the Jewish lobby in the United States."[61]

The President and his men could not quite believe their ears. Goldmann has devoted his long life to Zionism, had been a major player in the "Jewish lobby" since the Truman Administration, had, in fact, invented one of the lobby's most effective players, the Conference of Presidents of Major American Jewish Organizations, and here he was actually arguing that his own brainchild, the Presidents' Conference, had become a "destructive force" and "a major obstacle" to peace in the Middle East. Goldmann contended that despite the flak the White House would get in the beginning, eventually, if the Israelis compromised and a peace settlement were reached, Carter would emerge as "the hero of the Jews." The proposal was riddled with an irony that was probably beyond the people in the room. Goldmann had created the Presidents' Conference to prevent the kind of dissent among American Jewish leaders that he himself was now demonstrating. The *raison d'être* of the group was to present a united front to the White House on Middle East matters. But, of course, that was back in the old days when Goldmann's friends were running Israel.

Now that Begin was running the Jewish state, Goldmann was willing to do anything to undermine his policies—including destroying his own pressure group, which, like a Frankenstein monster, would soon be trying to destroy Goldmann when he went public with his own criticisms of Israeli policy.

Goldmann's proposal was unprecedented in the three-decade tug-of-war between American Jewry and the White House over Middle East policy. Given the Administration's difficult relations with Schindler, the current head of the Conference, the Carter people certainly agreed with the Zionist leader's assessment. Yet the President decided that, as much as he might like to "break the Jewish lobby," he could not afford the effort it would take to pull it off.

In an interview six years later, Cyrus Vance confirmed the Goldmann meeting.[62] "Goldmann did suggest we 'break the lobby,'" the former secretary of state recalled. "My reaction was that we couldn't break it. Rather, we had to recognize that it would continue to exist, that you could contain it so it didn't thwart what was good for our country. I believed that it was not only a waste of time to try to break the lobby, but it also risks opening the door to anti-Semitism."

The Carter Administration, however, was no longer in control of the peace process, and the lobby had nothing to do with that change of affairs. Sadat's announcement to the Egyptian parliament in early November that he was prepared to go to Jerusalem altered the lineup of potential peacemakers. The prime player in the peace process only a month before, the U.S. was now just another observer of the extraordinary events taking place in the Middle East. In one of his conversations with the Administration, Sadat made it clear that he thought his own efforts might lead to real negotiations on the issue of the West Bank. Sadat's critics, in Israel and in Egypt, have argued that the Egyptian president was eager from the beginning for a "separate peace" and cared little for the Palestinian issue and the final disposition of the West Bank. After all, Sadat was running into increasing opposition at home, and nothing would boost his popularity more than to be able to reclaim the Sinai—which the great Nasser had lost. Sadat also believed, according to Vance, that Begin would eventually have to step down, and whoever replaced him would be more prepared to negotiate a deal on the West Bank. Sadat wanted to push for peace. Again.

When Sadat addressed the Knesset in Jerusalem on November 20, he could not resist reminding the Israelis that this was not the first time he had made a move toward peace, noting, "I have shouldered the prerequisites of the historic responsibility and therefore I declared a few years ago—on February 4, 1971, to be precise—that I was willing to sign a peace treaty with Israel."[63]

But Sadat's peace efforts soon foundered on Begin's own "peace plan," which would eventually grant the Palestinian Arabs of Judea and Samaria and Gaza "administrative autonomy," while Israel would continue control over security and police functions, permitting Israelis to acquire land and settle in the territories. He also envisaged complete withdrawal from the Sinai. It seemed an extraordinary step for the ideologue Begin. Even the Labor opposition attacked him in the Knesset for giving up too much. Yet Begin knew exactly what he was giving up. The Sinai, after all, was not part of the Biblical Land of Israel, and thus expendable in Begin's version of the new Israel. The "autonomy plan" was Begin's way of appearing to make a move in the direction of the Palestinians while not budging on his belief that Judea and Samaria belonged to Israel by divine right.

As if to prove that Begin the peacemaker was the same old Begin, in January 1978, the prime minister decided to "bolster" existing settlements in the Sinai and break ground for six new ones. A leak to the press and the resulting furor in Israel, Egypt, and Washington forced Israel to back down on the new settlements. It seemed a curious and destructive strategy—to agree to negotiate withdrawal from the Sinai while creating new settlements there. Dayan and Ariel Sharon, in charge of settlement policies, were behind the move. Ezer Weizman condemned the strategy as "pernicious trivialities, capable of foiling the whole peace process,"[64] particularly when at that very moment Carter was with Sadat at Aswan trying to figure out how to deal with the Palestinian issue. The two leaders met again in early February in Washington, as public opinion began to shift against Israel. Sadat was treated as a major celebrity. Editorials began appearing attacking Begin as a liability to Israel and to American Jewry.

American Jewish leaders also wondered how long the Carter Administration, and its constituents, would permit Begin to get away with his inflammatory settlements policy. One prominent fund raiser —Laurence Tisch, the head of the giant Loews conglomerate and one of the UJA's most generous supporters—expressed his doubts, candidly and eloquently, at the end of February in an interview in the Israeli daily newspaper *Ha'aretz*, published in Hebrew.

> The Begin Administration played into the hands of the USA Administration. The only thing that Israel can offer is its righteousness, and the Jews in America are on the right side of public opinion when they can prove that they are fighting for something which is right. We can argue about border realignments, about the attainment of true peace, but when Israel falls in the wrong our strength is lost. If Begin continues to speak about the settlements, you will lose the war down to the last American. You have no justification for such a stance. . . . For thirty years we [American Jewish leaders] have been building for Israel the image of a peace-loving country. Begin destroyed this image in three months.[65]

Neither the President, the secretary of state, nor the national security adviser could have said it better. Trouble was, Tisch was unwilling to go on the record in the U.S., in English. Researching an article on Begin and American Jewry for *The Nation*, Arthur Samuelson, the former editor of Breira's magazine, came across the Tisch interview in *Ha'aretz*. Since the remarks would have been translated from English into Hebrew and now Samuelson was translating them back into English, he wanted to check the quote with Tisch himself. Tisch confirmed the *Ha'aretz* interview. "Can I quote you?" asked Samuelson. "No," Tisch replied. "I was speaking to the Israelis. The remarks were in house, not for the White House." Samuelson disputed that reasoning, pointed out that the CIA or the State Department was bound to report the quote to the White House and that it was odd that only Israelis were allowed to debate Begin's policies. Tisch stood firm. Samuelson eventually published Tisch's remarks anyway, based on *Ha'aretz*.[66]

The Israelis soon found out that Tisch was hardly alone. During early 1978, the Begin government commissioned the New York public-relations firm Ruder & Finn to survey 150 American Jewish leaders on their attitudes toward Israeli policies. Three to one, the Americans said they wished Israel would be more moderate. The results of the poll were never published, reportedly because they would have been too embarrassing to the Begin government.[67] The American Jewish leadership's Begin problem remained "in house," and the Administration was unable to turn this dissatisfaction with Begin among Jewish leaders into support for Jimmy Carter. Worse, just when prominent Israelis and American Jews were showing their frustration over Begin's intransigence, the Carter Administration turned suicidal, again: in February 1978 the Administration announced a proposal for selling F-15 jet fighters to the Saudis. Kissinger had promised the Saudis planes in 1975, and Crown Prince Fahd had reminded Carter about it in May 1977 when he was in Washington and again when Carter was in Saudi Arabia in January. Sadat's visit to Jerusalem forced the Saudis to make an inventory of their defense forces, and they apparently found them wanting in F-16 firepower (which the Israelis already had). The heat was off Begin and back on Carter.

It was time, once again, for the Jewish lobby to move into action. It seems incredible, in retrospect, that after all the trouble Carter was having with Begin and the American Jewish community that he would pour more oil on the fire. It was a congressional election year, not the best time to put congressmen on the spot by asking them to vote against Israel's interests. Moreover, Begin himself was scheduled to return to Washington in March. There were angry meetings in synagogues across the country. Pro-Israel crowds picketed the President on a trip to Los Angeles; the demonstrators were well organized and carried professionally lettered signs with such messages as "Hell No to the PLO" and "Aid to Israel! Best Investment for America" and "Carter Keep Your Promises."[68]

It was more proof of how far out of step the American Jewish community was with Israeli public opinion. Within a month, a group of three hundred young reservists in the Israeli Army and students who called themselves Peace Now collected sixty thousand signatures in Israel for a message to Prime Minister Begin beseeching him to refrain from establishing any more settlements in occupied Arab lands. A Peace Now newspaper ad in the Israeli papers, signed by 360 professors and intellectuals, charged that "the government's policy is not leading to compromise, but to loss of friends and the increasing of Israel's isolation."[69]

Jimmy Carter had more support for his policies in Israel than in the American Jewish community.

Some Carter critics saw the F-15 sale as proof positive that the President had been totally seduced by Sadat and gone over to the Arab camp. Among them was Carter's own liaison to the American Jewish community, Mark Siegel, who resigned. Siegel, a Brooklyn-born Ph.D. who had worked as an aide to Hubert Humphrey and as a top official at the Democratic National Committee where he helped party boss Robert Strauss piece the party back together after the McGovern debacle, realized his own influence was waning when he had not been warned of the U.S.–Soviet communiqué in October. Siegel argued in vain against the F-15 sale. Siegel, who was present for Nahum Goldmann's White House visit, was soon telling any reporter who'd listen that the F-15 sale was part of Brzezinski's plan to break the lobby's power in Congress.[70]

Then, also in March, Brzezinski and Schindler got into a public slugfest. Under attack as Carter's pro-Arab Svengali since the early months of the term, the national security chief, known for a fiery temper, finally popped. Brzezinski, whose father, a Polish diplomat, had helped Jews escape the Nazis, complained that Schindler had called him an "anti-Semite." Schindler was on the record as calling Brzezinski "antagonistic," but claimed he had never used the word "anti-Semite." The rabbi suspected a concerted campaign against him, and years later pointed to a column in *The New York Times* where William Safire, well known for his pro-Israel views, claims he had received a call from the White House asking him to attack Schindler.[71]

Upset by the White House's efforts to find Jewish leaders who were critical of Begin, Schindler decided to play rough too, and began organizing his own campaign to subvert Carter's Middle East plans. When Vance invited fifty or so members of the Presidents'

Conference and leaders of Jewish charitable federations from around
the country to a meeting at the State Department, Schindler learned
there would be federation people there who were believed to be sympathetic to the White House. Worried that Vance would try to get a
consensus out of the meeting that would undercut his organization,
Schindler arranged a premeeting at the B'nai B'rith headquarters in
Washington. "I found out who the hell was coming to that meeting
and I got all of them together at a prior meeting," Schindler recalled
years later. "I took that meeting away from Vance, in a sense, because we had everything planned in advance—every conceivable
point of view that we would make." Those who would speak were
designated beforehand, and, according to Schindler, Vance would ask
a question, and "I would nod to whomever was supposed to speak."

When asked whether he realized that the meeting had been rigged,
Vance replied, "It was fairly obvious that Schindler had engineered
it. It was naïve of me to think it could happen—that I could bring
together a large number of Jewish leaders and talk over our policies."
After the meeting, according to Vance, a friend in the audience came
up and advised him, "Don't ever make the mistake of meeting more
than five or so leaders at the same time."[72]

Vance, in fact, held other, smaller meetings, but it really didn't
matter. The May battle in Congress over the F-15 sale was nasty,
brutal, and not short enough. The Saudis had their own lobbyists on
hand, and the weeks before the vote turned into a festival of arm
twisting on all sides with the President finally getting enough arms to
be raised in favor of his side. Carter and Vance personally beseeched
Senate Democrats to support the sale. AIPAC lobbied more aggressively than ever to persuade them to oppose it, threatening to plug the
flow of Jewish campaign money to senators planning to run for re-
election. Advised by some Jewish leaders to ease up, that maybe the
plane deal wasn't worth antagonizing so many friends in the Senate
who felt they had to be loyal to the President, AIPAC's Morris Amitay, known to enjoy a good fight, put up one, and lost.

Immediately after the vote, National Public Radio broke a story,
picked up by *The New York Times*, that Carter's chief of staff Hamilton Jordan had said the Administration had "set out to break the back
of the Jewish lobby." The White House denied the remark. Carter, of
course, had beaten the lobby, barely; the trouble was that, finally, all
he really won was more animosity from the Jewish community.

AIPAC made sure that that animosity was contagious. Suddenly, senators who had considered themselves great friends of Israel—and had the campaign contributions to prove it in the past—were being portrayed as "enemies." George McGovern certainly did not have to support Israel to win votes in South Dakota, a region not known for its large Jewish population. But, like any politician, he could use as much financial support as possible, and with presidential ambitions McGovern was not eager to upset the Jews. During the 1972 presidential campaign, two-thirds of the people who lent him more than $100,000 were Jews, one of whom loaned the senator $390,000.[73] McGovern even had friends and supporters at AIPAC, where the politics of staffers can run from right to left. (The first lobbyist Sy Kenen hired in 1973—Ken Wollack—had been a McGovern aide.)

In 1978, when McGovern was raising funds for his 1980 re-election bid, friendly Jewish leaders helped set up four fund raisers in the major Jewish communities of New York, Chicago, Los Angeles, and Miami. He expected to raise $200,000 on this one swing—about 10 percent of his total campaign budget. But there was a slight problem: before he made this campaign tour, the F-15 vote came up. A member of the Foreign Relations Committee, McGovern represented a crucial swing vote for the Administration. According to a former aide, the senator decided to vote against the sale, and stuck to that decision—until twenty-four hours before the committee vote, when McGovern received phone calls from the secretary of state and the President, who said, "Be with me."

"George wouldn't use the word," recalls the former McGovern aide, "but he caved and voted for the F-15 sale. Afterwards the roof came down."[74]

At lunch with a McGovern fund raiser, Morris Amitay was so upset over the senator's flip-flop that he was soon stabbing his finger in the McGovernite's chest in anger. "Your guy deserted us, and we won't forget," Amitay reportedly said. McGovern's staffer pointed out that there was hardly a man in the Senate who had been a more reliable supporter of Israel over the past fifteen years. Was the lobby going to write off McGovern after one vote—particularly one that a Democratic President had begged him to side with the Administration on? "Not only that," Amitay threatened, "but we'll see that none of the Jewish groups will help you."

This was disastrous news. McGovern was fighting for his political life against an onslaught from the right wing led by the well-organized National Conservative Political Action Committee. NAC-

PAC had marshaled its forces and money to end the political careers of several "liberal" senators. The word went out, according to McGovern staffers, that the senator from South Dakota was "an enemy of Israel." Jewish groups were told to help all the liberal senators NACPAC was gunning for, except George McGovern.

Suddenly, McGovern's Jewish fund raisers were canceled. The senator appealed to his friend and longtime supporter Philip Klutznick, who had joined Carter's Cabinet as secretary of commerce, to help turn things around. Klutznick made some calls and reported that there was nothing he could do other than donate the legal limit for himself and his family, which he kindly did. McGovern called Howard Samuels for help; he could do nothing either. McGovern gave up and went forward with his campaign, without Jewish support, and was beaten.

IT was a truly extraordinary—and nasty—year and a half in U.S.–Jewish relations. In spite of his efforts to win over the Jews, Carter's words and deeds had only angered them. He might have been better off trying to follow Goldmann's advice to "break the Jewish lobby," because his efforts to win over American Jewry produced a result that was no more kindly to his Administration—and any intentions he might have of running for a second term. In June 1978, Carter conferred with a group of Democratic "wise men," party leaders well versed in political matters. He recalled in his book that their advice was to "stay as aloof as possible from direct involvement in the Middle East negotiations; this is a losing proposition."[75] Carter was in "a quandary": here he was trying to bolster Israeli security, and he was being attacked by American Jews, and warned by Democratic heavies that his Middle East policy was ruining the party. But Carter knew only he could keep the peace process going. He was right. And so were the "wise men": whatever the President did on the matter of Arab-Israeli relations, given the animosity toward him among American Jews, it was a losing proposition.

It was certainly a strange way to run a foreign policy. But if Carter had looked back at his predecessors' efforts to deal with the Arab-Israeli conflict with the interests of both sides in mind—JFK's Johnson Plan and Ford's "reassessment" come immediately to mind—he would have seen they were abandoned as politically dangerous.

The Administration was simply unable to convince American Jews that its own frustration with Begin's intransigence was the same as theirs. The problem was that while Jewish leaders knew that they could disagree with Begin without abandoning their support for Israel, they believed that the incompatibility of U.S. and Israeli policies was bound to push Carter into the arms of the Arabs. Meantime, the debate over the pros and cons of American Jews publicly dissenting from Israeli policy raged on—but always in private. In the fall of 1978, the American Jewish Committee published a "discussion guide" entitled "American Jews and Israel: Limits of Democracy and Dissent," outlining with admirable clarity the arguments for and against dissent.[76] Significantly, the "arguments" were against dissent and the "counterarguments" were for it. The document echoed Gruen's earlier argument, and is worth quoting extensively from to prove its good sense.

Argument: The solidarity of American Jews is important for Israeli morale.

Counterargument: Everyone—in Washington, the Arabs, the Israelis—is aware of our basic solidarity with Israel. Kneejerk support of every Israeli policy is unnecessary. On the contrary, true solidarity with Israel includes a responsibility to think carefully and critically about the possible results of her domestic and international politics.

Argument: Public criticism of Israel by Jews helps the Arabs drive a wedge between Israel and American Jewry.

Counterargument: Nothing, least of all Arab propaganda, can drive a wedge between American Jews and the Jewish state. The severest Jewish critics of Israel are among its most passionate supporters. They criticize, precisely because they care.

Argument: Public criticism by Jews gives ammunition and credibility to Arab criticism.

Counterargument: In a propaganda war, the side with the greatest credibility wins. By showing ourselves to be independent, we enhance our credibility and reduce that of the Arabs. Besides, the Arabs are quite capable of thinking up their own criticism. And they can find plenty in Israeli media.

Argument: It is the Israelis whose lives are on the line; therefore, only they have the right to criticize.

Counterargument: Israel has the final responsibility for making and carrying out decisions. *But that does not mean she cannot be wrong.* [Emphasis added.] Advice from a different perspective may very well be helpful to the Israelis, who have, in effect, lived in a pressure cooker for 30 years. When we find dissent necessary, we should voice it, precisely *because* their lives are on the line.

Argument: The Israeli government has expertise and information we do not have, and thus is better equipped to make vital decisions of war and peace.

Counterargument: Sometimes the Israeli government undoubtedly knows best, but to claim that it always does is unrealistic (as well as undemocratic). For example, Israel and the Arabs have confronted each other for 30 years; there have been so few human contacts between the two sides that they can't really understand each other.

Argument: American Jews don't understand and don't really want to understand Israel—least of all the complexities of her domestic politics and her policy-making process.

Counterargument: To achieve peace, Israel will need to make decisions that transcend domestic politics. Thus, greater American Jewish involvement in her affairs is needed.

It is an extraordinary document—and clearly not much attention was paid to it. Worried more about the effects of Jimmy Carter's policy toward Israel on the U.S.–Israel relationship than the effects of Begin's policies, more concerned about preserving the U.S.–Israeli relationship than the moral and democratic ties that assure that friendship, American Jewish leaders stifled dissent, and questioned the motives of anyone who dared criticize Israel, Jew, gentile, or President of the United States.

CARTER, however, did not give up, and finally did get Begin and Sadat together at Camp David in September 1978. By all accounts, Israeli and Egyptian, it was the President's personal touch and persistence that produced, in the last days, an agreement, the Camp David "Framework for Peace in the Middle East." The plan invited the Arab states to negotiate with Israel on the basis of U.N. Resolutions 242 and 338 (the three-paragraph cease-fire agreement after the Yom Kippur War in 1973 committing both sides to begin negotiating peace under the auspices of 242). At its core were arrangements for a transition to self-rule by the Palestinians of the West Bank and Gaza and for negotiations between Israel, Egypt, Jordan, and "representatives of the Palestinian People" about the final status of those territories. The solution, according to Camp David, "must also recognize

the legitimate rights of the Palestinian people and their just require-
ments"—precisely the phrase that Israel and American Jewish leaders
had created a furor over when it appeared in Carter's joint communiqué with the Russians in October 1977. There were also provisions in
the Camp David framework governing the negotiation of a peace
treaty between Egypt and Israel, the key being Israeli withdrawal
from the Sinai to the 1967 border.

Camp David would be the greatest achievement of the Carter Administration, yet, during the next two years, the President, who had
devoted more of his time in office to peace between Arabs and Jews
than any other President (and had achieved more success than any of
his predecessors), would never again be able to count on Jewish
voters. The hostility toward him was too strong, and tensions between Carter and Begin would not help matters much. The Israelis
were not prepared to face up to the Palestinian problem, as the failure
of the autonomy talks after Camp David proved; nor were American
Jews willing to voice their own dissatisfaction with Begin's settlements policy, which Carter had called "illegal."

According to an American Jewish leader, in 1979 Carter considered giving a major televised speech on the Middle East in which he
intended to outline the divergence of interests between Israel and the
U.S. and denounce Israel's intransigence. A few Jewish leaders sympathetic to his difficulties with Begin and the lobby sent word to
Carter, reportedly through Father Theodore Hesburgh, the president
of Notre Dame, that he might thus become the first U.S. President to,
as one leader put it, "risk opening the gates of anti-Semitism in
America." Carter decided that on top of all his troubles he could do
without that dubious distinction.[77]

Over the next year, Carter's Jewish aides, including Robert
Strauss, who became the White House's Middle East negotiator in
1979, Ed Sanders, the former president of AIPAC who replaced Mark
Siegel as Carter's liaison to the Jewish groups, and Washington lawyer Al Moses, who later took over from Sanders, tried to keep Carter
from pressuring Israel and to dissociate the President from the "pro-
Arab" views of Brzezinski and Vance. Trouble was that they were
genuinely Carter's views too. Besides, Jimmy Carter couldn't seem
to do anything right.

In August 1979, Carter was quoted as claiming that the Palestinian
issue was like the "civil rights movement here in the United States."[78]
The President claimed his remarks had been misinterpreted. Then

later that month another PR disaster struck. In the course of monitoring the PLO's observer at the U.N., where, as most U.N. diplomats will attest, the walls have ears, the Israelis found that the United States's U.N. ambassador Andrew Young, a close friend of the President's, had met with the PLO's man at the home of the Kuwaiti ambassador. It was not the first time Young had met with the PLO representative (nor would it be the last time an American representative would meet secretly with the PLO), but it was in clear violation of the 1975 Memo of Agreement that Kissinger had signed to persuade the Israelis to disengage from the Sinai, a pledge that the U.S. would not recognize or negotiate with the PLO until it recognized Israel's right to exist.

Vance and Carter had in fact been working on ways to get around the no-talk-to-the-PLO rule, but Young had been caught, had held the meeting without the State Department's knowledge, first claimed that it had never happened, then claimed it was accidental, and finally admitted to Vance that the Israelis had him dead to right. Vance was furious, and told Carter it was either Young or find a new secretary of state. Young was a goner. The Jewish community was happy to see Young's back, but the whole incident was disastrous for the already crumbling relations between blacks and Jews.[79]

Young's successor, Donald McHenry, another black with alleged Third World sympathies, had no better luck. Due to a so-called "breakdown" in communications," McHenry voted for a U.N. resolution in March 1980 that attacked Israel's settlement policy, "including Jerusalem." Carter had been told, the explanation goes, that all references to Jerusalem had been removed from the document. They had not been. Even Israeli doves who are willing to give back the West Bank aren't prepared to include Jerusalem.

The Jewish community was outraged, again—and in the middle of the New York presidential primary where Carter was fighting for his political life against Senator Edward Kennedy. Within days, Carter said the yes vote had been an error. But Carter's fate in New York was sealed when, a few days before the primary, Vance, testifying before Congress, confirmed that the Administration still viewed the settlements as "contrary to international law"; he also conceded under questioning that the Administration viewed East Jerusalem as occupied territory. True and true. But such views only served to remind Jewish voters in New York what they'd been hearing from their friends since April 1977—Carter was putting too much pressure on

Israel. And if that weren't enough, Begin's defense minister, Ariel Sharon, had urged American Jews to protest the Carter Administration's attitude toward the settlements. "I do not like to interfere with internal United States affairs," said Sharon, "but the question of Israeli security is a question for Jews anywhere in the world."[80] To be sure. Sharon, however, was not heard encouraging interference with Israeli policy among those American Jewish leaders who believed that Begin's (and Sharon's) eagerness to annex the West Bank was disastrous for Israel's reputation as a Jewish democracy.

Yet, clearly a growing group of American Jews shared Sharon's belief that they had an obligation to speak out when Israel's security was in the balance. Already, a full-page advertisement had appeared in *The New York Times* featuring the names of prominent American Jewish intellectuals and academics, topped off by the novelist Saul Bellow. More advertisements followed, sponsored by the right and the left, the West Bank annexationists and the dissenters. Still, as usual, it was the minority who were grumbling and shelling out for the ads. In mid-1980, the outgoing chairman of the Conference of Presidents of Major American Jewish Organizations, Theodore Mann, publicly criticized the Begin government's policy of continuing to allow settlements on the West Bank. But for most American Jews it was business as usual—a Sicilian-like *omerta* on the pros and cons of current Israeli policy remained the norm—while privately, they found themselves wishing Begin and his fellow ideologues would disappear from the Israeli scene.

That considerable bad feeling toward Begin did Jimmy Carter very little good. Israel's settlements policy had irked American Jewish leaders from the beginning, but never enough for them to band together and lambast the Israeli prime minister in public. Carter tried to tap this dissident element, but it was small, disorganized, and still inclined to keep its criticisms "in house." To most in Washington, the American Jewish community and its leadership seemed solidly behind the Israeli government (and opposed to Jimmy Carter), and neither Carter nor any member of Congress was willing to identify himself with the dissidents, who, after all, had no organization and, unlike AIPAC, could promise no help at election time. The President would certainly need all the help he could get.

Carter lost the New York primary. The man who was willing to take the heat back in 1977 was getting very burned. In those months before the election, Nahum Goldmann asked a mutual friend to arrange another brief meeting with Carter—twenty minutes would do—so he could pass on some scuttlebutt from Israel. Carter turned him down. The reason: Goldmann had become much too critical of Israeli policy, and the President feared another attack from the Jewish community if he talked to the renegade Goldmann. The intermediary was stunned by how gun-shy Carter had become.[81] After three years of ducking bullets from American Jewish leaders, Carter had good reason to opt for domestic tranquillity.

IN 1976, Jimmy Carter won 68 percent of the Jewish vote; in 1980, he got 45 percent—an all-time low for a Democratic candidate, not to mention an incumbent. In an effort to assure continued support for Israel, American Jewry not only lived with Begin, but became his enthusiastic supporter. At least publicly. Begin's adversary Jimmy Carter became their adversary too.

A former top aide to Carter recalled that after the election he and other top staffers went to Plains for a party held by the White House press at a local barbecue joint. A toast was made to the President's two legacies to Ronald Reagan: (1) Sam Donaldson, ABC News's dogged White House correspondent, and (2) Menachem Begin.[82]

They might have also included a third legacy: AIPAC. The pro-Israel lobby was determined not to lose another big one on Capitol Hill. What the partygoers in Plains did not know was that at that very moment, more than a month before Ronald Reagan was to be sworn in as President of the United States, AIPAC was already planning its strategy to block another sale of U.S. weaponry and planes to the Saudis.

5

"REAGAN OR BEGIN?"—THE AWACS BATTLE

BY the time Ronald Reagan was elected President in 1980, Jews had been lobbying in the U.S. on behalf of the Zionist state for thirty-five years. Both the Presidents' Conference and AIPAC had been operating as full-fledged pro-Israel pressure groups since 1954, though mainly in obscurity. Most Americans still knew very little about the "Jewish lobby," and Jewish leaders preferred to keep it that way, ever concerned about charges of "dual loyalty" and spurts of anti-Semitism. There was no dominant, or celebrated, personality—a Brandeis or Stephen Wise or Abba Hillel Silver—leading the American Jewish community. Few Americans, indeed few Jews, knew the names of those who wielded Jewish power in Washington and Jerusalem. And few Jews, in the U.S. or Israel, had ever even heard of AIPAC.

"In 1977 and '78, I would have to explain to Israelis what I did," recalls Leonard Davis, a former head of research for AIPAC and now a political consultant living in Jerusalem. "People in the Israeli press, the government, even the Foreign Office had no clear idea what AIPAC was, what the Jewish lobby did."[1] AIPAC, however, was famous on Capitol Hill, or notorious, depending on one's opinions about the Middle East, or about Morris Amitay, the lobby's swashbuckling director.

Amitay's eye-for-an-eye tactics during the F-15 battle in Congress not only offended many politicians who considered themselves longtime friends of Israel, but also concerned other Washington operatives of national Jewish organizations who saw their own good relationships with politicians and their staffs being poisoned by Amitay's overenthusiasm. A number of Jewish leaders in California went so far as to ask Amitay's opponent in the arms sale vote, Fred Dutton, a former aide to John F. Kennedy and ex-official at the Democratic National Committee who worked as a lobbyist for Saudi Arabia, his own professional opinion of the AIPAC leader's effect. "I know it sounds unbelievable, but it's true," says Dutton. "From my days in California politics and the Kennedy Administration, I have a broad network of friends and contacts in the Jewish community. After we won the F-15 fight, several of them flew me to California and wanted me to give them an off-the-record critique of what is wrong with AIPAC, which led to a change of leadership up there [at AIPAC]. It wasn't just me; they saw the problem too."[2]

Amitay insists he had never intended to stay on as long as he did and had already informed the AIPAC board a year before of his plans to leave. "I felt I had succeeded in changing AIPAC and after years of government service and lobbying, it was time for me to go out and make some money for my family," he says. Split over Amitay's leadership, "confrontational" style, and autocratic tendencies, the AIPAC board accepted his resignation and looked for a new leader.

Their choice, was, eventually, Thomas A. Dine, a Senate aide with a master's degree in Southeast Asian history and no experience in Jewish organizations. When Dine took over as director of Washington's fabled pro-Israel lobby in October 1980, many of his old colleagues on the Hill were stunned. "I didn't even know Tom was Jewish," recalled one legislative aide who had known Dine for almost a decade; a top AIPAC staffer under Amitay echoed that remark.[3]

Dine is a self-proclaimed "Brooks Brothers Jew" who grew up in Cincinnati with the leanest of Jewish educations; his family belonged to a Reform synagogue. After graduating from Colgate in 1962 and earning his M.A. at UCLA in Southeast Asian studies, Dine volunteered for the Peace Corps and served two years in the Philippines. He returned to Washington for a stint as the Peace Corps' congressional liaison. In 1967, he entered the Foreign Service and was posted to New Delhi as personal assistant to the U.S. ambassador to India, Chester Bowles. Three years later, Dine was back on Capitol Hill as a legislative assistant for foreign affairs to Senator Frank Church, then a senior member of the Senate Foreign Relations Committee. After a year's fellowship at the Center for International Affairs at Harvard's Kennedy School of Government, Dine returned to

Washington in 1975 as director of the Senate Budget Committee's national security staff. During 1979, he was a fellow at the Brookings Institution and then served as an adviser to Senator Edmund Muskie on the Strategic Arms Limitation Treaty (SALT). His next job was as deputy foreign-policy adviser to Senator Edward Kennedy. In 1980, AIPAC called.[4]

The differences between him and Amitay were obvious. Dine the lobbyist looked like an Ivy League diplomatist; Amitay, with his mustachioed intensity, was destined to be cast in the role of Iago. The new AIPAC director was handsome in a boyish sort of way, tall, with a jogger's leanness; his Midwesterner's ingenuousness and enthusiasms had just the right measure of Eastern veneer, but without any of that Cambridge "I'm smarter than you" arrogance. Dine, now forty-seven, is a man who likes being liked (Amitay seemed to enjoy being feared); he has a sense of humor that eases into an endearing sense of self-deprecation. He seemed a perfect choice: the man had Kenen's ease with politicians and the press, and Amitay's feel for Capitol Hill in the 1980s as well as an appreciation for Jewish political activism.

"Tom was aware of the problems—Morrie used to lobby him [when he was working as a legislative aide]," recalls a source who knows both men and their work well. "He was able to drop the negatives on both sides. Like Morrie, he could bring AIPAC into the twentieth century, and though he's assertive and very smart, like Kenen, he has that same empathy for members of Congress."[5] The word around Capitol Hill was that Dine was a good "political man." There was no question that he was well informed and, what's often more important, eminently friendly and presentable, albeit no expert on the Arab-Israeli conflict. Dine's wife, Joan, who is not Jewish, used to joke that her husband couldn't locate Israel on the map before he got the AIPAC job.

Tom Dine's sense of geography improved quickly. He took over as director of AIPAC in October 1980, and two months later, during the December transition period between Carter's departure and Ronald Reagan's entry into the White House, AIPAC got the word that there would be another attempt to sell arms to the Saudis. The package would be additional gear for the F-15 fighter planes the Carter Administration had sold in 1978 plus five airborne warning and command systems (AWACS), the state of the art in aerial electronic surveillance. Arms sales can be blocked only if a majority of both houses of Congress disapproves.

The "AWACS battle," as it became known, turned into one of the most bitter fights on Capitol Hill in recent memory. The American Jewish community and its lobbying arm, AIPAC, took on the President of the United States again, and the result was the end of AIPAC's national obscurity, and the beginning of a revolution in Jewish politics. The AWACS battle is a striking example of the current state of the art of Jewish political power, a self-contained picture of what Tom Dine likes to call "Jewish muscle" on the job. It also raised questions—in public—about the dominance of the pro-Israel forces in Washington without ever seeming to raise the fundamental issue of why the U.S. did not have a comprehensive (or comprehensible) Middle East policy.

In the mid-1950s, the pro-Israel lobby had been created to insure the goal of continued U.S. support of Israel; three decades later, the game of lobbying itself, initially a means to an end, seemed to have become the end. Critics charged that the pro-Israel forces had become an obstacle to American policy in the Middle East, and to peace itself. The lobby worked hard to counter those charges, though no one in AIPAC, and few Jewish leaders outside the group, seemed willing to raise the classic question of Jewish history: Is such an aggressive pro-Israel lobby good for the Jews, in Israel or the United States?

THE first hint of the Saudi sale had come in June 1980 when the Carter Administration announced that it was seriously considering a Saudi request for missiles, bomb racks, and fuel pods that would give the F-15s the Saudis had already ordered more lift and longer range. The Saudis were also interested in buying KC-135 tankers, which could refuel the F-15s in midair, and "airborne warning and command systems" aircraft, also known as AWACS, for directing the F-15s in combat.[6] During the F-15 sale, the President had promised that the planes would not be equipped in such a way as to be a threat to Israel, but the new gear would more than double the fighter planes' range to a thousand miles. "The only target would be Israel," declared Israel's ambassador to the U.S., Ephraim ("Eppy") Evron. Carter claimed the Soviet invasion of Afghanistan had "changed the regional security atmosphere." On July 8, Carter received a letter from a bipartisan group of sixty-eight senators urging him to reject the Saudi request. The additional equipment, the senators wrote, "would not be consistent with the assurances and understandings given" to Congress in 1978. The senators also told Carter he would not get congressional approval for such a sale.

On October 24, eleven days before the presidential election, Carter told a New York City radio audience that his Administration "will not agree to provide offensive capabilities" for the F-15s. The remark was taken as an implicit assurance to American Jews that the U.S. would not be equipping the F-15s to attack Israel. It was also electioneering as usual, because a few days before Carter's assurances, Secretary of Defense Harold Brown had ordered up a study on the extra gear. Reports cited that the Pentagon was hoping that the add-ons to the F-15s would help buy American access to military bases in Saudi Arabia. On October 27, "Administration officials" were reported to be still considering the Saudi request.

And then Ronald Reagan was elected President. Jimmy Carter may have returned to Plains, Georgia, his political career a memory, but the AWACS package remained alive and well in Washington. "We heard about it during the transition period," Tom Dine recalled. "Brzezinski and Brown finagled it after the election. It's a perfect time, and once you get it going, it's hard to stop something like that."[7]

The outgoing Carterites convinced the incoming Reaganites that it was important—to U.S. interests in the Middle East and to the Presidency—to keep their promise to the Saudis; Carter was willing to take the heat. The details of the package were delegated to a State and Defense interdepartmental committee headed by the Pentagon's undersecretary for policy, Fred Iklè. The Reagan Administration was quickly divided on the issue: Secretary of Defense Caspar Weinberger favored the sale, and thought he could get it through Congress; Secretary of State Alexander Haig, whose own presidential ambitions were no secret, was worried about the domestic political consequences of arming the Saudis.

Haig's political instincts were right, and his intelligence probably better. AIPAC had begun building opposition to the Saudi sale on Capitol Hill in December, and refined its strategy in January for what looked like a long fight. In February, the Administration seemed to be pulling away from the goals of Camp David. Haig met with Israeli foreign minister Yitzhak Shamir, and made it clear that the U.S. would not press for resuming the proposed next step after the Camp David accord—Israeli-Egyptian talks on Palestinian self-rule on the

West Bank. U.S. efforts, Secretary Haig declared, would be directed toward remedying the "deteriorating position of the West vis-à-vis the Soviet Union."[8] A State Department spokesman pointed to the causes: the invasion of Afghanistan, residual tensions from the seizure of the U.S. Embassy in Teheran, and the Iran-Iraq war.

The Reagan Administration was obviously not going out of its way to endear itself to the Israelis. In a speech to the Conference of Presidents of Major American Jewish Organizations, Shamir took a swipe at the Administration for walking away from the peace process, a fact that raised a few eyebrows in Washington since Shamir himself had disapproved Camp David in the Knesset. Israel's foreign minister had also reiterated to Haig Israel's opposition to any enhancements in the Saudi's F-15s. For their part, the Saudis were already warning that if the White House abandoned the sale, it would jeopardize future relations between the two countries. And if anyone doubted the issue was heating up, the same week, Tom Dine's old boss, Senator Edward Kennedy publicly warned that the additional equipment would disrupt the balance of power in the Middle East as well as violate Carter's pledge not to allow the F-15s to become an offensive threat to Israel. Such a breach, Kennedy declared, "would raise serious questions about the reliability of our word as a great power and as a guarantor of the peace process in the Middle East."[9] The next day most of the members of the Senate Foreign Relations Committee signed a letter to Reagan also contending that the F-15 gear violated the Carter promise. AIPAC was on the job.

Dine had already paid a visit to the Administration's new counsel, Edwin Meese, who was a close friend of the President's. Candidly (and arrogantly from the White House's point of view), Dine informed Meese that the American Jewish community was prepared to "fight all the way." The man from AIPAC explained a "scenario" of intense opposition from American Jews and their "friends" in Congress. The results, Dine noted, "would not be in the best interests of anybody." Dine emphasized to Meese the firm belief of the Jewish community and other Middle East observers that the Saudi regime was hardly the most stable in the region; he also reminded the White House aide of the Phoenix missile systems and F-15s that had been sold to America's friend the Shah of Iran, only to end up in the hands of America's sworn enemy the Ayatollah Khomeini.[10]

Over the next month, the lobby organized two "colloquies," in the

House and in the Senate, against the sale. According to Dine, "We fired our first warning shot across the Administration's bow. Our message to the White House was that, yes, there would be a winner and a loser, especially in the votes [in the House and the Senate]. But the fight would not be helpful to either side."

The Administration did not flinch. Reagan was still riding the top of his November mandate, and, like every new President, relishing his power. The President also, it seemed, was not giving the AWACS matter his top priority. The details of the deal were being worked on in the Pentagon and State Department interdepartmental committee. And before long it looked as though Secretary Weinberger, a fan of the sale, would be more persuasive than Haig, who was not crazy about it. By the middle of the spring, the President made it known that he was committed to the sale. Reagan's national security adviser, Richard Allen, had taken over directing the fight on Capitol Hill. While Allen may have been a close friend of the President's, he was not making friends in the Senate. "Allen seemed to have a talent for pissing people off over on the Hill," reported one observer who was rooting for the AWACS deal.[11]

The President's inclination to delegate authority was much in evidence in the beginning of the AWACS fight. Reagan seemed to take months to recognize that the Saudi sale was turning into a major event in his young Presidency. In retrospect, Reagan's behavior was typical of how he handled relations with Congress throughout his first term. In the beginning of Reagan's second term, the *New Republic* magazine published a cover story by Carl Bernstein raising doubts about Reagan's ability to run the country now that his crack staff was retiring from the front lines, or switching to other jobs within the Administration.[12] Bernstein quoted "one of the key Republican congressional figures throughout the last three Republican presidencies" (he sounds rather like the retired Senate majority leader Howard Baker) who reported "constantly bailing the President out, because decisions are made without thinking them through. Some people down there [at the White House] ought to be thinking about what happens next. . . . He gets in over his head."

That appeared to be Reagan's position on the Saudi deal. No one at the White House seemed to be paying attention to the juggernaut that the Israeli lobby was riding toward Capitol Hill. Reagan would have to be bailed out of this one too—by two Bakers, Senate Majority Leader Howard and White House Chief of Staff James.

IN early February, Dine had done a vote count in the Senate, and the numbers looked good. "Our friends in Congress," as Dine calls those who line up regularly behind pro-Israel policies, "were supportive." AIPAC knew it owned the House, if only on partisan grounds, with the Democratic majority eager to keep a Republican President in line. In the Senate, California's Alan Cranston, a loyal Israel supporter with presidential ambitions, and Oregon's Robert Packwood were collecting the names of opponents of the sale. Packwood, chairman of the Senate's Commerce, Science, and Transportation Committee, also held the influential post of chairman of the Republican Senate Campaign Committee. He had been laboring heroically to lure to the GOP the kind of generous support that wealthy Jews had bestowed traditionally on the Democrats, and with some success. Packwood now recognized that if the AWACS deal passed the Senate, checkbooks might very well close shut.

Meantime, AIPAC made sure that Jews were well informed about what was happening in Washington. Phone calls to Jewish "community relations councils" around the country alerted local leaders to AIPAC's needs. Letters, calls, and telegrams to members of Congress followed. Information on the capacities of F-15s with and without the proposed enhancements, the risks of AWACS to Israeli security, the instability of the Saudi regime contrasted to the stability of Israel—"the only Democracy in the Middle East"—poured into the offices of members of Congress.

Fred Dutton, the Saudi lobbyist, was no happier about how the Administration was handling things than Tom Dine, for different reasons. He watched in horror as Iklé's interdepartmental committee and then Richard Allen antagonized the very people on Capitol Hill whom the Saudis would need in order to win. Dutton found it curious, as did AIPAC staffers, that aides like Allen and Iklé (and even Haig) were carrying the ball on an issue that they were not personally comfortable with; all three were well known to Jewish leaders and to the embassies of Arab countries as "friends of Israel."

Dutton was in favor of matching AIPAC's efforts with a major Saudi offensive of his own, though he recognized that by March, as the Reagan Administration was preparing to go public with a formal announcement of the Saudi sale, AIPAC had been rounding up opposition for almost five months. His main opposition came from his clients. The Saudis were reluctant to push for a confrontation. After all, two American Presidents had made promises. What else did a small nation sitting on billions of dollars of oil need? In the desert monarchy of Saudi Arabia, the head man delivered. But, as Fred Dutton has said often, "The Saudis do not really understand the limitations of the U.S. Presidency."[13]

IN early 1981 while noodling around some ideas for how to move the Saudi arms deal through Congress against heavy American Jewish opposition, Dutton came up with a simple slogan that seemed to sum up the whole arms sale battle from the Saudi point of view—"Reagan or Begin?" "The only reason I thought of it was that the two names rhymed," Dutton insisted in an interview three years after the AWACS vote. "The American Jewish community said it raised all sorts of anti-Semitic nuances, but, hell, it had nothing to do with that. Sure it oversimplified the matter, but it did sum up the issue."

Dutton contended that the Saudis refused to buy his "Reagan or Begin?" brainstorm. "They didn't want to unleash a big effort," he recalled. But he later threw the line out in a newspaper interview about his role in the Saudi sale, suggesting that if "I had my way I'd have bumper stickers all over town that say 'Reagan or Begin?'"[14] The rest of the press, not surprisingly, picked up the phrase; Dutton had written a great headline for them.

Frederick G. Dutton might have been an amateur in the ways of the Arab world, but in the no less arcane world of Washington politics he was a pro. Dutton, fifty-seven, was particularly adept at dealing with the press; many of its most powerful men were old pals of his—Washington *Post* editor Ben Bradlee, the late columnist Joseph Kraft and political writer Richard Reeves, *New York Times* Washington bureau chief Bill Kovach, Carl Bernstein, NBC's Roger Mudd, to name only a few of the best known. The Saudis could not have hired a more skillful Washington agent. By most accounts (including some AIPAC staffers), whatever they were paying Dutton—reports cited $400,000 in 1981[15]—he was a bargain.

Dutton's résumé reads like a trip down memory lane in Democratic Party politics: campaign aide for Adlai Stevenson, executive assistant to California governor Edmund G. Brown, campaign aide to John F. Kennedy, special assistant to President Kennedy, assistant secretary of state for congressional relations in the Kennedy Administration. In 1968, Dutton was a top adviser in Robert Kennedy's presidential bid, and in 1972 he worked for McGovern, whose campaign was managed by Frank Mankiewicz, a former high-school classmate in Los Angeles. In 1970, Arthur Goldberg, the former Supreme Court justice and ambassador to the United Nations who was a respected figure among the American Jewish Establishment, sought Dutton's advice for his unsuccessful campaign for governor of New York. Dutton has remained close to Ted Kennedy in spite of his Saudi connections and Kennedy's pro-Israel positions. He has even maintained his friendships with prominent members of the California Jewish community.

Dutton, now sixty-three, works out of a modest two-office suite he shares with his wife, Nancy, also an attorney—Dutton and Dutton—on Connecticut Avenue in Washington, the capital's lawyers' row. In addition to his lobbying, Dutton is on call to the Saudi Embassy virtually around the clock, often extracting various Saudi princes from minor legal tangles. So often does the Saudi ambassador to the U.S. call on his services on short notice that Dutton prefers not to schedule appointments in advance for fear of standing people up.

In 1981, Dutton was busy giving his employers civics lessons. His memos to the Saudi Embassy often read like primers on the American political system, a fact that amused AIPAC staffers who had the opportunity to read enough of them to note also that the Saudis did not always take his advice. The first lesson Dutton quickly learned about lobbying for an Arab country was to forget all the lessons he had learned as JFK's special assistant and the State Department's liaison with Congress. He avoided the classic lobbying techniques of pitching members of Congress in person, warming them up with grass-roots support for your side back in their district or state, and generating thousands of letters and telegrams to Congress or the White House.

Nor does Dutton find it particularly efficient and effective to generate reams of op-ed–page pieces, editorials, and news stories about the Arab side of the issue, another textbook ploy of the congressional lobby. He is quite candid about the limitations of the "Arab lobby" in the U.S., in spite of the numerous stories about its increased power and influence. (Many generated by Dutton himself—"The publicity was useful for a while since we had to move from zero to one," Dutton explains matter-of-factly, which is his style, and a part of his charm for journalists.)

> Unlike AIPAC, the Saudis and the Arab countries do not have the means to reach out into the country. One has to be very sophisticated and shrewd about this. The Arab does not have a great image in this country. You cannot sell it on TV to the average housewife. The U.S. does have national interests in the Middle East—oil, big finance, trade. But these are not broad-based public appeal issues. To try to build up grass-roots support for things like that would be a bit like [Tom] Dine trying to make a big effort outside the Jewish community. It wouldn't be all that productive, and he'd probably stir up some wild animals against him in the process. You have to channel yourself, and the Arab channel in this country is paper thin.[16]

Dutton knew as well as Dine that the showdown would be in the Senate, but, unlike AIPAC, which had a tendency to charge up to Capitol Hill and begin putting pressure on members, Dutton's strategy was to pick the fence-sitters and work on them.

> AIPAC had 58 signatures. Our strategy was to get 52 names on our side—"Don't put too many people on the spot." Get 50 to 52—that's what we tried to do in '78 in the F-15 fight, and we tried to do the same in 1981. If your basic aim is to strengthen Saudi–U.S. relations, then you do more good inside the club of the Senate if you put the least number of people on the spot. Always look for 50 or 52, and don't go beyond that. Ronald Reagan understood that as well as anyone. He was looking for the senators who could help him.

On March 6, the White House announced that the U.S. would sell to the Saudis air-to-air missiles and fuel tanks for the F-15s. The Administration, however, rejected the Saudi request for bomb racks that would have made the fighter planes more effective against targets on the ground. To diffuse Israeli opposition, Reagan offered Israel an additional $600 million in military credits over the next two years. The White House also hinted the U.S. would relax restrictions on Israel's efforts to sell its new Kfir fighter plane abroad. (The Kfir had a U.S. engine, and the Israelis needed U.S. approval to export any planes.)

Israel stood by its principle of "No arms to Arab enemies." Begin's Cabinet protested that the F-15 enhancements would further threaten peace in the region by supplying additional offensive power to Saudi

Arabia, for whom, the Israelis noted, "has come a cry for *jihad* [holy war] against the state of Israel." The U.S. State Department replied that "circumstances in the region have changed dramatically," re-emphasizing that the Soviet invasion of Afghanistan and the Iran-Iraq war justified arming the Saudis.

On March 18, Secretary of State Haig testified before the House Foreign Affairs Committee on a wide range of foreign-policy issues, particularly the increased vulnerability of the U.S. and its allies to international terrorism and the Soviet tilt to "an imperial foreign policy," a trend that Haig described as "most alarming." Discussing the Middle East, Haig told the House committee that it was "fundamentally important to begin to develop a consensus of strategic concerns throughout the region among Arab and Jew and to be sure that the overriding danger of Soviet inroads is not overlooked." The next day, before the Senate Foreign Relations Committee, Haig stressed again the need for "a strategic consensus" in the Middle East. The secretary of state proposed that the U.S. route to peace was strengthening regional states like Israel, Egypt, Saudi Arabia, Jordan, Turkey, and Pakistan through military, economic, and political cooperation and assistance.[17]

Haig's remarks underscored the Administration's lack of any comprehensive Middle East policy, not to mention its misunderstanding of how those Middle East states viewed their own security interests. For Ronald Reagan "the paramount American interest in the Middle East is to prevent the region from falling under the domination of the Soviet Union."[18] The "paramount interest" of Israel and of Saudi Arabia, however, was not the Soviet threat—but the threat of each other.

WHILE Haig was outlining the Administration's policy to Congress in March, Tom Dine presented AIPAC's board of directors a memo outlining his strategy for defeating the Saudi sale, and then asked each member to destroy the memo in his presence. An experienced Washington hand who knows how fast "confidential" information can speed around town, Dine did not want to see AIPAC's strategy in the Washington *Post*. (In spite of his caution, Dine could not find his own copy of the memo three years later.)

Long before he was chosen to head AIPAC, Dine had given a lot of thought to Congress's role in the creation of foreign policy, and he treated his new job as a perfect opportunity to test out his theory of how Congress might check and balance a President's enthusiasm for foreign policy, the one area, traditionally, where a U.S. President could act virtually unhindered by Congress and special interest groups.

Saudi or White House spies would not need a copy of the strategy memo that Dine had submitted to the AIPAC board. All they had to do was get a copy of *The New York Times* of April 4, 1975, in which Tom Dine, then a fellow at Harvard, had published his first *Times* op-ed–page article, "A Primer for Capitol Hill." The piece was an eight-point manifesto of how Congress might "exercise its constitutional foreign affairs powers effectively" in the face of President Gerald Ford and Secretary of State Henry Kissinger's efforts to keep the legislative branch out of international affairs altogether.[19]

Dine proposed that legislators use their "purse string" power to press for alternative policies. Bipartisan appeal of such policies is, he argued, crucial, as is the support of congressional leaders. According to Dine, "External forces must be linked to domestic ones so that the objectives of both are similar." Congress had to counter the Administration's easy access to the press by cultivating its own friends in the media and by generating its own information on the issues, preferably through committee investigations "that use the pretrial technique" of putting witnesses under oath and grilling them. "Outside special interest groups should be mobilized on behalf of the issue," Dine suggested. Such groups would give a grass-roots legitimacy to alternative policies, and would provide a nationwide forum to publicize views and additional manpower for collecting information as well as "intelligence of member's voting patterns."

Dine saw the making of foreign policy as a kind of Super Bowl of lobbying: the Administration pressing its view, members of Congress selling theirs, while "outside special interest groups"—the professional lobbyists—backstopped committee members, feeding them information and "intelligence." Congress needed a professional staff of foreign policy experts to map strategy and keep members on the track, Dine the foreign policy staffer proposed. Above all, Congress had to exercise "persistence." Dine concluded: "By perennially and persistently criticizing a policy, there is a possibility of inducing the Administration to abandon or modify a program. . . ."

And thus AIPAC's strategy during the 1981 Saudi arms fight: "inducing the Administration to abandon" its policy.

• • •

THE President's personal attention to the difficult matter of getting the Saudi sale through Congress was diverted by an event out of Ronald Reagan's control. On March 30, 1981, Reagan was shot in the chest by a young assassin named John W. Hinckley, Jr. The President apparently issued the go-ahead for adding the five AWACS planes to the Saudi package from his bed in George Washington University Hospital. "His aides gave it to him to sign, and he did," claims Dine.

On April 5, during a trip made to the Middle East, Israeli Prime Minister Begin informed the U.S. secretary of state that the proposed AWACs sale to the Saudis and the additional gear for the sixty-two F-15s would jeopardize Israel's security and the overall strategic situation in the region. The following day, across the Jordan River in Amman, King Hussein told Haig that Israel's intransigence toward the Palestinians had "opened the door to turbulence, instability, and other problems" in the region. And as if to make sure Haig got the point before he left the Middle East, two days later, after meeting with Crown Prince Fahd, Foreign Minister Saud al-Faisal, and Prince Sultan in Riyadh, Prince Saud declared, at the airport before Haig's departure, that Israel was "the main cause of instability" in the Middle East, and not the Soviet Union, as Haig had claimed.[20]

In the first week of April also, after reports of the AWACS add-on had surfaced in the newspapers, Tom Dine paid a visit to Howard Baker, who was preparing to visit the Middle East during the upcoming Easter recess. Dine reiterated essentially what he had told Meese a few months before, though the evidence was by then much more obvious. The AIPAC director beseeched the majority leader to consider the consequences of a battle over the AWACS sale in Congress, and assured him that "we are going all out." The Administration would have to respond in kind to the opposition on Capitol Hill. "They may win," Dine conceded to the majority leader. "But in the end they would lose."[21] The lobbyist warned that the press would wallow in the controversy and "dissect the Administration and find it in disarray—because almost by definition every new Administration is in disarray." Reagan, whose popularity was now at an all-time high due to his courageous (and good-humored) recovery from Hinckley's bullet, certainly did not need that kind of bad publicity—especially amid concern over how fit the seventy-year-old President would be when he returned to work.

Baker listened, commiserated—he was not looking forward to the inevitable fight either—and pointed out to Dine that it was his job as majority leader to push the President's legislation through the Senate. Dine asked that the Administration postpone its final decision to bring the issue to a vote, "so that they at least be able to understand fully what they were doing." One of Dine's main arguments was that before the White House started changing U.S. policy in the Middle East, the President ought to have a Middle East policy.

Dine left the Baker meeting without anything more satisfying than the possibility of more time to build his case in the Senate. AIPAC had already decided not to bother lobbying the House very strenuously; Dine did not want the Saudi sale to be seen as a partisan issue. It was in AIPAC's interest—in the short term and long term— that arming the Saudis be seen as a threat to Israel. Even if AIPAC lost—and Tom Dine knew that no President had ever lost an arms-sale vote—he recognized the propaganda potential of a heavily armed Saudi Arabia.

ON April 18, the State Department disclosed that the Administration had tried to persuade the Saudis to settle for the F-15 gear and post-pone the AWACS purchase. The Saudis rejected any compromise intended to help ease Israel's fears. The Administration formally announced its decision to go ahead with the Saudi deal on April 21.[22]

Baker returned to Washington after Easter and advised Secretary Haig to postpone submitting the arms package to Congress for a vote until after the Israeli elections scheduled for June 30. Should the President try to submit the package to Congress for a vote before then, he would lose, in Baker's opinion. Begin was attacking the AWACS sale every chance he got. (In Israel, Baker had heard reports that Begin was warning fellow citizens that the Saudis would use the AWACS, for, among other things, peering through the windows of Israeli homes.[23]) Baker, however, knew that polls in Israel showed Begin's Labor opposition leading, and he was hoping that a new prime minister might be more reasonable about the new American President's desire to establish closer ties with the Saudis. Perhaps the prime minister would even be so kind as to help cool the enthusiasm

of Israel's friends on Capitol Hill for giving the President a beating
when the deal came to a vote. (In fact, the former Israeli foreign
minister Abba Eban declared that if the Labor Party, of which he was
a prominent member, did return to power, it would oppose the
AWACS sale as vigorously as had the Begin government.)

Baker, like Tom Dine, was trying to buy some time. He believed
that the Saudi deal was necessary and in the best interests of the U.S.
in the Middle East, but he was just not sure whether he'd be able to
peel off enough senators who had already signed on with Packwood
and Cranston (and thus AIPAC) to carry the vote.

Neither the White House nor the State Department had made
Baker's job any easier. "Whoever had designed the strategy [to win
the vote] over there at the State Department just sort of figured that
when the time came it would happen," recalled a Baker aide three
years later.[24] Internal bickering within the Administration over the
direction of policy between Haig, U.N. Representative Jeane Kirk-
patrick, and Reagan confidant (and foreign-policy novice) Judge
William Clark, along with differences of opinion between Haig and
Weinberger, diverted attention from the importance of the AWACS
fight. The Administration, of course, had other priorities, particularly on the domestic front where Reagan was eager to push through
economic measures to cut the budget and bring down inflation. Nevertheless, the Saudi arms package was the President's first foreign-
policy initiative, and, at the moment, it looked as if he was heading for a
major embarrassment.

"Nobody was in charge of the AWACS thing in the beginning," the
Baker aide recalled. "Which is ironic in view of Al Haig's famous 'I
am in charge!' line [after the assassination attempt on Reagan]. There
was not a central focal point that the AWACS strategy was coming
from. It was a classic case of too many chiefs and not enough In-
dians."

So when the job fell to good Indian Howard Baker, he told his own
staff, "I don't take something on to lose, but, boy, we've got big
trouble here." He also informed the White House that he required a
total commitment to winning. James Baker, Reagan's chief political
adviser and legislative liaison, took over the day-to-day coordination
of the AWACS fight, working closely with Howard Baker and the
Saudis. The signal went out to members of Congress that the President himself was lobbying this one, and he wouldn't take kindly to
losing.

There was no immediate response to the announcement from the Begin government. As much as Israel wanted to be self-reliant, as much as Begin pretended, as he often told his Cabinet, "the Americans need us more than we need them," the painful fact was that Israel would disintegrate into chaos the day after U.S. military and economic assistance was turned off.[25] Begin needed Reagan.

Yet Begin persisted, with amazing impunity, in stretching the limits of U.S. patience with its small friend in the Middle East. The Israeli prime minister had tested Jimmy Carter's good will throughout the Camp David negotiations, and afterward on the issue of Palestinian autonomy. On June 7, 1981, Begin gave Ronald Reagan a taste of Israeli unpredictability.

Israeli F-16s bombed and destroyed the French-built nuclear reactor near Baghdad. Without notifying the U.S. beforehand. There was an international uproar. Israel's government argued that the bombing was an act of "self-defense." The reactor had the potential to produce the material for nuclear weapons that Iraq could use against Israel. The Israeli prime minister warned that "Israel will not tolerate any country—Arab or otherwise—developing weapons of mass destruction." Begin added, "There will never be another Holocaust."[26]

The U.S. immediately protested that Israel's "unprecedented" move would only increase the threat of war in the Middle East; the State Department also pointed out that the evidence suggested that Israel had used U.S.–supplied aircraft in violation of the sale agreement that stipulated the F-16s were to be used only for defensive purposes. The Iraqis were signatories to the nuclear nonproliferation treaty, Israel was not, and, the State Department noted, the U.S. had no evidence that Iraq was building nuclear weapons.[27]

Many members of Congress worried that the Israeli raid would undercut ongoing U.S. efforts to encourage peace in the region. A certain unease drifted through the American Jewish community over Begin's talent for endangering the "special relationship" between the U.S. and Israel. The raid, however, was popular in Israel—though not among Begin's political opponents, who suspected the prime minister had timed the bombing to boost his standings in the polls for the upcoming elections. The U.S. joined a United Nations compromise resolution, initiated by Third World states and passed on June 19, that "strongly condemned" Israel's actions, but did not call for sanctions, though a shipment of F-16s to Israel was postponed. Begin escaped with a slap on the wrist.

In the midst of the furor over the attack, one irony went largely unnoticed: the F-16s, with their F-15 escorts, had flown over Jordan and Saudi Arabia eluding detection by U.S. AWACS patrolling northeast Saudi Arabia.

Begin put U.S.–Israeli relations to another test a month later. On July 17, Israel bombed PLO targets in West Beirut. Declaring regret over civilian casualties, the Israeli government again justified the raid on the basis of self-defense. Lebanese authorities charged that Israel had used U.S.–built F-4 Phantom jets. Again, the Reagan Administration, on the verge of lifting the ban on the F-16s, decided to postpone that shipment and a second one that was in the works.

On August 24, the Reagan Administration formally notified Congress of its decision to sell $8.5 billion worth of arms to the Saudis —five AWACS, ground stations to support them, and for the F-15s, 1,177 Sidewinder air-to-air missiles, fuel tanks, and six KC-707 tanker planes.

There was no immediate reaction to the announcement from Begin, who had beaten his Labor opponent, Shimon Peres, again in a close election. But Begin had other matters to attend to. The day of the AWACS announcement in Washington, Begin was beginning a two-day summit meeting with Egyptian President Anwar Sadat, during which they decided to resume talks in September about Palestinian self-rule. There were also, as usual, differences of opinion even within the Begin government, and definitely in the Knesset among the opposition party, over how far Israel should press its protest of the AWACS deal. Some saw it as a "no-win" situation: If Israel's lobbyists and friends in Congress succeeded in defeating the sale, the Begin government risked antagonizing the Reagan Administration. If the pro-Israel forces lost the battle, arming Israel's enemies would be a dangerous precedent. Though some Israelis even argued that the AWACS were not a real threat to Israeli security—one Israeli general had described the unarmed surveillance planes as "big buses," which the Israelis could blast out of the sky without much effort—there seemed to be a consensus in Israel that all arms sales to Arab countries ought to be opposed, as a matter of principle.

ISRAEL, however, could afford to remain silent about the AWACS announcement. AIPAC and the lobby's supporters in Congress were on the case. The head count looked good. On September 17, Senator

Packwood produced the names of half the Senate—fifty senators—as cosponsors of a resolution opposing the sale. The Administration, finally, recognized what was at stake; the gloves came off as the two Bakers set out to counterpunch that total down to a winning number for their side. Dutton stayed away from the Hill—he had not even registered for the right to lobby Congress—and spent his time keeping the Bakers informed on Saudi negotiations and which senators were on the fence or leaning toward the President. Dutton preferred to leave the arm twisting to James Baker and his aides. The Saudis, led by Prince Bandar, a politically savvy young fighter pilot and son of the Saudi defense minister, mounted a widespread campaign to persuade American corporations that the sale was not only in U.S. interests but in their economic interests too.[28]

The presidents of Boeing and United Technologies generated thousands of letters and telegrams supporting the sale from scores of corporations and executives around the country to members of Congress. Mobil Oil, according to one report, spent "more than a half million dollars on a media blitz," running a series of full-page ads in at least twenty-six newspapers. Though Saudi critics have made much of this corporate lobbying—particularly Steven Emerson in a series of *New Republic* articles that later became a book[29]—the extent of business interest in the Saudi sale seems less tied to pro-Arab (or anti-Israel) sentiment than to financial self-interest. American corporations may have thrown themselves into lobbying for the sale, but they certainly needed little prodding from the Saudis. Boeing, the main contractor for the AWACS planes, had billions at stake; United Technologies reportedly had about $100 million riding on the success of the sale. And, as one of the Mobil newspaper ads pointed out, "Saudi Arabia is far more than oil—it means trade for America, jobs for Americans, and strength for the dollar." The ad also estimated that the Saudi friendship was worth $35 billion to the U.S. balance of trade.[30] Mobil didn't even need to be asked to help out. "They moved on their own to get some brownie points in Riyadh," recalled one source familiar with the Saudi lobbying effort.[31]

Supporters of the sale began poking holes in AIPAC's headcount. "We did our own poll, contacting people who had allegedly committed [to opposing the sale] and discovered a large number who said they had not committed or were waiting though they were sympathetic to American Jewish opposition," recalled Ron Cathell, spokesman for the National Association of Arab Americans. "We were quite surprised because we really believed the AIPAC numbers, until we found weak spots or overexaggeration or misrepresentations." Founded in 1972 and registered as a lobby in 1978 to counteract the pro-Israel forces, the NAAA, and a gaggle of other grass-roots Arab-American operations, was light-years away from the kind of political clout and organization of the American Jewish community. During the AWACS fight, the NAAA consisted of one lobbyist and a total staff of eight; AIPAC numbered thirty-five, with reserve troops of thousands across the country eager to organize on its behalf at a moment's notice.

By mid-September, things had begun to take a turn for the better for the Administration. Begin had arrived in the United States, essentially to improve his public-relations image and affirm that Israel was with the President and the secretary of state in their anti-Soviet crusade. After some wrangling between the State and Defense departments over the propriety of inviting the Israeli prime minister to the White House—Weinberger had not forgotten the Iraqi raid and Beirut bombings—Begin did meet with the President. By most accounts, the meeting was strained, though Begin did agree not to lobby members of Congress against the AWACS sale.

But in a subsequent get-together with thirty-six senators, including Illinois's Charles Percy and Texas's John Tower, both supporters of the sale, Begin was asked about the Saudi deal, and answered what everyone already knew, that he was against it. The Israeli prime minister also stressed his opposition during a meeting of two-hundred Jewish leaders in New York, though he added that Israel would not intrude in the congressional debate. Privately, the White House charged that the Israeli prime minister had broken his promise to stay out of the controversy. AIPAC rolled its eyes; the fight was tough enough without Begin stirring up animosity in the White House. Dine claims several senators complained to him about the anti-Semitic undertones of the lobbying effort for the sale, a nasty residue from the "Reagan or Begin?" sloganeering. Senator Mark Hatfield told one reporter that "my mail has shown a definite increase in anti-Semitism."

There was some anti-AIPAC sentiment too. AIPAC had been lobbying against the sale for ten months. Dine had kept his promises to Ed Meese and Howard Baker. But now some prominent Jews expressed concern that AIPAC might have done its job too well. As one put it: "We've done enough. If we lose, we lose; if we win, we really lose."[32] Dine argued that they were falling into the "Reagan or Begin?" trap, while he, sticking to his "Primer for Capitol Hill" strategy, contended the AWACS fight was a classic struggle between Congress and the executive branch over the direction of foreign policy. Still, few Jewish leaders shared Dine's passion for political science; they were eager to protect Israel and the American Jewish community, and AIPAC's success on the Hill, in their opinion, was provoking a backlash. Dine was also getting some heat from Israel where he was being attacked for luring Begin into publicly supporting AIPAC's fight. There were air force generals worried about their relations with the U.S Air Force, and Foreign Ministry officials concerned that doors at the U.S. State Department would be slammed in their faces.

Dine had enough pressure on him on Capitol Hill. Meese and National Security Adviser Allen had appealed to all Republican senators to support the President. Haig claimed the list of opponents was "replete with soft spots." He could tick off a dozen senators who were "ready to reconsider," he said.[33]

On September 22, the Administration staged a separate press briefing to clarify "misunderstandings" about the alleged threat of the AWACS to Israeli security. National Security Adviser Richard Allen informed reporters that the planes were incapable of collecting photographic intelligence or pinpointing ground targets. Nor would the Saudis be up to coordinating an all-out multination Arab air attack on Israel because they would lack the sophisticated battle command equipment carried by the AWACS used by the U.S. and NATO forces. According to Allen, these AWACS would not even carry electronic countermeasure devices; the Israelis could jam their radar. The Saudis had already agreed not to fly the AWACS over Syria or Jordan.[34]

So strenuously had Allen stressed the limitations of the Saudi AWACS that reporters at the briefing joked that if the planes were that stripped, why would the Saudis even want to buy them? The Israelis knew the plane quite well; the Administration had already given a group of Israeli technical experts a nine-hour test ride on the plane to prove the restraints on the AWACS' offensive capability. The Israelis, however, were worried more about how the AWACS might hinder their own offensive potential. Since 1967 their best defense had always been the threat of a sudden air assault that swooped in so low to the ground that it eluded enemy radar. The Israelis feared that the "look down" radar on the AWACS would cancel out their most effective tactic, which had worked perfectly during the Iraqi raid.

The Administration and the GOP leadership had been working on several compromises with the Saudis and were impressed with Prince Bandar's willingness to make concessions.

On September 28, the new ambassador to Saudi Arabia, Richard Murphy, flew to Riyadh to gain Saudi approval for a proposal that AWACS missions be operated jointly by the U.S. and the Saudis. The Saudis were not happy about any reference to "joint control" of the planes, but they did seem amenable to Americans participating in AWACS flights "well into the 1990s," according to the testimony of Secretary Haig before the Senate Foreign Relations Committee. Defense Secretary Weinberger told the committee that the sale posed no threat to Israel. "I don't have the faintest idea why they have opposition to it," he said. "They could shoot down this plane in a minute and a half. It's not an armed plane. There isn't even a BB gun on that plane."[35]

To those involved in the AWACS battle, and many watching on the sidelines, it seemed as if the business of government in Washington had stalled while the White House and Congress focused only on the sale of five airplanes to Saudi Arabia. And, in a sense, they were right. As one Senate aide later put it: "If the deal did not go through —if there was not enough support for Ronald Reagan's first foreign-policy initiative—there was no doubt that the Administration would have not been able to regain any standing in the foreign-policy community for the remainder of the term."[36] AWACS was worth some undivided attention.

ON October 1, Ronald Reagan laid his reputation on the line. His Administration finally submitted its formal notice, in writing, to Congress of its proposed sale of arms to Saudi Arabia. Congress had thirty days to veto the proposal. Having racked up some success on the diplomatic front with concessions from the Saudis, the White House was now prepared to devote the month to winning a majority of the Senate.

The President had already called for reinforcements. A few weeks before, one Republican senator attending a dinner was summoned from the table by "a call from the White House." Ex-President Ford was on the line, and on behalf of the current President, he bluntly asked, "Are we going to let the Jewish lobby run American foreign policy?" Obviously shaken by the call, the senator returned to his table—at a dinner for Jewish leaders. (Presumably, the fabled White House telephone operators had tracked the senator down without informing Ford where.[37]) Yet Ford was simply (and carelessly) reflecting the anxiety at the White House. In a televised announcement of the sale, the President himself sent out the same message to Israel, though in less inflammatory words. In a sure shot at Israeli opposition and American Jewish lobbying efforts, Reagan bluntly declared: "It is not the business of other nations to make American foreign policy." Reagan said he was determined to defend Saudi oil fields against "anyone" who threatened them. Three days later, former President Nixon attacked the "intense opposition [of] the Begin government and parts of the American Jewish community" for interfering with the White House's aims to benefit the nation. A defeat of the AWACS sale, he argued, would be "a Pyrrhic victory" that would cause "serious embarrassment to Reagan, at home and abroad." A week later, Jimmy Carter called for support of his former opponent, warning of "the danger of a third worldwide oil shock."

On October 14, the House, as expected, voted overwhelmingly against the sale—301 to 111. The next day the Senate Foreign Relations Committee endorsed a resolution disapproving the Saudi deal by nine to eight. Senator Rudy Boschwitz, a Republican from Minnesota and a staunch friend of Israel, joined the eight Democrats on the committee. Two other Republicans whose positions had been up in the air—Maryland's Charles Mathias, Jr., and S. I. Hayakawa of California—supported the President. A third Republican, South Dakota's Larry Pressler, who had signed the September 17 resolution opposing the sale, switched after a phone call from the President that came in the middle of the debate preceding the vote. Howard Baker announced that "the momentum" was now with the President. Baker also reported that the full Senate would not vote on the measure until later in the month. Reagan was scheduled to attend an international conference of developing nations the next week, and the Senate felt it inappropriate to vote while he was out of town. The postponement would also be "convenient to members of the Senate." Indeed, Baker could use the time.

Throughout September and October, Baker had coordinated an intense lobbying effort on behalf of the AWACS deal. Baker himself

collared senators he thought he might be able to persuade; James
Baker canvassed the Senate Office Building, trying to win over
others. In several cases, Howard Baker invited a senator to his office,
where he *and* James Baker would lean on him. They also decided
which senators required a visit with the President, and Howard Baker
would, as one observer put it, "march him down to the White
House." A Baker aide recalled that "at one time or another, probably
half to two-thirds of the Senate went to the White House to discuss
the AWACS proposal, either in small groups of two or three or indi-
vidually."

Publicly, Reagan expressed his concerns about his own reputation
and the U.S. losing "all credibility" if the Senate blocked the sale. He
said he was confident about the outcome, and denied he was making
deals for votes. Senators emerging from the White House told a different story to colleagues, lobbyists, and reporters. The President had
appealed to their patriotism and respect for the office of the Presidency, but Reagan's main argument, in private, was really quite simple: the proposition that had once been "Reagan or Begin?" had
become "Reagan or else!"

"They used all the tools available to them to run this thing
through," recalls an aide to Howard Baker. Senator Dennis DeConcini, an Arizona Democrat, charged that someone "close" to the President had promised him Reagan would not campaign against him in
1982 if he voted for the sale. (DeConcini eventually voted against it.)
Iowa's Charles Grassley claimed he had been promised his choice for
a U.S. attorney for Iowa would be "expedited" if he voted "right."
(And "right" Grassley eventually did vote.) Senator John Glenn attacked such tactics as "political bribery" and "abhorrent." (He eventually sided with AIPAC.[38])

The vote now seemed up for grabs. AIPAC was trying to hold its
lead, and in the final weeks sent a copy of the novel *Holocaust* to
each member of the Senate. (One AIPAC staffer flying out of Washington noticed a fellow passenger, a Republican senator, reading the
book intently.) The lobby was not above some horse trading of its
own. Unlike the President, AIPAC really did not have to stress what
would happen if a senator voted for the sale. Some were still suffering the ire of Jewish constituents for voting for sale of the F-15s to
the Saudis in 1978. As Packwood and others who preferred to run
with some Jewish contributions in their campaign chests well knew,
AIPAC could shut off the tap as easily as it turned it on.

Edward Zorinsky, a Nebraska Democrat, had joined his fellow party members on the Foreign Relations Committee in voting to disapprove of the sale. On the day of the vote, Zorinsky, who is Jewish, stood with Tom Dine outside the Senate Chamber on a landing between the second and third floors, and informed Dine, "I'm going to vote for it." Dine, who had had Zorinsky to dinner at his home during the past month, replied: "I can't stop you. But I wish you wouldn't, because I want you to have a good relationship with the pro-Israel community. They are not going to forget this one." Zorinsky, who was up for re-election in 1982, told Dine: "You know, I just found out that the lampposts made in this country for the streets of Saudi Arabia are made in Nebraska."[39] AIPAC staffers, however, suspected Reagan had told the Democrat he would not interfere in his campaign if he voted for the sale.

For eleven months the AWACS debate had belonged to AIPAC. October was the President's month. "In my 19 years up here, I have never seen such 180-degree turns on the part of so many senators," Senator Edward Kennedy told a reporter the day of the vote.[40] All along the way, the White House had been looking for a key Democrat to go along with them. After trying unsuccessfully with several senators, they finally found their man in Oklahoma's David Boren, a former governor who confided in Dine that he believed a chief executive had to keep the promises of his predecessor.

But the *coup de grâce* was winning over Iowa Republican Roger Jepsen forty-eight hours before the vote. Jepsen, a first-term senator who would not be up for re-election until 1984, had always been a vigorous supporter of Israel in the Senate. He was one of the first senators to oppose the AWACS sale publicly. In May, giving the keynote address to AIPAC's annual conference, Jepsen had raised the issue of the AWACS sale, declaring: "This sale to an unstable government jeopardizes the security of our most advanced technology. In addition, this sale undermines the security of Israel. This sale must be stopped. . . . I pledge my efforts and my vote to block this sale." The day before the vote, Jepsen announced, in tears, that he had decided to vote for the sale.

What had happened? "We just beat his brains out," a White House aide explained in a two-page article on the AWACS battle and Jepsen in the Des Moines *Register*. "We stood him up in front of an open grave and told him he could jump in if he wanted to." The same day eight "uncommitteds"—four from each party—endorsed the sale.

Baker went into the vote hopeful but cautious. For the first time as majority leader, he kept a written tab of the roll call, making sure the vote was going according to plan. One Baker aide involved in the AWACS fight on a day-to-day basis recalled years later, "We were at the finish line ahead, but we still didn't know if we'd cross it a winner. It was a tough fight, believe me."[41] Just before the vote began, Tom Dine was standing outside the Senate Chamber in a group that included Virginia senator John Warner, who had been active in rounding up votes for the President. Dine was overheard asking Warner, as he headed into the chamber, "John, isn't there anything I can tell you that will change your mind?" Warner replied: "Tom, you've done an excellent job. You really did your homework. But today is not your day."

The Senate approved the AWACS sale 52 to 48.

THAT night Tom Dine threw a party for his staff, their wives, and friends. Senator Rudy Boschwitz, the Minnesota Republican who had defied a Republican President and voted against the AWACS sale, dropped by. Though AIPAC had just lost its second major battle in a row, the American Jewish community's pro-Israel lobby actually had plenty to celebrate: AIPAC had taken on the President of the United States, and almost, as Ronald Reagan himself had claimed, embarrassed him in front of the whole world. (What kind of President couldn't sell five airplanes to a small Arab country, particularly one sitting on billions of dollars of oil crucial to American prosperity?) Ronald Reagan had to apply political pressure to most of the Senate in order to win the vote. The issue of whether the AWACS were crucial to U.S. interests in the Middle East or a menace to Israel's interests in the region had been submerged by Ronald Reagan's interests—not to be embarrassed by the vote. "It was a ten-month marathon for us, and we finished standing up and strong," says Dine. "We had to win four out of four votes—two committees, both houses—and we lost the fourth vote. We all felt very good about it. I think we lost the vote but won the issue."

That remained debatable, but one thing was for sure: AIPAC had hurt the President, forced him to spend more chips than he had ever expected, exposed the Administration to more scrutiny than it needed during its first year in office, and tainted the White House, at least among the American Jewish community, with the image of wanting to win so badly that "anti-Semitic" comments were not ruled out. The White House was bound to be more gun-shy in the future.

And while the press wrote its stories about the Jewish lobby (weakened), the Arab lobby (getting stronger), and corporate lobbying (getting dangerous and maybe even illegal), the fact was that the AWACS fight was just business as usual on Capitol Hill—the American system at work, the *Federalist Papers* in action, constitutional checks and balances just chugging along. Whether the system was working well was less clear, particularly on matters relating to the Arab-Israeli dispute. American policy making had turned into a kind of battle of champions—powerful special-interest groups dueling one another for the heart of Congress. There were actually three lobbies at work during the AWACS battle: the pro-Israel lobby, the Saudi lobby, and the biggest and most powerful lobby of all, the White House.

But what had happened to the debate and analysis so necessary to a genuine Middle East policy? Apparently slogans and public-relations techniques and propaganda and charges of anti-Semitism had taken over. The old questions remained: Were U.S. interests in the Middle East the same as Israel's? Why did the American Jewish community differ so strongly with U.S. policy? Were the current President of the United States and his three predecessors all really anti-Semites? No one seemed willing to raise such questions. The game of lobbying, and ducking the lobbyists, seemed predominant.

The morning after the AWACS vote, Tom Dine put in a call to Howard Baker's office, asking for an appointment. He got it. ("If the nature of the job [of lobbying] is working from access, that was access," Dine explained in an interview three years later.) When he met with Baker, Dine assured him there were no hard feelings on his side. He congratulated the majority leader on his victory, and "for knowing your colleagues." Baker might have congratulated Dine on the same grounds, though he didn't. But Dine knew Baker's colleagues too. He also knew they would continue to be vulnerable on matters relating to Israel, because, as he had told Zorinsky the day of the AWACS vote, American Jews "are not going to forget this one."

6

AIPAC: "THE WAR
FOR WASHINGTON"

THREE days after the AWACS battle, Hyman Bookbinder, the Washington lobbyist for the American Jewish Committee, sent a letter to half of those members of the Senate who had voted with the President. Bookbinder expressed strong disappointment in their vote but added that "we intend to continue working with you" on future Middle East issues. In an interview four years later, the AJC lobbyist recalled that he didn't want those senators to think that the AWACS vote was "a litmus test of our friendship."[1]

It was a generous sentiment, doubtless comforting to those who had voted with the President—and against AIPAC—and were up for re-election in 1984. Yet Bookbinder's note failed to take into account what perhaps the AJC lobbyist had not yet realized, though most denizens of Capitol Hill were getting the picture: while the American Jewish Committee might not have considered the AWACS vote a test of Jewish "friendship," AIPAC did. The reality of Jewish politics in the 1980s is that on all issues relating to Israel, what AIPAC says goes—and after the AWACS fight, AIPAC was saying that several members of the Senate had to go. And while Bookbinder was inclined to be conciliatory and look forward to the next inning in the lobbying game, Dine was now telling Jewish audiences, "Like the Indian elephant, we don't forget."[2]

For a quarter century, AIPAC had been the official Capitol Hill lobbyist for the American Jewish community, the only organization in Washington registered to lobby on Israel's behalf, and a loyal middleman between the member groups of the Presidents' Conference and members of Congress. From the beginning, AIPAC's *raison d'être* had been to keep U.S. aid flowing to Israel. The Israeli economy now depended entirely on congressional beneficence (a stingy Congress could destroy Israel faster than any Arab army), and AIPAC was the master of Congress. Or so AIPAC contended.

The lobby was now in a position to dominate the American Jewish community on the matter of Israel, which, of course, had become the dominant issue among American Jews. The pro-Israel lobby, once a small, underfinanced group of propagandists, following the AWACS "loss" began its impressive metamorphosis into what Tom Dine began calling "a mass movement" to politicize American Jews, already members of the most highly organized community in the nation. Traditionally, the Jewish lobby had been a small group of well-connected (and -heeled) Jewish leaders; Dine was now inviting Jews across the nation to become active, dues-paying members of the pro-Israel lobby. Equally important, AIPAC would keep local political action committees informed about how their representatives and senators were performing on the pro-Israel scoreboard.

"The AWACS fight was the bench mark," says Dine.[3] "We lost the vote but won the issue." Perhaps. But what the lobby had definitely won was the propaganda battle. American Jews perceived the sale of arms to the Saudis as evidence of the growing power of the "Arab lobby." The "enemies of Israel" were clearly on the rise. AIPAC, of course, knew better: it was Ronald Reagan—not the National Association of Arab Americans or Fred Dutton and Prince Bandar's "Saudi lobby"—who had muscled the sale through the Senate. But Dine was not about to argue the point that served his immediate goals perfectly: Jews were rushing to join AIPAC and support the lobby financially.

"AWACS was the most effective battle AIPAC ever lost," says one American Jewish activist familiar with the lobby's history and current strategy. "Proof was that unlike after the F-15 fight nobody said, 'That S.O.B. Dine put pressure on me.' And there was plenty of pressure."[4]

In fact, Dine had, as he later put in an interview, "wounded" the President of the United States.[5] Reagan aides were soon coming by to patch things up. Secretary Haig was on the phone asking for AIPAC's help in getting the Administration's foreign-aid bill through Congress. Tom Dine, a political professional who had never worked for a Jewish organization in his life, was now positioned to become *the* most effective leader of the American Jewish community.

The time was right. "There is not a single American Jew who can galvanize the Jewish community," says a prominent figure in that community. "Eighteen years ago, [former Supreme Court justice] Arthur Goldberg could have done it. [But didn't.] Now there's a real crisis in leadership." The concern on his face is canceled by a smile and a moment of candid self-knowledge: "When I become one of the most quoted 'Jewish leaders' in the press, then I know the Jews need leadership."[6]

Once there were Brandeis and the rabbis Wise and Silver. Goldmann dominated the 1950s, America's foremost genuine Zionist, a disciple of Weizmann, an adversary of Ben-Gurion, a cohort of Sharett. Such prominent Jews were friends of Presidents and members of Congress, major irritants to the State Department, and celebrated among their Jewish rank and file. They were religious and political figures who had a deep sense of Jewish history (except for Brandeis, a latecomer to Jewish concerns). The names of the current leaders of organized Jewry in America are unknown to most Americans, and to most Jews. "Today's Jewish leaders are dwarfs," says another Jewish professional who deals with them daily on behalf of his own organization. "Jewish politics these days has been reduced to 'photocracy' —your power depends on what major political figures you've been photographed with lately. What kind of Jewish leader is it who cannot even read the street signs in Tel Aviv?"[7]

Similarly, Arthur Hertzberg, speaking to the subject "American Jews and Israel," posed this question to an audience at the American Enterprise Institute, the Washington-based conservative think tank: "How does a dentist in Shaker Heights become a political figure?" By becoming, according to Hertzberg, head of the AIPAC chapter in Cleveland and thus an interlocutor with Ohio's senators, perhaps even the Senate Foreign Relations Committee. And if he's successful, he might become president of AIPAC or another major national Jewish organization and find himself on the White House invitation list. "Not for my charm, not for my brilliance, not for my sweet character have I been invited to dinner at the White House," Hertzberg explained. "I was invited to dinner at the White House a half dozen times in the six years that I was president of the American Jewish Congress."[8]

It is an irony of Jewish history: though the American Jewish community has rejected the *sine qua non* of Zionism—finding a refuge from anti-Semitism in the "normalcy" of a Jewish state—support for Israel has made American Jews powerful Americans, with more political clout, in fact, than Jews have ever had in their history of living in the Diaspora. "To put it crudely," Hertzberg told his AEI audience, "through Zionism American Jews can become big bangs on the American political scene."

Tom Dine is a case in point. "It's quite incredible," says one Dine watcher in the Washington headquarters of B'nai B'rith. "But you actually hear people say things like 'Tom Dine spoke at our synagogue' in the reverential tones that I'd imagine once were used by Jews for the likes of Rabbi Stephen Wise."[9]

In his speeches, Dine often talks about the "new Jew"—the politically active Jew, the Jew who masters the American political system in order to protect Jewish interests. It is an easy image for him to conjure because Dine himself is the embodiment of that "new Jew": American-born, no serious Jewish education, not religious, no Hebrew, non-Zionist, gentile wife, 100 percent political animal. The difference between Dine and the more traditional European-style Jewish leader like Hertzberg is striking. Hertzberg is Polish-born, a rabbi (Conservative branch) descended from six generations of rabbis (Hassidic branch), fluent in Yiddish and Hebrew, a lifelong Zionist and former member of the Zionist Executive, former president of the American Jewish Congress, current vice president of the World Jewish Congress, professor of religion and modern Jewish history at Columbia and Dartmouth, the author of the most popular book on Zionism in English, and an outspoken critic of Israeli policy, which has earned him one more distinction in the Jewish community—the American Jewish leader AIPAC loves to hate.

"I'm too much an old Jew for the new Jews," says Hertzberg with a wicked grin. "The AIPAC people are barely Jewish. They certainly don't know anything about Judaism, or Zionism for that matter. What kind of Jewish education do they have? They're lobbyists who could lobby for just about anything, except perhaps the Arabs. When it all comes crashing down thanks to AIPAC, it'll be the old hildagos, the traditional quiet diplomats, who'll be there to pick up the pieces. Tom Dine isn't in this for the long run." Hertzberg has publicly declared that it is time for the Jewish community to shut the lobby down. "It's creating more anti-Semites than it's scaring away," he says. "Being Jewish is not just about supporting Israel or being an anti-anti-Semite."[10]

Yet part of Hertzberg's annoyance with AIPAC is the recognition that the lobby has pushed his sort aside, at least for now. He has become a dinosaur—"the last of the Mohicans" as in the headline in an Israeli Sunday supplement profile of Hertzberg that portrayed him as the last of the breed of Jewish leaders in America who have successfully combined the roles of rabbi, intellectual, and politician. It was, after all, the "new Jew" Tom Dine who had challenged the President on the AWACS, and boosted his organization into the leadership of American Jews. AIPAC now had access to the White House, and to the State Department, that traditional nest of "Arabists."

But there was one problem: Menachem Begin. The Israeli prime minister was making it very difficult for the lobby to argue that the interests of the U.S. and Israel in the Middle East were identical. Though the Reagan White House and Congress seemed unwilling to face up to it, the policies of Begin's Israel were incompatible with U.S. policy in the Middle East. By authorizing and establishing Jewish settlements in the Occupied Territories, Begin pursued his policy of Greater Israel, which, if achieved, would leave no land to trade for peace, the basis of the U.N. and U.S. peace proposal. After Camp David, the Israeli premier had neatly sidestepped the issue of Palestinian rights on the West Bank and in the Gaza Strip and pursued his settlement policy aimed at annexing those very areas. The Carter Administration had denounced the settlements as "illegal" and an obstacle to any negotiations based on U.N. Resolutions 242 and 338.

What were U.S. interests in the region? On this matter, there is a surprising degree of unanimity among Middle East experts, pro-Israel and not so. U.S. interests in the Middle East are (and have been since the creation of the State of Israel) basically these, not necessarily in order of importance: (1) insuring access to Arab oil; (2) curbing Soviet expansion and influence, thus avoiding a superpower confrontation in the region; (3) ameliorating local conflicts and preventing the rise of anti-Western radical regimes; (4) increasing American economic and political influence in the Arab world; (5) supporting the independence and security of Israel.[11]

Yet, during the first half of Reagan's term, there was no evidence that he had transformed U.S. interests into a Reagan Middle East policy. While Carter had seemed driven from his first days in office by the hope of bringing peace to the Middle East, Reagan's entire foreign policy, such as it was, centered entirely around the Soviet Union as the source of America's problems around the world, including the Arab-Israeli conflict. It was "us against them," and Reagan believed that Israel would be useful to us against them. He had declared that "the fall of Iran has increased Israel as the only remaining strategic asset in the region on which the U.S. could truly rely. . . ."[12]

Reagan and Haig saw Israel as a check on Soviet designs on the oil fields in the Persian Gulf. They probably had never bothered to ask Haig's mentor, Henry Kissinger, his opinion of Israel's role in U.S. policy. In 1975, Kissinger, then secretary of state to Gerald Ford, informed a group of Jewish leaders with uncharacteristic simplicity and lack of diplomacy: "The strength of Israel is needed for its own survival but not to prevent the spread of Communism in the Arab world. So it doesn't necessarily help United States global interests as far as the Middle East is concerned. The survival of Israel has sentimental importance to the United States. . . ."[13]

In Kissinger's opinion the best defense against the Soviets in the Middle East is to strengthen moderate Arab governments—precisely what Israel and AIPAC have been afraid of since the Eisenhower Administration. Haig was trying to have it all ways. During 1981, Reagan's secretary of state was eager, to the amazement of Arab leaders, to forge a "strategic consensus" with Egypt, Jordan, Saudi Arabia, *and* Israel against Soviet encroachment in the region. How that would be possible without peace between Israel and the Arabs was unclear. The moderate Arab states wanted no part of Haig's "strategic consensus," and Begin, the prime minister, remained Jabotinsky's loyal disciple, a man who viewed America's "friends," the moderate Arab states, as his sworn enemies.

After his re-election in June 1981, Begin left little doubt that he would go his own way, and U.S. interests, or even dismay, be damned. And thus the June 1981 bombing of the nuclear reactor in Iraq, which the U.S. condemned; the bombing of PLO sites in Beirut in July, for which Reagan sent "stern" messages of disapproval; and the total rejection of a Saudi proposal for negotiating peace in August—the Fahd Plan, which the U.S. praised as "welcome." In the fall of 1981, Begin's defense minister, Ariel Sharon, decided to take a "new" approach to administering the occupied West Bank that sounded more liberal but turned out to be more rigid than the *laissez-faire* policies that Moshe Dayan had established a decade before. The result was increased Arab violence on the West Bank, a general strike, and Jewish terrorism against Arab mayors. Israeli policy seemed aimed at destabilizing the region and was thus counter to U.S. interests every step of the way. Relations cooled during the AWACS battle in October, and any prospects that Americans had that things might get more peaceful in the Middle East were shattered when Sadat was assassinated that same month.

For anyone who was still eager to argue that U.S. and Israeli interests were identical, 1981 ended on a shattering note. In November, Reagan's strategic consensus was reduced to a consensus of one Middle East state: Begin's defense minister, Ariel Sharon, met with U.S. secretary of defense Caspar Weinberger and worked out a "strategic cooperation" agreement "to deter all threats from the Soviet Union in the region."[14] While Begin cited the accord as a personal political achievement and more evidence of Israel's special relationship with the U.S., his Labor opposition denounced the deal, pointing out that it put Israel right in the middle of the U.S.–Soviet conflict. Did Israel, with all its homegrown problems, want to be dragged into an American war with the Soviet Union? Begin's critics asked. No matter—the agreement lasted two weeks, as Begin followed his own strategic designs: on December 14, Israel annexed the Golan Heights.

The Reagan Administration denounced the move as a violation of U.N. 242, and supported a U.N. Security Council resolution declaring Israel's jurisdiction over the Golan Heights "null and void and without international legal effect." The President also suspended the strategic cooperation agreement. Begin was furious, and typically intemperate in his public response: he pointed out that the U.S., after Vietnam, had no moral right to preach to Israel, or punish it, particularly after "an ugly anti-Semitic campaign" that resulted in the AWACS sale. "Are we a vassal state of yours?" the Israeli prime minister asked. "Are we a banana republic? Are we fourteen-year-olds, who, if we misbehave, we get our wrists slapped?"[15] Labor winced, but Begin's constituency loved it; the "Boss" certainly knew how to stand up to the Americans.

Israel argued that the Golan action had nothing to do with the strategic cooperation agreement. Yet what kind of strategic asset was this that ignored totally U.S. interests in the region? The Reagan White House, like every one of its predecessors since 1967, viewed U.N. 242 as the basis of any negotiated peace in the Middle East, and here was Israel extending its legal jurisdiction to Syrian territory that was supposed to be part of any negotiated settlement for Arab territories occupied in 1967. Why? Begin's foreign minister, Yitzhak Shamir, gave his own unequivocal answer: "Much as we want to coordinate our activities with the United States, the interests [of both nations] are not identical. We have to, from time to time, worry about our own interests."[16]

The Begin government proceeded to pursue those interests during the next year by invading Lebanon. Alexander Haig has insisted in his own memoir of the events leading up to the Israeli invasion that he had been informed as early as October 1981 of Begin's intention, as repeated to him in February 1982, to "push into the southern suburbs of Beirut" in an effort to wipe out "the PLO infrastructure." In May, according to Haig, Begin's defense minister, Ariel Sharon, shocked a room full of State Department bureaucrats with his plans, in Haig's phrase, to "rewrite the political map of Beirut" by establishing a Christian government in Lebanon that would ally itself to Israel. Alexander Haig has been criticized by both U.S. and Israeli writers for giving Sharon "the green light" to launch what turned out to be Israel's ill-fated and divisive invasion of Lebanon.[17] But the former secretary of state insists in his memoir that he challenged the Israelis from the first time he had heard of Sharon's grand plan from Begin at the Sadat funeral, contending that such a move "would have a devastating effect on the United States."[18]

Sharon's response was blunt and undiplomatic. "No one has a right to tell Israel what decision to take in defense of its people," Israel's defense minister informed the U.S. secretary of state. When Haig later wrote to Begin warning that an Israeli attack "could have consequences none of us could foresee," Begin too set the general straight: "Mr. Secretary, my dear friend, the man has not yet been born who will ever obtain from me consent to let Jews be killed by a bloodthirsty enemy and allow those who are responsible for shedding of this blood to enjoy immunity." Haig claims that after reading this note from Begin he "understood that the United States would not be able to stop Israel from attacking." Begin—and the U.S.—allowed Sharon to invade Lebanon, and drag Israel into the most divisive war in its history. Few American Jewish leaders criticized the invasion at the outset.

It now turns out that from the planning stages of the invasion Sharon apparently misled Begin, who in turn was misinforming the United States. Begin had assured Haig that Israel would not draw

Syria into the attack. During the invasion itself, according to a book by two eminent Israeli military correspondents, Begin's Cabinet informed the Knesset that Israel wouldn't take on the Syrians unless attacked first.[19] The U.S. told Syria the same thing. Israel then devastated the Syrian air force and a missile complex.

That Syria would be sucked into the fight was inevitable, of course, as Israel's own general staff studies had indicated. According to Arye Naor, Begin's former Cabinet secretary, the original decision to push twenty-five miles into Lebanon was based on faulty information. When a Cabinet minister raised the possibility of provoking a Syrian attack, Begin waved a hand, while Sharon and his chief of staff, Rafael Eitan, never mentioned the disagreement among their fellow generals. Naor claims that Sharon never informed the Cabinet that the chief of staff, the deputy chief of staff, and the commander of the air force all had serious reservations whether an attack on Syrian missiles was in Israel's interests.[20]

The reason why became clear to everyone after the attack. Their own equipment and pride destroyed, the Soviets quickly rearmed Syria with their most advanced weapons. And to make sure they were well cared for and protected, Moscow sent along seven thousand troops to guard them. Sharon's muscle flexing had undercut one of America's most fundamental interests in the Middle East—keeping the Soviets out.

By August, Israel was bombarding the city of Beirut. The United Nations Security Council unanimously ordered a cease-fire and asked for U.N. observers. Israel refused to allow U.N. observers, and ignored the cease-fire, moving into West Beirut. On August 4, President Reagan called the bombardment "disproportionate," and in a note to Begin questioned whether Israel was using American weapons, as required by law for all arms sold to other nations, for "legitimate self-defense."

Once again, Begin lived up to his reputation for being his own man. The prime minister told a group of American Jewish leaders in Jerusalem to be briefed on Lebanon: "Nobody, nobody is going to bring Israel to her knees. You must have forgotten that the Jews kneel but to God."[21] And in case anyone in Washington was considering leaning on Israel to comply with U.N. and U.S. wishes to stop shelling Beirut, Newsweek quoted a "senior Israeli official"—journalistic code for top policy makers usually of Cabinet level—who warned that any U.S. pressure on Israel would provoke an "unpredictable" response.[22]

So much for the pretense of "strategic cooperation" between the United States and Israel, which seemed willing to cooperate only when it was in its interest to do so. Israel, with some justification, viewed its own security as paramount. With no justification—indeed against all evidence to the contrary—the Reagan Administration continued to view Begin's Israel as a loyal U.S. agent in the Middle East, indeed a strategic asset. However, reservations were already building among a few Jewish leaders. Philip Klutznick, for one, was impressed with neither Begin nor Reagan. Klutznick publicly urged the Reagan Administration "to face the realities of the Middle East as boldly as did the Carter Administration."[23] He suggested that Reagan put a stop to the conflict in Lebanon, force Israel to withdraw its troops, and then enlarge the peace process by bringing all parties in the conflict to the table, "including the Palestinians." Once again, Klutznick became a target of abuse; an editor of AIPAC's *Near East Report* had to be restrained from attacking a former president of B'nai B'rith International, who was also the president emeritus of the World Jewish Congress and the co-founder with Nahum Goldmann of the Presidents' Conference, for pandering to the Arab cause.[24]

But by September 1982, Reagan had a new secretary of state, George Shultz, and seemed ready for a "fresh start" in the Middle East. For Begin, however, it was the same old story. What immediately became known as the "Reagan Plan" was one more gloss on U.N. 242 that would force Israel to negotiate what Begin was ideologically opposed to negotiating. Reagan opposed an "independent Palestinian state" in the territories, which was good news, but the bad news was that he also opposed "annexation or permanent control by Israel." The President also called for a "freeze" of Jewish settlement activity, which he noted was "in no way necessary for the security of Israel." Reagan's solution was a self-governing entity in association with Jordan. While Reagan positioned his peace points in the "framework" of Camp David, he sidestepped the role of the Palestinians in determining their own fate.[25]

The Reagan Plan received the immediate support of a number of American Jewish leaders, including AIPAC's Tom Dine, who immediately, and publicly, praised the President's initiative as having "a lot of value," especially for its promise to bring Jordan's King Hussein to the peace table to discuss the Camp David framework. "Its beauty is that it's open-ended," Dine told *The New York Times*.[26] AIPAC staffers later claimed that the lobby had been informed beforehand that Shultz had Hussein ready to jump aboard "within 72 hours" of the President's speech.

Menachem Begin, however, found nothing beautiful about the Reagan Plan. He denounced it immediately and categorically. Why anyone believed he would do otherwise is a mystery. Begin, after all, had quit Golda Meir's National Unity Government over Israeli acceptance of 242; he had frustrated Moshe Dayan's efforts to activate the second step of Camp David, which sought to move toward Palestinian "autonomy" on the West Bank. And the prime minister now viewed the Reagan Plan as more of the same; worse, it explicitly opposed his own goals for the West Bank. He would soon be ranting that the U.S. was "selling out to the Arabs."

The Arabs generally applauded the President's move, though cautiously, mainly because it had left out any explicit role in negotiations for the Palestinians or the PLO. Nevertheless, the Saudis called the plan "a breakthrough," the Egyptians said it was "positive and constructive,"[27] the Palestinian mayor of the West Bank town of Bethlehem extended his support, and a week later Hussein called the plan "the most courageous stand taken by an American Administration ever since 1956."[28] Yet the Administration had not delivered Hussein, as AIPAC had been assured. The king, of course, was hardly eager to attach himself to a plan that the Israelis rejected out of hand. Besides, Hussein told the U.S. that he needed the Arab states on his side and the Palestinians. Tom Dine began to back off his public support of the plan. But his move had its public-relations advantages: he had established himself as independent of the Begin government, if only for a few days.

The prime minister of Israel, however, poured contempt on Reagan's position. Four days after the President had declared his opposition to annexing the West Bank and called for a settlements freeze, the Begin government allocated $18.5 million to build three new settlements in the West Bank and approved the construction of seven others. The U.S. called this turn "most unwelcome," and insisted in its most diplomatic manner that it would try to help Israel understand "how damaging the settlements are to peace." The continued settlement activity, the Administration pointed out, "can only raise questions about Israeli willingness to abide by the promise of U.N.

Resolution 242 that territory will be exchanged for peace."[29] (Five years before, Jimmy Carter had confided to his diary his amazement that Begin seemed to want to "throw 242 out the window.")

Was anyone paying attention, or had diplomacy blurred everyone's memory? Begin had opposed trading territory for peace since those Arab lands were "liberated"—his phrase—in 1967. In spite of Begin's hostile response to the U.S. initiative, one which bore Reagan's own name and thus his prestige, the U.S. failed to apply pressure on Israel, and, worse (and more curious), neither Reagan nor Shultz personally pushed for their own plan. The Americans took comfort in the fact that Israel's Labor Party supported the Reagan Plan. Trouble was, Begin's Likud was running Israel, and Israel's army was besieging Beirut.

The consequences of that rocked the world on September 18 when the story broke that women and children had been massacred at Sabra and Shatila, two Palestinian refugee camps just south of Beirut. Few Jewish leaders, understandably, were willing even to consider that the Begin government may have been at least "indirectly responsible" for the tragedy—as an independent commission in Israel would conclude in early 1983. But the combination of Sharon's invasion, the sight of bombs exploding in Beirut on television, and the massacre were enough to break the silence of American Jewish leaders. Finally.

The first to strike out at the Begin government was Arthur Hertzberg. The weekend of Sabra and Shatila, he wrote a blistering attack on the policies of Begin and Sharon which was published the following week as a *New York Times* op-ed piece headlined "Begin Must Go."[30] Howard Squadron, a prominent New York attorney, and Rabbi Alexander Schindler, both past chairmen of the Conference of Presidents of Major American Jewish Organizations, called for an independent commission to investigate the events leading up to the massacres. (In Israel, 400,000 demonstrators—ten percent of the country—also demanded an inquiry.)

Hertzberg, still vice president of the World Jewish Congress, quickly became Begin's most vigorous and articulate American critic. In speeches to Jewish audiences and in the pages of Jewish publications he pointed out that "I am not in the dissenting minority; it is Begin who is in the minority, in Israel and the U.S." In the pages of *Foreign Affairs* and the *New York Review of Books*, he called for a return to the U.N. partition plan as a way of settling the Arab-Israeli dispute. Hertzberg also charged that Sharon had invaded Lebanon as part of a plan to scare Palestinians out of the West Bank, thus making it safe for annexation. The American rabbi also pointed out that occupation of the West Bank would make any settlement of the Palestinian question impossible.[31]

By October 1982, even Rabbi Schindler, once one of Begin's most loyal supporters in the American Jewish community, attacked the prime minister. On a trip to Israel, he told Begin to fire his defense minister, Sharon, and then repeated this view on Israeli television. Begin reportedly let the rabbi know that he now considered him "more American than Jew." An aide to the prime minister called Schindler "a traitor."[32] When he returned to New York, Schindler made it clear that his days of slavish adherence to Israeli policy were over. Echoing a criticism by Moshe Sharett, the late Israeli prime minister, that American Jews were treated like cows only good for milking, Schindler told *New York* magazine, "We were used like cows. We were milked, both for financial and moral support—and for the influence that we could bring to bear on Washington—and when we were used up we were put out to pasture. Yes, it is fair to say that we have been treated with contempt—and we've gone along willingly. But we've crossed a watershed now, and our open criticism will continue and increase."[33]

The man who had made life miserable for Jimmy Carter now turned to the task of putting the heat on Begin. Suddenly, Schindler, his tenure as head of the Presidents' Conference over, joined Hertzberg in publicly attacking Begin. In a major address in Denver to his own organization, the Union of American Hebrew Congregations, Schindler attacked Israel's invasion of Lebanon—for starting a war "for the first time . . . when it was not under immediate attack." He strongly declared his opposition to annexation of the West Bank, which, he argued, "will corrode the Jewish character of the state and thereby rupture world Jewry." Moreover, Schindler finally met head on the issue that had been dogging the Jewish community all along: "Is it therefore proper under certain circumstances to disagree with a particular leader or government policy?" Yes, was his answer—support for the nation of Israel was not necessarily undercut by dissenting from a specific policy.

The Reform leader now admitted that special missions, the sort that he made over and over again as head of the Presidents' Conference, were "of doubtful worth." Public dissent was now required, he concluded: "Somehow American Jews, the largest Jewish community in the world, must find a way to communicate more openly and honestly with Israel. We do not serve her cause when we censor or sanitize or stifle our opinions." Schindler raised the idea of a Parliament for the Jewish People that would force Israel to pay attention to Diaspora opinions and criticisms. He suggested that Jewish senators and representatives might meet periodically with Israeli politicians to discuss American political realities.[34] Schindler warned that "if either the Israeli leaders or the institutions of American Judaism suppress honest dissent and smear the dissenters, I predict that the Jewish people will be spiritually impoverished and Israel's cause intolerably diminished." Regardless, though, after Lebanon, Schindler declared that "relations between Israel and world Jewry will never be quite like they were."

Schindler was only half right. While it was true that more American Jews were inclined to criticize Begin, they still preferred to do it "in house," still resented those who spoke out, and still attacked any politicians who dared to echo the kinds of criticism of Begin that had become common "in house" and in Israel. Meantime, Begin pursued his policies, with American Jews—AIPAC included—looking on uncomfortably.

"BEGIN was a major disaster for Israel, and thus a real problem for AIPAC," explains a source extremely knowledgeable about the lobby's operations.[35] Ignored for decades as a right-wing threat to Ben-Gurion's dreams for the Jewish state, Begin had never forgiven American Jewish leaders for their support of the Labor Party. But he needed them, and he was the only prime minister they had. Reluctantly, both sides embraced. "Begin viewed us Americans as 'fainthearted Jews,'" notes Tom Dine. "I spent most of my time arguing with Begin."[36]

They were arguments that Dine, of course, could never win. Nor could he publicly break with the Israeli government and remain effective (and thus keep his job) for long. American Jewish leaders are useful middlemen and lobbyists for Israel (and the U.S.) as long as they have the support of the Israeli government. AIPAC's official stance under Dine, as it had been under Amitay, is that the lobby does not take sides on Israeli political matters, that it is an "American organization" that merely supports "the elected government in Israel."

As the only registered lobbyist for Israel, AIPAC's position is understandable. The consequences, however, are troubling, for American Jews and U.S. foreign policy. By backing Begin, AIPAC was forced to count itself out of the most important issue concerning Israel for Diaspora Jews—whether Israel would annex the West Bank and Gaza and risk the democratic and Jewish character of the state. Furthermore, by branding any American critic of Begin's policies, whether pundit or U.S. senator, an "enemy of Israel," AIPAC was smothering the kind of debate that is supposed to fuel American democracy, and its foreign policy.

Begin had told Arthur Hertzberg in 1977 that his mandate was to repair "twenty-nine years of bad Zionist education." He did essentially that, and AIPAC became Begin's most active American teacher. While privately many American Jewish leaders hoped the Israeli prime minister would become more moderate, or better still, disappear, publicly they supported Israel totally, and thus the very policies —annexation and opposition to negotiations—that they were most uncomfortable with. By his second term in office, Begin was managing to accomplish what his more talented mentor Jabotinsky could never do: transform American Jews into Revisionists Zionists, though most hadn't a clue what was happening. Suddenly, by supporting the Begin government, American Jews were not just supporting Israel, but an ideologically charged vision of its future opposed by hundreds of thousands of Israelis and the Labor politicians whom most American Jewish leaders had supported since the creation of the state.

There were, in fact, AIPAC staffers, including Tom Dine, who were as uncomfortable as many Israelis with the prospect of an Israel that was either a secular state of Arabs and Jews or the South Africa of the Middle East. The lobby's dilemma was agonizing: AIPAC could oppose Begin and risk losing its job as Israel's defender of the faith, or support Israel and hope that no one would notice what was going on. With luck Labor would resume power, reverse the settlements, and press for negotiations with the Arabs.

But while Begin remained in power AIPAC decided to back Israel, in effect, "right or wrong," and come up with a strategy that would make Begin's Israel palatable to American Jews and Congress. While Israeli political and military strategists made their contingency plans for annexing the West Bank and the next Arab-Israeli conflict that was likely to result from it, AIPAC had already begun its own, as

Dine has called it, "War for Washington." AIPAC's war would take thousands of devoted troops, and the lobby intended to find them in Jewish communities throughout the nation. The Jewish community had already been "Zion-ized"; it was now time for them, as Americans, to become "politicized" around the issue of Israel with AIPAC as their leader.

Events in the Middle East had given the "enemies of Israel" the best ammunition they ever had in their own propaganda battle to prove to U.S. policy makers that it was Israel and not the Arabs who was rejecting peace. AIPAC's task was to maintain U.S. support, indeed increase it—in spite of Begin. "The best offense," says Dine, "is the best offense." And the best offense AIPAC could come up with in 1982–1983 was to fasten onto the one notion that both Reagan and Begin could agree upon, in spite of what had happened in the Middle East in the past two years—that Israel is a "strategic asset" to the U.S.—and bolster it with facts, figures, and the kind of academic analysis that makes for better Ph.D. dissertations than foreign policy.

AIPAC's plan was to beat not the Arabs but "the Arabists," as the pro-Israel lobby likes to call the Middle East experts in the State Department and their allies spread throughout various university departments, foundations, and independent think tanks around the country. The so-called "Arab lobby," mainly imitations of Jewish groups led by the National Association of Arab Americans, the American Arab Anti-Discrimination League, and the Saudi Embassy, has no significant grass-roots strength; Arab-Americans have not rushed to form PACs. The Arabists, however, do have power, at least in AIPAC's opinion; proof is the extent to which the lobby has gone to battle them.

It's all-out war, a propaganda war. The term is now pejorative: our side tells the truth, the enemy shovels "propaganda." But the Latin word "propaganda," in this context, means nothing more than what our side believes. Long ago, the Catholic Church institutionalized the notion of getting the good word out to the world by calling the department of the Roman Curia responsible for missionary activities in non-Christian countries Sacra Congregatio de Propaganda Fide. "Propagation of the Faith" is what the pro-Israel lobby is now up to, the faith according to AIPAC.

As an old graduate student and former fellow at Harvard's Kennedy School and Brookings, Tom Dine respected the value of a well-documented argument. He knew that those who write the books and papers and pamphlets and "studies" that U.S. policy makers read will own the policy makers. Policy makers need arguments, and those who supply those arguments will be most appreciated. When Dine had taken over at AIPAC he had hired two experienced Middle East hands sympathetic to AIPAC's lobbying efforts, Steven J. Rosen, a Ph.D. who had been at the Rand Corporation, and Martin Indyk, a young Australian academic who has written extensively about the Arab-Israeli conflict.

"It was Tom's strategy that the premier American Jewish organization vis-à-vis Israel has to develop an ideology and the research to back it up," Indyk explained in an interview. "The Arabists try to delegitimize us just like they try to delegitimize Israel—that it's a strategic liability to U.S. interests. They write the papers but are not accountable to public opinion. We have to combat them by ideas and arguments."[37]

Traditionally, Israel had been something of a charity case for U.S. politicians. Support was based on a moral and humanitarian commitment to a group of democratic pioneers seeking a new life in their own land free from anti-Semites. Guilt over the Holocaust was ever present, and after 1967, the nagging fear of another Holocaust at the hands of the Arabs was never far from anyone's mind. Add widespread and embarrassing ignorance among members of Congress about the Arab world and how Israel fits, or doesn't fit, into it, and the result is an American policy constrained by guilt, sympathy, emotion, and few facts and open debate.

Enter an argument—debatable perhaps but an argument nevertheless—that the U.S. needed Israel more than Israel needed the U.S. The "strategic asset" argument would not work for all Presidents. But for Ronald Reagan, the Sovietophobe, it was a natural. As Reagan had said during his campaign: "Israel is the only stable democracy we can rely on in a spot where Armageddon could come . . . we need an ally in that area. We must prevent the Soviet Union from penetrating the Mideast. The Nixon Administration successfully moved them out; if Israel were not there, the U.S. would have to be there."[38]

While the Arabists tried to portray Israel as a liability in the region, AIPAC would prove it a strategic asset. Israel deserved U.S. aid, not out of charity, the argument went, but because the U.S. was, in effect, paying for its political stability, military skills, and intelligence.

And for those services rendered, the more than $2 billion that the U.S. sent to Israel each year, much of it in grants that did not have to be repaid, was, as AIPAC would soon begin arguing, a "bargain." That many Israelis disagreed was not the sort of information that AIPAC was inclined to pass on to its friends on Capitol Hill. The Labor Party opposed "strategic cooperation" because it worried that if the U.S. viewed Israel only as a rapid deployment force in the region, with the Begin encouragement, the odds of Israel's being dragged into an American-made foreign policy disaster only increased. That many Israelis, including some politicians in Begin's Likud, believed that Israel would be better off in the long run without huge infusions of U.S. aid—how else to create an independent economy?—was another matter that AIPAC left up to U.S. policy makers to find out for themselves. The lobby, after all, was in business to keep U.S. aid flowing to Israel.

Reagan's commitment to the strategic asset argument was a blessing to any pro-Israel lobby that had to show up at work every day with the unpredictable Menachem Begin in Israel's top job. The only thing that would make AIPAC's task easier would be for Israel to be a genuine, signed-on-the-bottom-line ally. And didn't Ronald Reagan himself say in that campaign speech, "we need an ally in that area"? AIPAC dreamed about such a possibility. What better way for the Arabs to be forced to face up to the reality of Israel—not Israel the enemy, but Israel the ally of the U.S., that generous donor of foreign aid needed as much by Arab states as Israel.

"Our primary goal is for the U.S. to hang in there with Israel," says Dine. "There are two theories for getting the Arabs to the peace table: (1) that the U.S. distance itself from Israel and deal with the Arabs; (2) prove to the Arabs how close Israel and the U.S. are so that they have to deal with the reality that they can't undermine this relationship. If they want to be close to the U.S., they have to deal with Israel."[39]

Number two, of course, is AIPAC's preference, but the result has been the opposite: instead of forcing the Arabs to come to terms with Israel, the growing strategic intimacy between the Israelis and the Reagan Administration has distanced the Arabs from the U.S., jeopardizing its role as a potential peace broker in the Middle East. The lobby is, in effect, stockpiling Israel's negotiating chips in the U.S. "When the time comes for Israel to sit down with the Arabs at the

negotiating table, it is our aim that it will have so much on its side
that even if it has to give up a few things, it will not matter," says
Dine.[40]

IN 1982, AIPAC began publishing a series of "position papers" under
Rosen's editorship that focused on Israel's strategic value to the U.S.
in the Middle East, and each was copiously footnoted. With descrip-
tive titles—*Israel and the U.S. Air Force, Israel and the U.S. Navy*
—the pamphlets argued persuasively for the strategic help the Israelis
could offer to the U.S. in the region.[41] That Israel had frustrated U.S.
interests in the Middle East throughout 1981 and 1982 seemed beside
the point. So was the fact that as long as Israel felt threatened, as
long as there was not peace in the Middle East, Israel would be
inclined to pursue its own interests.

Nevertheless, Rosen argued in the AIPAC monograph *The Strategic Value of Israel* that Israel offers the U.S. four main advantages
against Soviet aggression: (1) its "geostrategic position" midway between Europe and the Persian Gulf gives the U.S. an opportunity to
move into three theaters of operation—the Gulf, the Mediterranean,
and NATO's southern and central fronts; (2) "political stability" of a
sound democracy that is not as susceptible as Arab states to a coup or
revolution; (3) "political reliability"—today's Arab friends can be
tomorrow's ex-rulers, whereas, explains Rosen, "Israel's strategic interests and the values of its people are permanently aligned with
those of the Free World"; and (4) "Israel is the one politically and
technologically advanced country in the region."[42]

The AIPAC strategic papers were a quantum leap in the lobby's
"informational" efforts. Aimed not at AIPAC's membership, but at a
small group of U.S. policy makers in the White House, State Department, and Pentagon, the lobby's pamphlets were challenging the Arabists on their own turf, an ivy-covered spot where specialists thrive
on such information as Israeli hospitals have "4.7 beds per 1,000
people versus .64 in Egypt"[43] and swoon to such prose as "In short,
tank farms in Israel would give USAF both a 'fall-back' facility for
Persian Gulf operations and a 'swing' facility for Mediterranean con-
tingencies."[44]

Yet the strategic asset argument, in its more blatant anti-Soviet
form, has wider public-relations implications. While AIPAC was romancing hardline policy makers with arguments about "preposition-

ing" and "lift-times" to "CONUS" (better known as the "Continental United States"), the lobby was also seeking to create a new pro-Israel coalition with the far right in the U.S. whose commitment to Israel has little to do with the U.S. government's traditional support of the Jewish state.

An AIPAC insider candidly explains the strategy:

> It looks like the Israelis will be holding on to the West Bank for a long time to come. Tom is not crazy about that. Steve Rosen doesn't seem to mind. [The problem of creeping annexation of the West Bank] has hurt the moral authority of Israel—the thing that most Americans respect and admire about Israel. The other side is playing up the Palestinian issue as a human rights problem—a concern that touches Americans. We want to offset that with the argument that Israel has been forsaken by the left [because of the invasion of Lebanon and the West Bank]; therefore we're becoming more 'neo-conservative.' We want to broaden Israel's support to the right—with the people who don't care about what's happening on the West Bank but care a lot about the Soviet Union.[45]

These are, namely, the millions of American Protestant fundamentalists who support Israel as a key to the political—and spiritual— survival of the U.S. Their commitment to the Jewish state is based on the belief that the re-creation of Israel is a fulfillment of Biblical prophecy; many Protestant fundamentalists believe in the notion of the Jews as God's "chosen people." Millennialists among them support annexation of the West Bank because they believe that the re-creation of the Biblical Land of Israel signals the Second Coming of Christ.

Begin himself embraced the "Christian Zionists," as they call themselves, and solidified the relationship when he awarded one of its most visible leaders—the Moral Majority's Jerry Falwell—the prestigious Jabotinsky Award for service to Israel. Begin once described Falwell as "the man who represents 20 million American Christians" in a land of only 6 million Jews. It is difficult to find accurate figures on the followers of Falwell and his fellow evangelicals. One guess puts the evangelicals at about 30 million; Protestant fundamentalists all together may number more than 50 million Americans. The best estimates may come from the ratings figures for the television audiences that watch Falwell and the other "Pray TV" figures, as *Time* magazine has called such TV preachers as Jimmy Swaggert, Jim Bakker, Oral Roberts, and Pat Robertson. According to a 1985 Nielsen survey, Christian TV is reaching 61 million American households—and that's counting only the ten biggest among sixty-two nationally syndicated shows. Robertson's Christian Broadcasting Network alone reaches 27 million homes. Falwell's religious ventures earned $100 million last year, while Swaggert takes in $140 million in donations. This tends to be an audience that is inclined to vote as its ministers tell it.[46]

Begin was eager for as many American supporters as he could get, the more non-Jews the better. AIPAC agreed, and signed on as a permanent staff member a former legislative aide with ties to the fundamentalists. The Capitol Hill branch of the Jewish lobby was soon cosponsoring "prayer breakfasts" featuring such fundamentalist worthies as Swaggert and Robertson breaking bread with local Washington rabbis, the Israeli ambassador, and that old Peace Corps alumnus and "Kennedy liberal" Thomas A. Dine.

Tens of millions of Christian Zionists have their advantages, but there was one big problem with this particular Zionist connection: for the fundamentalists, Greater Israel was only a means to an end—the Second Coming. The next step on their agenda was the conversion of the Jews—a theological point that the pro-Israel forces and the Likudniks preferred to ignore. "What are we supposed to say to those millions of American Protestants who support Israel so strongly? Don't?" asked Israeli Cabinet minister Moshe Arens, the former defense minister who grew up in the U.S.[47]

To Jews concerned about a new pro-Israel coalition with a group of Americans who, traditionally, have been no friends of the Jews on such crucial domestic issues on the Jewish agenda as civil rights, opposition to school prayer, and support for abortion, Nathan Perlmutter, the director of the Anti-Defamation League of the B'nai B'rith, has answered, "Praise God and pass the ammunition."[48]

The Israelis' pragmatism about the Christian Zionist connection borders on cynicism. Lenny Davis, formerly AIPAC's chief of research who now runs a political consulting company in Jerusalem, echoes the view of many Zionist hardliners of the new Protestant-Jewish coalition: "Sure, these guys give me the heebie-jeebies. But until I see Jesus coming over the hill, I'm in favor of all the friends Israel can get. Let the defense organizations [American Jewish Committee and the Anti-Defamation League] worry about the domestic issues [school prayer, abortion, and anti-Semitism among this group]." Though Davis didn't say it, imbedded in that view is a bit of

Zionist ideology: If things really get bad for American Jews, maybe they'll become good Zionists and move to Israel.

AIPAC's main constituency remains the American Jewish community, and the AWACS vote had given the lobby a perfect recruiting advertisement for joining its "War for Washington"—the "enemies of Israel" were getting stronger every day. In 1983, the lobby published the third pamphlet in its series, *The Campaign to Discredit Israel*. Rosen was coauthor. In his preface, Dine explained that the publication's aim was to update for AIPAC's members the activities of anti-Israel groups and individuals and "to analyze the intellectual and political strengths and weaknesses of their political positions."[49] Since 1977, AIPAC had been sending out annually a Xeroxed "Who's Who" list of "anti-Israel" organizations and personalities. Though the latest broadside was wrapped in paperback book form and claimed to be a "more complete and convenient analysis of this anti-Israel activity," *The Campaign to Discredit Israel* was nothing more than a campaign to discredit critics of U.S.–Israeli policy—a hit list for local Jewish leaders to refer to whenever anyone came to town to discuss the Middle East.

If George Ball, for instance, were scheduled to speak, an AIPAC member could turn to pages 98–99 and learn that Ball is a former undersecretary of state and U.N. representative, and author of books and articles, including one of his "best-known," which appeared in the April 1977 edition of *Foreign Affairs*, entitled, "How to Save Israel in Spite of Herself." The curious reader would also learn that Ball argues that, as the pamphlet puts it, "sympathy should be felt for the Jewish need for a homeland," but he believes the U.S. should put "disciplinary restraint" (Ball's phrase) on Israel. Ball is also for imposing peace in the Middle East. It's all true, and Ball wouldn't question the facts. But does dissent from the Begin government's policies make one an "enemy of Israel"? Why does a former top American official have less right than a top Israeli official to criticize Israeli policy?

Some of AIPAC's readers begged to disagree too. Anthony Lewis, *The New York Times* columnist, questioned the facts in AIPAC's review of Walid Khalidi, a Palestinian scholar who teaches at Harvard. In 1978, Khalidi wrote an article, again in *Foreign Affairs*, supporting an independent Palestinian state. AIPAC quoted selectively from the article in a way that made it seem as if Khalidi was in favor of the destruction of Israel. What steamed Lewis was that Khalidi, a well-known Palestinian "moderate" who has risked the anger of Arab extremists, had actually advised, as Lewis wrote it, "peaceful co-existence between Israel and a Palestinian state."[50]

A skeptical AIPAC member checked out Lewis's contention, found him correct, and allowed the *Times* columnist to publish his letter to Dine demanding an apology to Khalidi from AIPAC. Dine stuck to his guns, and in his reply charged that "Khalidi demands that Jerusalem be turned over to Arafat and that Moscow be party to the arrangements." Lewis, who happens to be Jewish, noted that "Joe McCarthy could not have produced a nastier distortion" of Khalidi's argument; he also suggested that Israel's supporters should be "gladdened" by a major Palestinian intellectual's interest in negotiations instead of trying to "smear" him. (A similar "enemies of Israel" list published by the Anti-Defamation League at about the same time branded the Harvard professor a "pro-Palestinian propagandist," which is true but trivial. Were Dine and Rosen not "pro-Israel propagandists"?[51])

In 1983, AIPAC also intensified its pro-Israel campaign on college campuses, sending out a questionnaire on anti-Israel campus activity. The answers formed the basis of another pamphlet, published the following year, *The AIPAC College Guide: Exposing the Anti-Israel Campaign on Campus*. "American college students are being exposed to a steady diet of anti-Israel vituperation . . ." the first line of the pamphlet begins.[52] The authors concede that the college campaign against Israel has not gained widespread support. In fact, a Gallup poll indicates that students are more sympathetic to Israel than to Arab countries by five to one, an actual increase over past years. But pro-Arab success has come in gaining attention for the Arab side, and, they argue, "in defining the parameters within which much of the campus debate about Israel takes place." AIPAC is particularly worried about efforts to bring to the campus "expert propagandists who sugarcoat its [*sic*] radical message with idealistic and sometimes poetic rhetoric."[53]

Five years before, the lobby had established its Political Leadership Development Program for training students in the fine art of increasing pro-Israel attitudes on campuses across the country. AIPAC's college liaison is Jonathan Kessler, a tall, good-looking,

articulate twenty-nine-year-old who claims that the leadership program is affiliated with five thousand students on 350 campuses in all
fifty states. AIPAC works closely with B'nai B'rith's Hillel Foundations, the nonprofit Jewish centers on most college campuses, generally headed by a rabbi. (Hillel, of course, is tax exempt; AIPAC is
not.) These college contacts keep AIPAC informed on "pro-Palestinian" or "anti-Israel" speeches and professors, and Kessler advises
them how to handle upcoming speakers based on AIPAC's files on
their past performances.

Just as on Capitol Hill, AIPAC prefers to set the limits of the
debate on campus. The *College Guide* gives a detailed rundown on
the anti-Israel campaign on campus and provides arguments for
countering such "propaganda" ploys as "Israel is oppressive," "Israel
is Goliath," "Israel has no right to exist." But often in its efforts to
set the limits of the debate, AIPAC stifles it. The lobby's campus
crusade is its strategy in Washington writ large. Any speaker who
might differ with AIPAC's views of the U.S.–Israel relationship is
immediately branded as "anti-Israel." During leadership workshops
in the Washington area, AIPAC aides brief students on how to undercut the efforts of anyone who might disagree with the AIPAC line.
"You need to create muscular Jews, not just the UJA-type," Kessler
told his audience at a workshop on building campus coalitions during
the 1984 leadership conference. "Don't be afraid to show your Jewishness and assertiveness for Israel." Kessler has adopted an evangel-
ical style, a sort of Jimmy Swaggert in the guise of a Yuppie Jewish
activist. "We're called the sexy lobby," he pointed out. "Jews have to
spread the gospel—the word, the gospel of pro-Israel."[54]

But like any gospel, the word according to AIPAC has little room
for dissent. A few tips from some AIPAC campus leaders offered in
workshops for pro-Israel activism: Suppose you have the "hidden
agenda" of endorsing a candidate—AIPAC is not allowed by law to
endorse candidates—all you have to do is hold a symposium on the
main issue of the campaign. Or put up a sign-up sheet for those who
support the candidate and then call up the congressman's campaign
office and identify yourself as "Campus Friends of Israel" eager to
work for him. ("Don't say AIPAC," advised the AIPAC moderator,
"because AIPAC doesn't endorse candidates.")

Students were advised to organize symposia on campuses—and
then stack the deck: Don't invite any professor "who might be ago-

nizing over the plight of the Palestinians." Know what your speaker will say, or, as one leadership moderator put it, "You don't want any surprises."

One befuddled student raised a hand. "What do you do when someone like Edward Said [the eminent Columbia literature professor who has close ties to the PLO] comes to speak on campus or may be on the faculty?" The answer: "Don't even try to ruin Edward Said's credibility." A young Capitol Hill staffer related an anecdote about a meeting of three hundred people in which someone challenged Said, and the Columbia professor "tore him to shreds." One useful strategy was suggested: "Don't challenge Said head on; perhaps suggest another speaker."

And so it goes in the propaganda war on campus where the "sexy lobby" might be signing up students by the thousands to work on its behalf or for local political campaigns, but AIPAC is certainly not winning friends and influencing people for Israel among faculty appalled by the lobby's efforts to crush academic freedom and the sort of debate that universities are supposed to be all about.

No one, however, knows the risks of dissent or debate on matters relating to the Arab-Israeli conflict better than members of Congress —and the leaders of their local political action committees. PAC power has evolved into a formidable memory aid with which AIPAC can remind politicians that supporting Israel is definitely the "litmus" test" of AIPAC's friendship, and the lobby's friends' friendship.

7

PRO-ISRAEL PAC POWER

Two years after AWACS, the lobby seemed to own Capitol Hill. Indeed, Tom Dine was so good at his job that there were members of Congress and their staffs who feared him *and* liked him. Addressing an AIPAC conference in 1983, Lawrence Eagleburger, then the State Department's top political officer, put his arm affectionately around Dine and informed the audience, "This is a guy who can hurt you."

It's the kind of remark any lobbyist would love as his epitaph. Tom Dine confirmed Eagleburger's opinion during the 1984 elections. AIPAC also proved that the AWACS vote had been a test of Jewish friendship by sending several members of Congress into retirement, with the help of PAC power.

AIPAC is not a political action committee, and would be breaking the law to act as one. Dine is quick to emphasize that his organization is "an information-gathering group." As he has often said publicly, "This organization doesn't touch political money."[1] True, but AIPAC treats PAC money as if it were a Playboy bunny—the lobby never touches but does it ever look. As one of the best "information-gathering groups" on Capitol Hill, AIPAC knows whom the PACs favor; more important, the lobby, as an information dispenser, alerts its members—and thus their PACs—to which politicians deserve their support. The lobby also encourages its members to supply the totals of PAC money contributed to candidates so that when a crucial vote comes up in Congress, AIPAC, the ever-vigilant elephant, can remind wavering politicians of the generosity of the American Jewish community. Each election year, AIPAC is proud to point out,

hundreds of candidates for the House and Senate solicit the lobby's
support. "If money talks, early money shouts" is a favorite slogan at
AIPAC conferences.

PAC money positively screamed during the 1984 campaign. "No
one can run for national office without Jewish support," says a
former Democratic fund raiser.[2] That has been true since the 1960s,
but the rise of PACs—and the costs of running for office on television—has made that estimate indisputable. According to Federal
Election Commission figures, it took an average of just short of $3
million to win a Senate seat in 1984.[3] In the 1984 North Carolina
Senate race, Governor James Hunt reportedly spent more than $7
million to lose to the incumbent, Jesse Helms, who is said to have
spent the amazing sum of $16,155,157 to keep his Senate seat.[4] The
average price of a seat in the House of Representatives was a bargain
$325,000.

No wonder then that whoever puts up money to support the campaigns of his poorer bretheren will be a big man in Washington. It
happens that American Jews have been the most dependable big
donors, in spite of their small numbers. "One of the problems about
raising political money from rich Arab-Americans," notes one who
has tried hard and often, "is you constantly run into the complaint,
'But I don't even know the guy.' Jews don't care about that as long as
they think the candidate will vote their line."[5] The willingness to give
money to an acceptable candidate in any state explains why even
candidates with minuscule Jewish constituencies are uneasy about
risking anything that might shut off the flow of funds from outside
the state. "There's not a political campaign in the country where the
role of the Jews—and the lobby—is not discussed," says a well-
known Democratic power broker. "In every campaign I've been in,
we'd have two meetings—one with AIPAC and then another after the
AIPAC meeting."[6]

According to an analysis of the Federal Election Commission figures, pro-Israel PACs in 1984 contributed nearly $3.6 million to can-
didates for the House, Senate, and Presidency—twice the amount
contributed in 1982. The number of Jewish PACs also doubled, to at
least seventy, and contributed $1.5 million to candidates for the
House of Representatives—more than a third of it to members of the
House Foreign Affairs Committee and the Foreign Appropriations
Subcommittee. Senate candidates received a total of $1.8 million.

The big winner among Republican incumbents was Minnesota's Rudy Boschwitz, AIPAC's "rabbi" in the Senate and chairman of the Senate Foreign Relations Committee's subcommittee on the Middle East. But 44 percent of the pro-Israel PAC money for the Senate was marked for the opponents of five Republican senators who voted for the AWACS sale. Illinois congressman Paul Simon received more Jewish PAC money—$270,000—than any other candidate in the 1984 race.[7] Simon was running against Charles Percy.

Percy, the chairman of the Senate Foreign Relations Committee, had voted for Jimmy Carter's F-15 deal with the Saudis, and afterward had spent a great deal of time explaining himself to his Jewish constituents in Illinois. Percy might have been forgiven the F-15 vote, but a second sale to the Saudis?

Percy was a marked man. Ironically, Chuck Percy had begun his career in the Senate in 1967 as an enormously popular figure among Jewish voters in Illinois, particularly for a Protestant Republican. Percy was a well-known moderate, and quite liberal on some issues; he also emerged in the late 1960s as a national figure with justifiable presidential ambitions. Percy numbered many influential Jews among his most loyal supporters, with Philip Klutznick in the lead. In 1972, Chuck Percy won re-election by carrying every county in Illinois— and 70 percent of the Jewish vote in a state with the fourth-largest Jewish population in the nation.

Percy's Jewish problem began in 1975, after a trip to the Middle East. He charged that Israel had missed opportunities to negotiate and urged its leaders to talk to the PLO, provided the group recognized Israel's right to exist behind secure borders. Percy also described PLO leader Yasser Arafat as "more moderate, relatively speaking, than other [PLO] extremists [such as George Habash]."[8] The senator's mail quickly underscored the seriousness of his remarks: within a week, twenty-two hundred telegrams and four thousand letters arrived—95 percent of them hostile to Percy's prescription for peace in the Middle East. His correspondents threatened to withhold votes and support if Percy didn't shape up.[9]

But his name was not on the AIPAC-inspired "letter of 76" pro-Israel senators opposing the Ford-Kissinger call in 1975 for "reassessment" of U.S.–Israeli relations. The letters and cards kept coming in, though Jewish voters in Illinois stuck with Percy in his race for re-election. Of the seventy Jews asked to sign an advertisement on behalf of the Percy campaign, sixty-five signed, and though Percy received only 53 percent of the vote in the state, he ended up with 61 percent of the Jewish vote.

But after the AWACS vote, AIPAC decided that Percy was too dangerous in his role as chairman of the Senate Foreign Relations Committee. Jewish constituents soon began to organize on behalf of Percy's GOP primary opponent Congressman Tom Corcoran. Letters went out all around the nation, their envelopes emblazoned with the question, "CAN YOU NAME *ISRAEL'S WORST ADVERSARY* IN CONGRESS?" An enclosure seeking support for Corcoran declared that "more than any other officeholder in Washington, Percy has worked to destroy the special relationship between the United States and Israel. . . ."[10]

The evidence for Percy's "anti-Israel stance" was his two votes for the Saudi plane sales plus "his endorsement of a terrorist PLO state on the West Bank and his description of Yasser Arafat as a 'moderate.'" Corcoran's voting record on Israel was described as "100 percent." The mailing also included a brief "interview" with Corcoran about his support for Israel by Morris Amitay, the ex-head of AIPAC. The Corcoran forces ran a full-page ad featuring a photograph of Arafat with the headline: "Chuck Percy says this man is a moderate." While Percy and his campaign aides tried to explain that he had actually described Arafat as "more moderate, relatively speaking" than others in the PLO, and pointed out he had argued that peace in the Middle East required "a Palestinian entity," not necessarily an independent state, such elaboration was considered sophistry.

The troops were marshaled against Percy, and Corcoran's war chest was enriched by $285,000 from fifty-five pro-Israel PACs. What Percy considered disagreement, AIPAC saw as coming down, as Tom Dine later put it in a speech, "on the side of the Arabs."[11] In a newsletter devoted to evaluating the candidates in the 1984 Senate races for contributors to his pro-Israel PAC—the Washington Political Action Committee—Morris Amitay noted that though Percy had shown support for Israel by voting for U.S. aid to the Jewish state, "he has displayed insensitivity and even hostility to our concerns."[12] Nevertheless, Percy managed to win the primary. The PACs—the total eventually reached seventy—began sending their checks to his Democratic opponent, Representative Paul Simon.

A California businessman named Michael R. Goland reportedly spent more than $1 million for anti-Percy billboard, television, radio, and newspaper ads. He contended that he was personally opposed to Percy and acting on his own; therefore, Goland argued, he had not violated the campaign spending limits. Early in the campaign, Percy supporters complained to the Federal Election Commission that Goland was acting on behalf of Corcoran supporter Morris Amitay. The former AIPAC director conceded that though Goland was once on the advisory board of his PAC, Amitay had only given him legal advice and got him in touch with a direct-mail company specializing in Jewish donors. Percy tried to marshal his traditional Jewish support in Illinois against the outside attack. No less than Senator Boschwitz and former New York senator Jacob Javits, a Jewish politician with the purest pro-Israel credentials in the land, made appearances in Chicago on Percy's behalf. A hundred prominent Illinois Jews sponsored a full-page ad declaring that Percy had "delivered for Illinois, delivered for America and delivered for Israel." Thousands of Jews from all over the nation, however, donated $3 million to Simon's campaign—40 percent of his total funds.

In the fall "Citizens for Percy" sued the FEC for failing to thoroughly investigate Goland's campaign spending practices. A U.S. district court found that there was "reason to believe" that Goland's spending in Illinois violated federal law. Unfortunately, Percy did not learn of the decision until *after* the election, but by then Percy had lost to Simon by 89,000 votes. The judge in the case criticized the FEC's "routine," "casual," and "dilatory" treatment of Percy's formal complaint as "unacceptable" and "contrary to law."[13] Percy, who was, after all, the head of the Senate Foreign Relations Committee, refused to apologize for having opinions on the Middle East; he insisted on his right to criticize Israeli policy. "A U.S. Senator," the ex-senator told *The Wall Street Journal*, "should have the same right as a member of the Knesset or the editorial board of an Israeli media outlet to disagree with any government when its actions may not be in the United States's interest."[14]

AIPAC claimed credit for beating Percy, and held the race up as an example to any member of Congress contemplating criticism of Israel. Tom Dine told a Jewish audience in Toronto, "All the Jews in America, from coast to coast, gathered to oust Percy. And the American politicians—those who hold public positions now, and those who aspire—got the message."[15]

• • •

UNLIKE Percy, Roger Jepsen, a senator from Iowa, was perceived as a loyal friend of Israel. In his campaign newsletter, Amitay noted that Jepsen, a member of the Senate Armed Services Committee, "has been supportive on a number of issues affecting U.S.–Israeli relations." In fact, Jepsen was viewed as such a good friend of Israel that the Iowa senator had been invited to be the keynote speaker at AIPAC's annual policy conference in May 1981 where he attacked the AWACS deal. Five months later, Jepsen tearfully changed his mind, and, in effect, at the urging of his President and party leader, fell on his own sword.

Early in the 1984 Senate race, a fund-raising letter went out across the country under the signature of Gary Rubin, a Des Moines–based supporter of Jepsen's opponent, Congressman Thomas Harkin. Page one of the letter discussed the grave threat of the Saudi sale to "the very survival of Israel" and pointed with pride to the fact that "my Senator . . . Roger Jepsen of Iowa . . . not only agreed with our side, but promised to lead the fight in the Senate to block the sale of these dangerous weapons to Israel's enemies. And lead the fight he did . . . at least until the going got tough!"[16]

In the rest of the letter, Rubin performed a neat backflip and asked friends of Israel to throw their support to Harkin, who had been described in Amitay's scorecard in this way: "Somewhat worse than [the other Democratic candidate ex-Senator Dick Clark] on our issues, Harkin signed a particularly offensive anti-Israel newspaper ad in 1980 in which he was joined by some of the most virulent foes of Israel in the U.S." According to Amitay, Harkin's name had appeared on an ad with the likes of James Zogby, an Arab-American activist; Noam Chomsky, the eminent MIT professor who, although Jewish, is an outspoken critic of Israeli policy; and ex-Congressman Paul Findley, who was the Chuck Percy of the 1982 campaign. (Findley had suffered the ire of the Jewish community for his own "pro-Palestinian" sympathies, lost his seat, and published a book in 1985 about the Jewish community's inability to accept differences of opinion.) Yet the anti-Jepsen letter delcared "Tom Harkin is a strong supporter of Israel." Harkin had voted against the AWACS deal.

When the Israeli minister without portfolio Moshe Arens was informed in October 1984 about Jepsen's battle with the American Jewish community to stay in office, he was surprised. "He's a friend of mine," said Arens, a former ambassador to the U.S. and Begin's defense minister. "If American Jews are attacking someone like Jepsen—it's obvious why he was unable to vote against Reagan's AWACS deal—then that's not good for Israel or American Jews, in the long run."[17]

Jepsen certainly could have used the endorsement. Tom Harkin—signer of "a particularly offensive anti-Israel ad," according to Amitay—received $108,330 from pro-Israel PACs and was elected the junior senator from Iowa.

THE growing power of PACs in the early 1980s stirred up discussion about the inevitability of political corruption, of "special interests" buying votes. Common Cause, the citizens' lobby, and other groups organized to abolish PACs. Mark Green, the consumer and political activist who has denounced PACs as "legalized bribery" and set up a "PAC to end all PACs" called UNPAC, is only one of the many Jewish critics of PACs who are even more uncomfortable with the increasing prominence and growth of Jewish PACs. Participating in a conference on the pros and cons of PACs, sponsored by the American Jewish Congress in 1983, Green had warned:

> Many Jewish groups must realize that if we enter the PAC race and become just another monied special interest lobby, we may be squandering an asset that very few other groups have: a moral authority in the Middle East and in this country. . . . Also, many military contractors and oil interests hostile to Israel can always outraise us in PAC funds. Finally, it is unfortunately true that many anti-Semites would attack our PACs as another example of Jews trying to control things with money.[18]

"Moral authority has very little influence in politics," declared Morris Amitay, the former head of AIPAC addressing the same conference. Amitay noted that he—the former head of the pro-Israel lobby—would not try to persuade congressmen to vote for a particular bill on the basis of Israel's "moral authority." Instead, he said, he would point out Israel's "value." Getting to the point—this was, after all, a conference on PACs—Amitay added, "I would also remind Congressmen about the help and support American Jews have given candidates over the years because they feel Israel is important to them and to the United States." Amitay, who admitted that he himself had warned three years before that high-profile PACs would bring the anti-Semites out of the woodwork, now, with no evidence of an increase in anti-Semitism due to Jewish PAC power, considered the pro-Israel PACs "a very positive development in Jewish life."[19]

And while many Jews have often argued that their own efforts as lobbyists for Israel were puny when compared to the lobbying power of the oil companies on behalf of Arab interests, Amitay, unlike Green, dismissed the oil lobby. "When oil interests and other corporate interests lobby, 99 percent of the time they are acting in what they perceive to be their own self-interest—they lobby on tax bills," Amitay explained. "We very rarely see them lobbying on foreign-policy issues." And then this former skeptic proved how much a believer in PAC power he had become: "In a sense, we have the field to ourselves," Amitay pointed out. "I think we should take advantage of that."[20]

8

"AN AGENDA FOR A CITIZEN LOBBYIST"

IN a speech to the United Jewish Appeal Young Leadership Biennial Conference in Washington in 1984, Tom Dine defined what he called "an agenda for a citizen lobbyist," pro-Israel division. "Our first major priority for 1984 is to convert all U.S. aid to Israel—military and economic—to grants rather than part grants/part loans," Dine declared. Number two was to press for passage of bills in the Senate and the House to move the U.S. Embassy in Israel from Tel Aviv to Jerusalem. Three: To encourage "strategic cooperation" between the U.S. military and Israel. Four: To establish Israel as a Free Trade Zone by eliminating all tariffs on trade between Israel and the U.S., thus boosting Israeli exports to the U.S. Five: To block all arms sales to Jordan until King Hussein is willing to enter peace talks "under U.N. Resolutions 242 and 338." Six: To pursue peace through a process that excludes the PLO and sees Hussein "without pre-conditions . . . sitting with the head of Israel's government, at the same table."[1]

For AIPAC, 1984 was a busy and very successful year. In March, the House Foreign Affairs Committee voted enthusiastically for $2.5 billion in military and economic aid to Israel for fiscal 1985, and a few weeks later the Senate Foreign Relations Committee voted (16–2) for $2.6 billion. For the first time the aid money would be in the form of a total grant that Israel would never have to repay. Included in the military aid was $400 million to help Israel develop the Lavi, a multipurpose fighter plane that Israel hoped to be able to sell on the international arms market in the 1990s. The U.S. first agreed

to fund the Lavi in 1983, and the project moved forward with virtually no opposition in Congress.

Few joint ventures between the U.S. and Israel were more illustra-
tive of how eager American politicians had become to please Israel
and AIPAC, which had argued that the Lavi would promote stability
in the Middle East.[2] Congress kept doling out more funds for the
Lavi, in spite of opposition from the Pentagon and counter lobbying
from high-tech labor unions warning about the loss of jobs. Secretary
of Defense Caspar Weinberger warned about transferring sensitive
technology outside the United States. Major American aircraft manufacturers complained that the Lavi would compete with the F-16s and
F-20s on the open market. Even some Israeli politicians and defense
analysts opposed the Lavi, pointing out that it would be cheaper to
buy F-16s from the U.S. Two former chiefs of the Israeli Air Force
—Ezer Weizman and Matti Hod—opposed the project as too expen-
sive and risky for an already shaky economy. (The original estimates
for research and development had doubled by 1983—to $1.5 billion
—and would leap to a total of more than $9 billion in 1985.) AIPAC
had turned a potential Israeli economic scandal—a classic cost over-
run—into a test of American support for Israel.

The lobby, under Dine, was becoming a master at transforming the
dubious and the debatable into the incontrovertible. Spring 1984 gave
AIPAC plenty of practice. Before both houses in March were bills to
transfer the U.S. Embassy in Israel from Tel Aviv to Jerusalem,
Israel's official capital since 1949.* The embassy issue became the
hottest topic in the Democratic race for the Presidency, as candidates
Walter Mondale and Gary Hart both seemed to be competing for the
title of who was more in favor of the move—and the more pro-
Israel. Since the creation of the Jewish state, the U.S. had finessed
the Jerusalem issue, claiming that the United Nations viewed the city
as international territory and its "final status" was a matter for negotiation. After the 1967 war, the Johnson Administration had reiterated
that Jerusalem still enjoyed a "special status" that the Israeli occupation had not changed. In spite of protests that Israel was the only
country in which the U.S. Embassy was not in the "administrative
capital," the Nixon, Ford, and Carter administrations stuck to that
policy, and so did Reagan. In his Middle East peace plan of Sep-

---

*The Old City in East Jerusalem had remained under Jordanian control until Israel captured it
in the 1967 war; Begin formally annexed East Jerusalem in 1980.

tember 1982, the President stressed that the U.S. continued to believe that Jerusalem remained an issue to be discussed over the peace table.

Significantly, the Israeli government did not press for the embassy transfer in 1984. Nor had AIPAC encouraged the legislation, which had been initiated in the House by Tom Lantos, a representative from California who is the only Holocaust survivor in Congress and known to have senatorial ambitions, and in the Senate by New York's Daniel Patrick Moynihan. In fact, AIPAC privately was miffed that Moynihan had introduced the bill without conferring with the lobby beforehand. The Jerusalem issue was hardly a priority for either AIPAC or Israel, which, after all, currently occupied Jerusalem and had no intention of ever giving it up. The Shamir government was hardly eager to stir up the issue and jeopardize U.S. aid. But once Moynihan and Lantos forced the point, AIPAC was obliged to help out. "What else could we do?" said Dine at the time.[3]

But what was Mondale's and Hart's excuse? Their appeal to Jewish voters was so unabashed that it provoked the American Jewish Committee to hold a press conference at the end of March criticizing the candidates for pandering to Jewish voters. The president of the committee pointed out that Jews cared about other issues and didn't "want to be patronized by just being talked to about Israel."[4] The same day, the by-line of the committee's Washington lobbyist, Hyman Bookbinder, appeared under a *New York Times* op-ed–page article entitled "The Wrong Appeal to Jewish Voters."[5] Bookbinder admitted that the embassy transfer was a legitimate political issue, "but for heaven's sake," he pleaded, "it is not the central issue of our times—and should not be the central issue of the 1984 campaign." Bookbinder too stressed that though Jews were committed to Israel's security, they still cared about such things as civil rights, equal opportunity, anti-Semitism, school prayer, and other domestic and international issues.

The committee's public criticism of two presidential candidates for being *too* pro-Israel was proof of how concerned some Jewish leaders had become about Israel's total domination of American Jewish life. Privately, several Jewish leaders expressed concern that such "pandering," as Bookbinder had called it in print, to Jews on the embassy issue was bound to stir up the anti-Semites. Yet Hart and Mondale are hardly political novices; clearly, they believed that some pandering was necessary, and gave it all they had, with unforeseeable consequences. Hart had gone on record supporting U.S. policy toward Jerusalem in February, and now he looked as if he was flip-flopping to compete with Mondale, whose pro-Israel credentials had managed to survive his tenure as Jimmy Carter's Vice President. (Former AIPAC chief Morris Amitay was one of Mondale's unofficial advisers on the Middle East.) Even some of Hart's Jewish supporters winced, while the press began to deride his self-proclaimed role as the candidate with "new ideas." (After Hart's defeat, some would point to the embassy issue as the beginning of his end.)

The candidates had gotten one thing right, though. In spite of the AJC's protestations, support for Israel had become, in the eyes of the lobby, the test for *the* Jewish vote.

AIPAC soon took up the cause of the embassy transfer as if it were its own, urging its members to force their representatives to "recognize reality"—that only in Israel was the U.S. Embassy not in the nation's capital. (The rest of "reality" they failed to mention was that every other major nation also had their embassies in Tel Aviv, and that the U.S. maintained a consulate in West Jerusalem.) The Reagan Administration refused to budge. Secretary Shultz argued that the issue was the President's to decide and warned that moving the embassy would provoke a wave of anti-American hatred and violence throughout the Arab world.[6] The bills' sponsors pressed ahead.

Then the lobby came up with a face-saver for all sides, and in the process racked up another item on Dine's 1984 agenda. The White House had announced earlier that the U.S. would sell $140 million worth of Stinger antiaircraft missiles to Saudi Arabia and Jordan, a move that Israel and AIPAC opposed. In fact, as Dine boasted in his UJA speech on March 12, the House Middle East Subcommittee, with AIPAC's encouragement, had passed an amendment preventing Jordan from using U.S. aid to buy arms unless the White House "certified that Jordan is publicly committed to recognition of Israel and to prompt entry into peace talks under U.N. Resolutions 242 and 338." The day after Dine's speech, the President, in his own speech to the UJA, asked American Jews to support the Stinger sale. The day after that, in an exclusive interview with *The New York Times*, King Hussein, annoyed that a U.S. President, as Hussein saw it, would have to ask permission from American Jews to sell weapons to Jordan, savaged American policy. "The U.S.," said the king, "is not free to move except within the limits of what AIPAC, the Zionists and the State of Israel determine for it."[7]

Suddenly, AIPAC had, as one staffer put it, "a new cosponsor [for the bill to kill the Stinger sale]—King Hussein." Hussein's attack on the Reagan Administration now made it easier for AIPAC to strike a deal with the White House. After a series of head-to-head negotiations with Undersecretary of State for Political Affairs Lawrence Eagleburger, AIPAC agreed to settle for a "resolution of Congress" that the embassy eventually be moved, which saved both sides from a nasty battle in Congress and committed Reagan to move without handcuffing him to it; in return, the Administration agreed to dump the arms sale rather than risk an AWACS-type battle in Congress over it. It was another impressive victory for AIPAC.

Critics at the State Department and on Capitol Hill privately began to echo King Hussein, wondering whether AIPAC had taken over setting U.S. foreign policy. The Dine-Eagleburger talks, they charged, undermined any genuine effort to pursue an "evenhanded" policy in the Middle East. State Department dissenters bitterly pointed out that the White House had notified AIPAC that the deal was off twelve hours before anyone informed Richard Murphy, assistant secretary of state for Near Eastern affairs and supposedly in charge of U.S. policy in the Middle East.[8] Tom Dine was exultant. The king of Jordan was now doing AIPAC's public relations! (And check off Number Five on the AIPAC agenda: no arms sales to Arab countries.)

Formal military ties between the U.S. and Israel were also strengthened in 1984. Slightly more than a year after the embarrassing flap over annexation of the Golan Heights and suspension of the Sharon-Weinberger strategic cooperation agreement, in December 1984, Foreign Minister Shamir and Reagan signed an agreement for a Joint Political Military Group to work out a strategic *quid pro quo* between the two countries. It was the AIPAC strategic papers come to life: air force and naval cooperation in the region, sharing intelligence, prepositioning of U.S. equipment on Israeli territory, ammunition storage facilities, potential medical supplies and Israel hospital beds. Israel had retrieved its reputation—in spite of the invasion of Lebanon—as a strategic asset. For AIPAC, the agreement was almost as good as a formal alliance.

The lobby was eager to strengthen Israel's trade relationship with the U.S. as well, and in 1984 began pressing the Administration and Congress to consider making Israel a Free Trade Zone. Finally, after months of meetings between U.S. and Israeli trade representatives,

the White House agreed in March 1985 to eliminate all tariffs between the two countries within ten years.[9] In fact, nearly 90 percent
of Israel's U.S. exports had been duty-free under an existing "preference" system for imports from developing countries. But there were
limits under that system, which was due to expire anyway, and the
new deal would give both sides a better chance of predicting trade for
the future. Israel also hoped the agreement would provide an incentive to its export industries. For AIPAC, there was significant sym-
bolic value in the trade deal: it was the first such free trade agreement
the U.S. had ever made—and thus another signal to Israel's enemies
and the Arabists of the *de facto* alliance between the two old friends.

The pact was a major triumph for AIPAC in a year studded with
victories—sullied only by a mini-scandal involving the security of
the trade talks. A copy of the classified document featuring the U.S.
strategy for the negotiations found its way into the hands of the lobby
during the late-summer preparations for the talks. AIPAC contended
it "did not solicit" the document, and that Dine had known nothing
about it until U.S. Trade Representative William Brock telephoned
about it. The FBI was investigating the source of the leak.[10]

Though the Free Trade Zone agreement had the President's support
all along, opposition was strong. The AFL-CIO, one of Israel's most
loyal supporters in the U.S. and a major purchaser of Israel bonds,
argued that the agreement threatened U.S. jobs. Industries that enjoyed some protection against Israeli imports—fruit growers, jewelry
makers, textile and apparel manufacturers—also opposed the deal.

On the peace trail, AIPAC's success was largely a negative factor,
helping to sidetrack the President's own efforts to broker peace in the
Middle East. While Dine had been one of the first to support the
Reagan Plan, AIPAC staffers were now claiming—in private—that
the State Department had "snookered" the lobby into backing Reagan
by promising that Hussein was about to metamorphose into another
Sadat. There was something disingenuous in this excuse since AIPAC
surely knew that Hussein had stayed clear of Camp David precisely
because Sadat had stepped out on his own, negotiated for the Sinai,
and left the Palestinian issue and the West Bank—Jordan's prime
concerns—on hold.

Memories are short and selective in Middle East diplomacy, but
central to Camp David and the Reagan Plan's visions of peace were
negotiations about the future of the West Bank and Gaza between

Israel and Jordan, along with the Palestinians. Had AIPAC been concentrating so much on Israel's role as a strategic asset in the region that it had forgotten what Begin had signed at Camp David? The document had declared that the final sovereignty of the West Bank and Gaza would be determined not by Israel but by Egypt, Jordan, *and* the Palestinians, who would actually have the right to veto the agreement. (The reason why many Jewish leaders had preferred the Reagan Plan to Camp David was that it left the role of the Palestinians in the peace process vague; indeed, Camp David had given them such a strong position that it is a wonder they rejected such a pro-Palestinian document—and even more curious that Begin signed it.)

In spite of his talk about Israel's—and AIPAC's—commitment to the Camp David process, Dine was regressing into a familiar characterization of U.S. policy in the Middle East. In his UJA speech in March, the AIPAC director derided efforts by U.S. policy makers who feel, as he phrased it, "the only way to woo Arab friends is to beat up on Israel." The language was as old as efforts of the Eisenhower Administration to prevent the Arabs from becoming a Soviet client, JFK's Johnson Plan, the Rogers Plan, and U.N. 242 itself, all of which sought to come to terms with what used to be called "the refugee problem." The Palestinian issue was no less central to peace in the Middle East in 1984. Evidence of Reagan's effort "to beat up on Israel" at the time was slim, and proof of the Administration's pro-Israel stance impressive: record aid to Israel, strategic cooperation, cancellation of the Stinger package, and support for the Lavi, where the President was bucking the opposition of the Pentagon, major U.S. aircraft companies, and aerospace unions worried about competition and jobs. But then AIPAC preferred to take credit for those achievements.

The lobby did have a problem, however. Many experts on the Arab-Israeli conflict, including Israelis, believe that peace is not possible without the participation of the Palestinians in some form or another. Even Begin and Moshe Dayan were willing to welcome Palestinians in a Jordanian delegation at a Geneva-style international peace conference, as long as they were not obviously members of Arafat's PLO. But by 1984, the Israelis had hardened on PLO participation; the Labor Party was no more eager to talk to the PLO than was the Likud. AIPAC followed that lead. As Dine told his audience, "Please communicate the message to the Administration and to Congress that the PLO wants Israel destroyed, and that it is structurally incapable of genuine moderation as manifested by its pathetic inability to say simply 'We recognize Israel.'"

In his speech, Dine attacked secret meetings between Arafat and an American academic that had the blessings of the State Department and the White House. When word of the meetings hit the press, the White House virtually apologized for that breach of U.S.–Israeli etiquette. AIPAC pursued legislation that would make sure it would never happen again. The reason, of course, for secret meetings between the PLO and the U.S. via an intermediary with no official U.S. government ties was the 1975 Memorandum of Agreement between Henry Kissinger and Israel promising that the U.S. would not talk to the PLO until Arafat repudiated terrorism, recognized Israel's right to exist, and agreed to negotiate under the umbrella of U.N. 242 and 338. Yet how could the U.S. persuade Arafat to do all of the above if no one was allowed to talk to the PLO?

But talk about the "enemies of Israel" and the dangers of the PLO was precisely what stirred up "citizen lobbyists" to join AIPAC's War for Washington. "Politics is the favorite sport of our community," Tom Dine said in an interview in March 1984. "I want grass-roots strength. I want strength in 435 Congressional Districts. AWACS gave us visibility, and I've been stomping the country rallying troops."[11] When Dine took over in October 1980, AIPAC had eleven thousand dues-paying members; by the end of 1984, there were more than fifty thousand. Membership tripled after the AWACs vote. "We're a mass movement," Dine was boasting of an organization that had been established in 1951 with a staff of five and a ledger book that would be written in red for the next twenty years.

In July 1984, Bob Asher, a Chicago businessman who had just been elected president of AIPAC, addressed the annual policy conference—the twenty-fifth—and declared that his dream for the only Jewish group registered in Washington as a lobbyist for Israel was 250,000 members, Jews and non-Jews. He and Tom Dine were eager to make AIPAC into the preeminent Jewish organization in America. AIPAC's 1985 budget was $3 million.

Along the way, AIPAC had picked up the kind of clout that Hussein had lamented in his *New York Times* interview. For several years now, congressional opposition to giving U.S. arms to Jordan has rested on King Hussein's alleged inability to "enter the peace process"—a constant refrain in Dine's public speeches. Yet few leaders in the Middle East have lobbied for peace as often and as persistently as the king of Jordan. No Arab leader has met with as many Israeli leaders as Hussein, in private. A secret meeting with Hussein has become something of a badge of eminence in Israeli politics. In spite of his difficulties with the Israelis and the Palestinians, the latter constituting a political majority in his country, and the Islamic fundamentalists, who threaten his future, and the Saudis and Syrians and Egyptians, Hussein has supported every U.S. peace move since 1967, except Camp David. Dr. Akram Barakat, head of the Jordanian Information Bureau in Washington, summarizes Hussein's contributions to the peace, and his frustrations at the results:

> U.N. 242 raised the issue of territory for peace for the first time, and the King persuaded Nasser to accept it. The Israelis resisted 242, Begin resigned from the government over it, and nothing happened. The King cooperated with the Jarring Mission. Nothing happened. The Rogers Plan. He accepted it—in spite of the political upheavals in Jordan and the internal pressure not to cooperate. And the Rogers Plan vanished. Jordan accepted U.N. 338 too. The King played an active role in the peace process until after the disengagement between Syria and Israel engineered by Kissinger. Because Jordan didn't enter the [Yom Kippur] war in 1973, we were told we had no right to play a role in disengagement. The U.N. role was also reduced, but the King still hoped that the U.S. could put pressure on Israel on the issue of withdrawal. But once the PLO became the accepted representative of the Palestinian people, Jordan's role became secondary, up to Camp David. The King also accepted the joint U.S.–Russian call for a peace conference in Geneva [mooted when Sadat announced his plan to go to Jerusalem].[12]

Jordan refused to get involved in Camp David, mainly because the king saw Sadat making a separate peace with Israel without pressing very hard for Palestinian rights on the West Bank. But Hussein supported the Reagan Plan, though never as enthusiastically as the Reaganites had expected when they announced it. The king has explained that Syrian, Saudi, and PLO opposition and Reagan's inability to force the Israelis to withdraw from Lebanon made it impossible to go all out for the peace plan; he also pointed out that strategic agreements between the U.S. and Israel have brought both countries closer than ever, and thus have jeopardized the U.S.'s ability to act as an objective peace broker.

Like the Israelis and all the other players in the Middle East arena, Hussein has his own political problems at home and abroad. With more than half his subjects Palestinian, the king is caught between

the historic rejection of Begin's Herut (and its most recent manifestation in the Likud) of any compromise on the West Bank and the
PLO's covenant, which calls for the destruction of Israel.

Nevertheless, Hussein has also labored to bring Arafat into the
peace process. In 1983, according to a series on the king in *The Wall
Street Journal*, Hussein almost got Arafat to sign a document endorsing "all international efforts, including the Reagan Plan." Arafat
agreed in theory, but when a draft was presented to him for his signature, he backed off. The *Journal* correspondent—Karen Elliot
House, now the paper's foreign editor—reports an "American official privy to part of this process" saying "the king did a hell of a job
with Arafat. He got that slippery fish right up to the side of the boat
and almost had the gaff in him."[13]

It was the closest the PLO leader has come to putting the Israelis
on the spot by actually agreeing—in writing—to the terms Israel has
always demanded as a precondition for negotiations. Yet Arafat continued to talk as if he was ready to face up to the reality of Israel and
his own political problems, and adopt a political rather than military
solution to the Palestinian problem. When John Oakes, a former senior editor of *The New York Times*, asked the PLO chairman in an
interview in March 1984 if he was committed to the destruction of
Israel, Arafat replied, "You're joking. How can we destroy a state
which has 30 atomic bombs?" An evasion to be sure, but perhaps
also some evidence—hyperbolic though it is—of why Arafat has
been moving toward a political solution. When Oakes pressed him on
why the PLO had not recognized Israel's right to exist, Arafat was
more candid: "I have to be careful. I'm not Sadat. He committed
suicide. I have but one card—recognition—and I'm not so stupid as
to throw it away unless I get something substantial in return. Give me
a package deal."[14] Arafat added, "I've sent my signals to open a
dialogue, but without response." He pointed out that Prime Minister
Shamir was on the record against recognizing the PLO even if the
PLO recognized Israel.

Arafat sent a few more signals over the next few months. In a May
interview in the French magazine *Le Nouvel Observateur*, the PLO
chairman said, "I would propose direct negotiations between the
Israelis and us, under the aegis of the United Nations." In the same
interview, Arafat also said, "I would be for mutual recognition between two states [i.e., Israel and a Palestinian state]."[15]

It was an extraordinary public concession for the PLO leader. Implicit in those remarks are both recognition of Israel—one cannot, after all, negotiate with someone who does not exist—and acceptance of U.N. 242 and 338. News of Arafat's remarks were not even reported in the American press.

AIPAC certainly was not listening. In October 1984, the lobby urged friends in Congress to tack onto a "continuing resolution"—legislation that allows a Congress that has been unable to agree on new appropriations for the next fiscal year to continue federal spending at current levels—Section 535, which tightened the Kissinger restrictions one notch further.

No employee of or individual acting on behalf of the United States government shall recognize or negotiate with the Palestine Liberation Organization or representatives thereof, so long as the Palestine Liberation Organization does not recognize Israel's right to exist, does not accept Security Council Resolutions 242 and 338, and does not renounce the use of terrorism.[16]

Hussein kept plugging. Elections were scheduled in Israel in the summer of 1984, and there was a chance that the Likud might be replaced by a Labor government led by Shimon Peres, who seemed more eager to return Israel to its old policy of being willing to trade territory for peace. Peres, however, failed to win the kind of majority needed to form a government; the compromise solution reached in October was a National Unity Government in which Labor and the Likud would share power over the next four years—Peres serving in the top job for two years, after which it would rotate to Shamir. Hussein continued to meet with Arafat, trying to hammer out an agreement that would satisfy the U.S. and Israel and bring him into negotiations that Hussein could not safely enter without him.

Yet few who had followed events in the Middle East since 1967 were sanguine about the prospects of peace under Israel's new government. The National Unity Government, after all, was made up of two halves—the Likud coalition, led by Begin's Herut, and Labor—which had despised each other's vision of Israel since before the creation of the Jewish state. "There is little likelihood that this government will take any major steps toward peace," said former secretary of state Cyrus Vance shortly after the government had been formed. "On the matter of foreign policy there is no way of reconciling their differences." Vance saw little prospect of the peace process moving ahead during the tenure of the new Israeli government.[17]

THAT American Jewish groups sat in silence in the face of Likud intransigence mystified many Israeli politicians to the left of Begin, Shamir, and Sharon. Almost half the citizenry of Israel was opposed to annexation of the West Bank. While the Israeli public began to denounce the Begin-Sharon adventure in Lebanon, American Jewish groups were still defending Israeli policy. The fact is, so were almost half the American Jewish public and a clear majority of its leaders who remained supporters of Israel's Labor party. Though the American Jewish community rallied around the Begin and Shamir governments in public, private conversations with pollsters expressed their dissatisfaction and concern about the Likud's vision of Israel, particularly the Begin-Shamir policies on the West Bank. Indeed they were so concerned that they claimed they wanted to do some thing about it. A Gallup Poll of Jewish opinion conducted on September 23–24, 1982, found that more than a third surveyed recommended that American Jews play a more active role in affecting Israeli policies, an unwelcome trend in the opinion of Israeli leaders.

In a 1983 American Jewish Committee poll, American Jews expressed precisely what they did not like about the policies of the current government of Israel led by the Likud. Contrary to the policies of Begin and Shamir, 42 percent of the Jewish public (74 percent of their leaders) believed that "Israel should offer the Arabs territorial compromise in . . . the West Bank and Gaza in return for credible guarantees of peace." On the issue of Jewish settlements in the Occupied Territories, American Jews were even more anti-Likud: 51 percent said that "Israel should suspend the expansion of settlements in . . . the West Bank . . . to encourage peace negotiations." American Jews thus proved they backed U.S. policy to trade land for peace and to oppose Jewish settlements in the Occupied Territories.

They also proved that almost half of them disagreed with AIPAC —even on the issue of negotiating with the dreaded PLO *and* the prospect of a Palestinian state next door to the Jewish one. In the 1983 American Jewish Committee poll—I dwell on this survey because these opinions come after five and a half years of Menachem Begin—70 percent of the public (73 percent of the leadership) agreed that "Israel should talk with the PLO if the PLO recognizes Israel and renounces terrorism." And just as AIPAC was gearing up to pressure the U.S. government to keep the PLO out of the peace process altogether, almost half the American Jewish public—48 percent—and more than half of their leaders (51 percent) told the AJC pollsters that "Palestinians have a right to a homeland on the West Bank and Gaza, so long as it does not threaten Israel."[18]

These are strong views, too strong, in fact, for many Jews to utter in public for fear that such dissent would play into the hands of the "pro-Arab" politicians and anti-Semites eager to cut U.S. support for Israel. Even Israeli moderates were unable to persuade Jewish leaders that dissociating themselves from Likud policy was in Israel's best interests.

In early fall of 1984, Mordechai Virshubski, a Tel Aviv lawyer who had just won a seat in the new Knesset as a member of the left-of-center Shinui Party, known for its dovish views on Israeli foreign policy, traveled around the U.S. speaking to Jewish groups. He had two goals, Virshubski explained in an interview at the Shinui headquarters in Tel Aviv in November 1984, a few weeks after his return from the U.S.: "to explain Arab-Israeli opinion to American Jews" and point out that "the consequences of settlements on the West Bank would not help strengthen Israel," as its Likud sponsors had long been arguing. Virshubski was startled by American attitudes toward Israeli society and politics. "There is no deep understanding of what Israel is facing and we [Israelis] do not make any effort to get people interested in the real Israel, which, in spite of its problems— actually because of them—is a fascinating place, one of history's great social experiments."[19]

Virshubski was particularly upset about his meeting with Steven Rosen, AIPAC's head of research and prime mover of the lobby's policy to sell Israel to Congress as a strategic asset. Around the lobby's offices, where political opinions on most matters range from the left to the right, on U.S. and Israeli issues, Rosen is known as a hardliner in favor of annexing the West Bank. Though his boss, Tom Dine, is personally opposed to annexing the West Bank, Rosen, who reportedly has the support of some of AIPAC's most powerful board members, is in charge of supplying pro-Israel information to U.S. policy makers. Virshubski was not pleased with Rosen's stance on Israel. "Rosen's behavior toward me indicated his mind was made up and his attitude was 'Don't inform me of the facts,'" Virshubski recalled. "I found it quite obnoxious. I had the feeling he not only opposed my very presence in the United States, but perhaps my very existence—as if I were taking his Holy Works and sullying them." With the characteristic candor of Israeli politicians (and the anger of a lawyer whose arguments have been ignored), Virshubski recalled, getting angrier at the memory, "I was elected by Israelis; I'm from a center party. What I'm saying is not even in opposition to the government of Israel. I am part of that government, part of what one side of it is thinking. We should have had it out. If he's for annexation of the West Bank, he should have owned up to it, and discussed it."

Virshubski was accompanied by another Knesset member, Haika Grossman, a famous Israeli politician who's a heroine of the Warsaw Ghetto Uprising and a survivor of Auschwitz. Grossman excused herself during the meeting, pleading a former engagement. When Virshubski met her back in Israel, she confided that she did not have another meeting but simply could not stomach the one she was sitting in on.

"Now this was not just any American Jew," notes Virshubski. "This is a very important man—Steve Rosen, head researcher of AIPAC, the pro-Israel lobby. And he wouldn't even talk to two Israeli Knesset members—one of us a major figure in Jewish history who survived the Holocaust and created a life based on Jewish Humanism. I find that very dangerous. It won't do much good for Israel."

AIPAC's official stance is that it doesn't play Israeli politics; the lobby, as both Amitay and Dine are on the record saying, simply supports the government of Israel. Yet by supporting the government of Israel under Begin and Shamir—and urging Congress and American Jews to do the same—AIPAC was, in effect, supporting a particular Israeli ideology, and ignoring the views of a sizable portion of the Israeli parliament and electorate. By discouraging debate in the U.S. on the issue of settlements on the West Bank, AIPAC was, as Virshubski noted, supporting only *half* of the current government of Israel. Begin, it seems, had given the conservative tendencies of American Jews an outlet; AIPAC was now busily trying to transform the most progressive ethnic community in America into anti-Russian neo-conservatives, at least on the issue of the Middle East.

Meantime, Israeli policy on the West Bank was becoming an obstacle to the kind of negotiations that American Jews claimed they were in favor of. West Bankers and Israelis feared there soon would be nothing to negotiate. In 1984, the former deputy mayor of Jerusalem Meron Benvenisti concluded in an analysis of Israeli policy that "processes working toward the total annexation of the West Bank and the Gaza Strip outweigh those that work against it."[20] The goal of that settlement policy, according to Benvenisti, was to establish a "strong domestic lobby" in Israel of settlers who have an economic interest in not letting go of any land. The result, says Benvenisti, is "a barrier to any political alternative espousing political compromise."

In the face of such rejectionist attitudes toward peace negotiations, Virshubski's frustration with the Jewish lobby and AIPAC did not seem much different from King Hussein's.

IN February 1985, Hussein and Arafat signed an agreement in Amman that outlined a joint PLO-Jordanian approach to peace, and seemed to offer some concessions from the PLO. The pact called for "total withdrawal" from the Occupied Territories, which was not so surprising, but then called "for comprehensive peace as established in the United Nations and Security Council resolutions." Jordan said that meant 242 and 338. Even more significant (and less vague) was the agreement's call for the right of self-determination of the Palestinian people "within the context of the formation of the proposed confederated Arab states of Jordan and Palestine."[21] It was the first time that Arafat had not insisted on an independent Palestinian state. The PLO also had agreed to participate in peace talks within a "joint Jordanian-Palestinian delegation," another shift in PLO policy. Arafat, with radical Palestinians lined up against him, seemed to be making an effort.

Certainly a growing number of well-informed and influential Israelis began to think so. By spring of 1985, there was considerable discussion in the Israeli press about the need to recognize Arafat's existence and start talking to the enemy, which, as several writers pointed out, is the only party to negotiate peace with. In no less than six articles in the Hebrew press in March and April 1985, editorial and op-ed–page writers argued that Israel had to confront seriously the peace overtures from Egypt, Jordan, and the PLO. "It is clear today that our Palestinian partner in the peace process is the PLO" and not local Palestinian leaders on the West Bank, argued Pinchas Inbari in *Al Hamishmar*. Inbari argued that after the PLO's eviction from Lebanon, Arafat was so eager for a political solution that he by now regarded the PLO as only "a means to an end." Inbari wrote:

"The closer he comes to a solution of the Palestinian problem, the less importance he attaches to the organization as such."[22]

Two other writers pointed out that while the Israeli government—its Likud *and* Labor halves—had been reluctant to talk to *any* Palestinians, the coalition has given plenty of lip service to the need to stick to the Camp David process, somehow forgetting that the peace treaty between Israel and Egypt establishes explicitly that "Egypt, Israel, Jordan and the representatives of the Palestinian people should participate in negotiations on the resolution of the Palestinian problem in all its aspects." Camp David also specifies that "the delegations of Egypt and Jordan may include Palestinians from the West Bank and Gaza or other Palestinians mutually agreed upon."[23]

Neither Begin nor Dayan had doubted that such Palestinians would be PLO members. But by 1985, "most Israelis remain obdurate" on the issue of PLO representation, explained the Jerusalem *Post* editorial writer Meir Merhav in an op-ed–page article in *The New York Times*. The article was adapted from a piece Merhav had written for his own paper in which he derided the apparent widespread rejection in Israeli political circles of talking to the PLO or their representatives. Merhav attacked this as "a consensus of nonsense."[24] The writer, like many other Israeli journalists, politicians, and intellectuals, noted the dangers and absurdity of "negotiating with Palestinians who represent no one but themselves." Merhav concluded:

> True, the PLO is Israel's mortal enemy. . . . But if Israel wants peace, it must make peace—with its mortal enemies above all. To try to settle with proxy negotiators would be futile at best, and potentially dangerous. Israel must insist on speaking directly to those who can make peace. How long must it take, how many more wars must be fought, how many lives must be wasted and how much treasure spent before we recognize that the PLO is the genuine representative of the Palestinian people and the key to any settlement of the Arab-Israeli conflict?[25]

It is a question that few American policy makers are willing to answer, at least publicly. Yet, as the Israeli PLO watcher Matti Steinberg, a member of the prestigious Truman Institute at the Hebrew University, pointed out in the Israeli daily *Ha'aretz*, by refusing to deal with the PLO, Israel is only playing into the hands of Arab rejectionists. "The way out of the deadlock being sought by the Arabs," he argued, "is to convince the United States to put pressure on Israel to change its attitude toward the PLO."

Another Israeli critic of his government's policy against talking to the enemy suggested that "America is the only major power that can help Mr. Peres in his effort; as a proved friend, it could apply discreet pressure on Israel's leaders and at the same time provide ample incentives to the Arabs. Yet Washington refuses to budge."[26]

Why? That these Israeli writers do not offer the answer themselves is more proof of how little even the most sophisticated Israelis understand about the American political system, and the role of the pro-Israel lobby in it. Thanks to AIPAC and "the friends of Israel" on Capitol Hill, no American policy maker or his representative can talk to the PLO, officially or unofficially. By law.

Hussein got another taste of AIPAC's power in the last week of May 1985. During what was billed as a routine visit to the White House to discuss a $750 million arms sale plus $250 million in U.S. economic aid to Jordan, the king placed on the table a package deal that met every U.S., Israeli, and AIPAC requirement for going ahead with negotiations. Or at least seemed to.

Hussein announced in Washington that the PLO had finally agreed to peace talks on the basis of "the pertinent United Nations Resolutions 242 and 338," and called the PLO's decision to negotiate "a historic breakthrough."[27] After his four-day visit, the king told the press, "For our part, and I speak for both my people and the representatives of the Palestinian people, we want peace."[28] The next step, said Hussein, was for the U.S. to meet with a joint Palestinian-Jordanian delegation to prepare the way for negotiations with Israel. Secretary of State George Shultz said he thought that the king had moved the peace process forward "in a very significant way.[29] Of course, Arafat himself had said nothing, and the Jordanian king and the PLO leader had come together before only to part again. But there was the February agreement between him and Hussein, which indicated a shift in PLO policy, and Arafat did not dispute the king's claims on his behalf; he was reportedly in Amman awaiting Hussein's return.

More problematic was that Hussein wanted negotiations to begin under the "umbrella" of international talks, which would include the Soviet Union, a sticking point for both the Israelis and the White House. Yet it was a start—an extraordinary one, all things considered. Congressional opposition to U.S. arms to Jordan had rested on King Hussein's inability "to enter the peace process." And then Hussein stepped forward as a seemingly willing "Arab negotiating partner." The Israelis rejected his offer. Foreign Minister and Deputy Prime Minister Shamir refused to treat Hussein seriously. On a visit to Washington, Yitzhak Rabin, the former prime minister who is Israel's defense minister, attacked the proposed arms sale to Jordan. Prime Minister Peres was also cool, but, unlike his fellow ministers —both longtime political opponents of his—Peres seemed to leave a crack in the door.

The U.S. Senate slammed it shut. The king had barely left town before sixty-nine senators introduced a resolution opposing aid and the arms sale until Hussein actually began negotiations with Israel. The White House called it "a serious mistake," pointing out it was not the best way to encourage peace in the region. Both the Senate majority leader, Robert Dole, and the chairman of the Senate Foreign Relations Committee, Richard Lugar, agreed that pressing such a resolution was, in Lugar's words, "not a good idea." Shultz was more visibly upset; Hussein had made a major move toward direct negotiations, and the Senate had greeted him by "sticking its finger in his eye."[30]

The Senate group pressed the resolution, picking up three more allies. Within days, the Administration announced that it was dropping the proposed arms sale but still wanted to encourage the king by giving Jordan the $250 million in economic aid. *Newsweek* quoted an anonymous "senior Pentagon official" who called the retreat on military aid a "failure of nerve." The newsmagazine added its own gloss on the outcome: "In the eyes of Arab moderates, it may well appear that the powerful pro-Israel lobby in Washington had beaten back the administration—without even trying very hard."[31]

But the reason why *Newsweek* did not offer. Anyone inclined to disagree with AIPAC had not forgotten what had happened to Senators Percy and Jepsen. "The White House called around and quickly discovered it couldn't get twenty votes," an AIPAC insider boasted in a confidential interview.[32] The White House was not willing to face another battle in the Senate. Lucky for AIPAC, because the lobby too had just stepped out of the way of a speeding bullet. There are two things that AIPAC goes to war on as a matter of policy: arms to the Arabs and recognition of the PLO. And here was the prime minister of Israel indicating he was willing to entertain both. The Hussein deal would have put AIPAC in the unprecedented public position of opposing an Israeli prime minister.

Actually, no one had more to gain by Hussein's move than Shimon

Peres. For weeks there had been reports in the Israeli press that Peres, working under the liability of sharing government with the Likud, was looking for an opportunity to break the coalition, call for new elections, and run as a peace candidate in a nation exhausted by the war in Lebanon. Shamir was scheduled to take over again as prime minister in October 1986, according to the deal that had formed the National Unity Government, and true to Likud policy, he would be unwilling to yield a stone on the West Bank. Neither Peres nor Hussein had any time to lose.

According to a source familiar with the Reagan-Hussein negotiations, before the king arrived in Washington, an agreement had been worked out among him, Shultz, and Peres. If the king delivered the PLO and if he announced publicly that he was adopting a policy of "nonbelligerency" toward Israel, Israel would drop its opposition to the arms sale to Jordan. It was an extraordinary concession by Peres. Traditionally, Israel opposed all arms sales to its Arab enemies until direct negotiations are under way. But then, in his statement in Washington, Hussein did not say he would negotiate with Israel on the basis of a policy of "nonbelligerency." Instead he referred to negotiations in an "environment free of belligerent and hostile acts."[33] The Israelis balked. An "environment" was hardly a policy. And thus the agreement, like so many others in Middle East diplomacy, had crashed against a phrase. To AIPAC's relief, Rabin came out strongly against the arms sale, and the Israeli Defense Ministry started kicking up a storm. The deal that was almost done was dead. Not even "nonbelligerency" would now bring the Israelis to accept the arms sale, according to this source.

Worse, the hijacking of a TWA airliner by Shiite Muslim "terrorists" in late June 1985 knocked all discussion of peace prospects in the Middle East out of the newspapers. Indeed, Israel's reluctance to help meet the Shiites' demands by turning over the more than seven hundred Shiites in an Israeli prison introduced a chill into U.S.–Israeli relations. The White House was waiting for its "strategic asset" to help resolve the issue, while Peres, Shamir, and Rabin treated the hijacking as, in Rabin's words, "an American problem."[34] Once again, U.S.–Israeli relations were sidetracked by domestic political concerns in Israel, as its top three leaders danced around the issue for fear of jeopardizing their own political futures. Curiously, the public-relations winner in the crisis turned out to be Syria, top man on Israel's and Ronald Reagan's enemies list, which arranged for the release of the hostages, apparently with the help of the dreaded Ayatollah Khomeini.

Still Peres, like Shultz, remained interested in getting Hussein to the table, and both were willing to give the Jordanians arms to get him there. AIPAC was not. In fact, the lobby was willing to jeopardize its good relations with Shultz to pursue its own agenda. Even more surprising, the lobby was contemplating opposing the prime minister of Israel.

Apparently, AIPAC has its own frontiers to protect. "What most people don't realize," explains a source familiar with the inner workings of the lobby, "is that the agendas of AIPAC and Israel are different."[35] While Peres may be seeking peace, while Shamir may be trying to block any withdrawal from the West Bank, AIPAC is primarily concerned with protecting the "special relationship" between the U.S. and Israel—from an Israeli government, if need be.

According to two sources familiar with AIPAC's strategy, the lobby cannot afford to be "flexible" in the way Peres can be flexible.[36] AIPAC sees its role as a limit on U.S. policy in the Middle East. That means making sure that the White House is committed to pressing for direct negotiations between the Israelis and the Arabs instead of imposing terms on negotiations that might hurt Israel. It means never allowing the U.S. to talk to the PLO. "If Arafat becomes a legitimate player," explains one AIPAC insider, "and for some reason—it happens all the time—relations between the U.S. and Israel cool, the U.S. might side with the Palestinians to bring Israel around. AIPAC cannot afford that option." And, finally, it means persuading Congress to oppose all arms sales to the Arabs.

As one of the sources puts it, "AIPAC does not want an evenhanded Congress because it sees Congress as a countervailing force to evenhandedness in U.S. policy."[37] AIPAC's job, as it sees it, is to make sure Israel will always have the upper hand on the Arabs, especially in any negotiating situation.

AIPAC's critics call that being "an obstacle to peace." Nastier critics call it protecting a job. "AIPAC is going to wake up one morning and discover peace in the Middle East," says Arthur Hertzberg, "and then what will it do? Its job will be over. The fact is that what 'PLO Inc.' is to Palestinian nationalism, AIPAC has become to American-Israeli relations."[38] Hertzberg has publicly called for AIPAC to be disbanded. "AIPAC is stirring up the anti-Semites," says Hertzberg. "The lobby has become the Sorcerer's Apprentice."

But unlike the Sorcerer's Apprentice, AIPAC seems likely to remain in charge. In fact, one of the reasons for such animosity toward AIPAC among Jewish leaders like Hertzberg—he is not alone, though he is alone in his candor—is that the Washington lobby has pushed them out of the picture. On the issue of Israel, the leader of the American Jewish community, in the eyes of Washington, is AIPAC. Since there is no more important issue for American Jews than the security of Israel, that makes AIPAC the *de facto* leader of the American Jewish community, much to the annoyance—and envy —of the other national Jewish groups whose influence in Washington has slipped badly since 1977.

The traditional leaders—the American Jewish Committee, B'nai B'rith, and even the Presidents' Conference, which represents more than thirty Jewish organizations—are annoyed that AIPAC seems intent on dominating the Arab-Israel issue. AIPAC staffers have called themselves the "sexy lobby," and some Jewish leaders are worried about the effect of sex appeal on young Jews who in the past gave their time to or sought careers in Jewish life. "AIPAC is skimming off the cream of the bright young activists in the American Jewish community," complains one executive at the American Jewish Committee.[39]

Dine himself is aware of the bitterness, as well as the "secret" meetings to determine future relations between organized Jewry and AIPAC, once its servant on Capitol Hill, and now "the spearhead of the American Jewish community," to borrow a phrase from Dine. "I wish they didn't feel that way," he says, "but my response is let them catch up. We've got a job to do."[40]

Critics and fans alike have noticed that AIPAC has been slipping in the one job that made it famous, and very useful on Capitol Hill. "The service aspect of the organization has fallen by the wayside," writes David Silverberg, a former AIPAC staffer who covers Jewish politics for *Washington Jewish Week*. "As AIPAC lifted its research sights to lofty international vistas, the kind of information it used to provide on a moment's notice to the Hill and the Jewish community is no longer emphasized."[41] Saudi lobbyist Fred Dutton, a less objective source, agrees: "I get the sense that Dine is devoting himself more to being a public figure than to the legislative side of things. AIPAC is building itself at the expense of the client. Lobbyists ought to keep a low profile."[42]

But Dine points to the indisputable results of "Jewish muscle": in spite of Israel's attack on the Iraqi nuclear reactor, the annexation of the Golan Heights, the rejection of the Reagan Plan, the invasion of Lebanon, proof of "Jewish terrorism" on the West Bank, intransigence during the TWA hostage crisis, Israel's "special relationship" with the U.S. has flourished during the Reagan Administration, and U.S. aid has flowed to Israel in record amounts. No foreign-policy lobby in Washington is more successful in keeping American military aid and economic assistance flowing to Israel, the record holder in both departments. For 1985, AIPAC had helped win $2.6 billion for Israel—for the first time a total grant—and was working for an additional $1.5 billion in "emergency" aid over the next two years to help prop up an Israeli economy crumbling under high defense costs, an occupation of Lebanon, and expenses from settlements on the West Bank.

No one doubted that AIPAC would be able to persuade Congress to keep raising the ante. But even AIPAC recognized that Israel would have to do something about its economy. The lobby had informed the Unity Government that it, as one AIPAC staffer put it, "had better gets its act together to improve the economy, if it expected to receive more U.S. aid." There were politicians and economists in Israel who argued that U.S. aid was precisely what was destroying their economy (or Israel's ability to create one). But that was one bit of information about Israel that AIPAC, the Indian elephant, was quick to forget. The implications were disconcerting: if U.S. aid was helping to destroy the Israeli economy, and AIPAC was responsible for those billions every year, then wasn't the lobby instrumental in helping Israel to hurt itself?

9

U.S. AID: HELPING ISRAEL TO HURT ITSELF

FOR the past three decades, it has been AIPAC's primary role to assure that U.S. aid flows to Israel in increasing amounts. To say that the lobby has been phenomenally successful in this part risks understatement. It is impossible to understand the relationship between the U.S. and Israel—and AIPAC's special role in it—without examining the issue of U.S. aid to Israel and its effects on U.S. politics and the Israeli economy.

The engine that has run the Israeli economy for decades has been American aid. One might even say that the U.S. owns Israel. There is no deed, but there is a mortgage. Israel is heavily in debt to the U.S. Treasury, its commercial banks, and its Jews and other citizens and organizations that have purchased millions in Israel bonds or donated money to Jewish causes.

The special relationship between the U.S. and Israel features some very special numbers. Since 1948, the U.S. has given Israel $28 billion in economic and military aid—slightly more than half of it ($14.6 billion) in outright grants that never have to be repaid.[1] According to one academic study, upwards of $1.4 billion a year in non–U.S. government funds flows into the Israeli economy—about $500 million of it in tax-deductible donations to Jewish charities and purchases of Israel bonds that are lost to the U.S. Treasury.[2] When one factors in those nongovernment dollars, the total figure of American money that has ended up in the Israeli economy since 1948, according to estimates, jumps to $40 billion.[3]

For 1985–1986, the Reagan Administration budgeted $4.5 billion for Israel in military and economic assistance—about $1,500 for every man, woman, and child in Israel; $6,000 for a family of four. (That amount of money becomes all the more striking when one considers that in 1985, Israel's finance minister, Yitzhak Moda'i, took home $580 a month[4]; a postman or grocery check-out clerk in Israel makes about $200 a month; a top photographer working for a foreign news service earns the princely sum of $600 a month.)

In 1970, Israel's foreign debt was $2.6 billion. In 1984 it was $23 billion, and rising. About one-third of it is owed to the U.S. That external debt could reach as much as $41 billion by 1988.[5] Every year that debt costs Israel about $1 billion in interest payments. The U.S. has loaned money to Israel under the most generous terms, with thirty-to-forty-year repayment periods. In 1985, the first big loan passed its ten-year "grace period," when only interest is paid; as more of the principal comes due in the 1980s and 1990s, Israel's annual payments will only become more crushing, particularly if its leadership continues to spend the money it borrows on imports instead of high-return investments. Israel already has the highest per capita debt in the world. Without U.S. aid, Israel would default immediately.

Foreign aid to Israel, most of it from the U.S., generates most of the nation's growth. Because of its growing loan payment, Israel now requires annual increases in foreign aid to maintain its *status quo*. The government's domestic deficit is covered by additional borrowing from commercial banks abroad, its own banking system, and bond issues to citizens, creating a massive inflationary spiral.

The U.S. pays for nearly all Israel's military imports, which amount to one-half its defense budget—more than 25 percent of all Israel's expenditures. For the past several years, Israel has been importing more than it has been exporting. Export earnings are barely enough to cover the interest and amortization of Israel's accumulated debt. The result: Whatever import goods Israelis are buying—cars, televisions, VCRs, appliances—it is foreign aid that is paying the bill.

Israel has one of the most generous welfare systems in the world. Created to care for the large numbers of immigrants pouring into the country, the government's "entitlement's" for education, maternity leave, hospitalization, the handicapped, child rearing, and other social services, according to one estimate, now amount to upwards of a third of the nation's GNP.[6] There is no "means test" for these benefits. According to one Israeli study, the top 20 percent of the population in terms of income was benefiting twice as much as the bottom 20 percent. Therefore, people needing it least were getting twice as much in welfare as those who needed it most.

It is difficult to overstate the mess that the Israeli economy has been in. One prime indicator of economic crisis is the amount of foreign reserves a nation has on hand. By July 1985, the government announced foreign reserves had fallen under $2 billion, down $70 million over the previous month.[7] Actually, the situation was even worse because the Israelis had borrowed money simply to maintain their cash reserves at a level that wouldn't scare off their short-term lenders whose faith in Israel continued only because more U.S. aid had been promised. Businesses were struggling and failing right and left. That same summer, 782 Israeli companies had landed on the Dun and Bradstreet "blacklist" of companies in "financial distress"— that is, with either severe liquidity problems, unable to pay bills and supply goods and services promised, drastically reducing business operations, ceasing business entirely, or being in receivership. Every sector of the economy was represented: trade and services, construction, electronics, metals, and electricity.[8]

In 1985, by virtually every measure available, Israel was flat broke and on the verge of economic collapse. Yet between 1973 and 1983, the standard of living in Israel had risen 70 percent.[9] Between 1981 and 1983, Israeli consumption had increased by 27 percent.[10] In fact (and incredibly), Israelis were consuming 80 percent of what Americans consumed—while earning a fraction of the average U.S. income.[11] *The Israeli Economist* reported in 1984 that Israel had the highest per capita rate of VCRs in the world. "Is this what the Zionist dream was all about?" asked the magazine.

While spending was up 27 percent, for the same period, growth increased a mere 5 percent. The fastest-rising indicator was inflation. In the fall of 1984, shortly after the new National Unity Government of Shimon Peres and Yitzhak Shamir took office, the inflation rate hit 1,000 percent. By mid-1985, the annual rate of inflation stood at about 500 percent. In 1977, it had been about 60 percent. Gad Ya'acobi, Israel's minister of economic coordination and one of the prime minister's oldest, most loyal friends, reportedly warned Peres that few democracies have survived triple-digit rates of inflation lower than Israel's.[12]

HOW do the Israelis survive in such an economy? Protecting the Israeli standard of living from the ravages of inflation—and contributing to it in the process—is a mysterious invisible shield called "indexation," whereby wages keep pace with the Consumer Price Index. When prices at the supermarket go up, so does the amount in a worker's pay envelope at regular intervals during the year.

Then there is U.S. aid. During one of Prime Minister Peres's visits to Washington, an American breakfasting in an Israeli coffee shop asked the man behind the counter his opinion of the prime minister's trip. The American spoke Hebrew well so the Israeli was engaged, and candid in his brief answer: "He's gone to pick up the check," said the counterman.[13] Actually, the prime minister doesn't even have to pick up the check. It's easier than that. Israel used to receive aid in quarterly payments, but for fiscal year 1985 the House approved a measure disbursing economic aid in a one-shot electronic cash transfer. According to Deputy Assistant Secretary of State Robert Pelletreau, the change costs the U.S. $50 million, since "we have to borrow funds to disburse at an earlier date."[14]

Israel has become a foreign-aid addict. The Georgetown economist Thomas Stauffer, in a forthcoming book, argues that nations inevitably become addicted to "unearned resources"—whether it is easy oil money or U.S. foreign aid. "Just like the oil-addicted economies of the Middle East—only Kuwait seems to have escaped by good management—Israel has developed grossly inflated economic expectations," Stauffer explains.[15]

Yet the prospect of economic disaster was predictable to anyone who bothered to examine the Israeli economy, a task that few top Israeli—or American—politicians seemed to have bothered with. The Jewish state's problem is simple and well entrenched. Israel and its citizens have always been inclined to spend more than they make. Like most of us, Israel has been living beyond its means. The huge increases in U.S. aid have only increased Israel's habit. But then Israel seems to have been turned into a foreign-aid junkie at a very early age.

DURING the first two decades after its miraculous birth, Israel was one of the world's most successful economic stories. Throughout the 1950s and 1960s, the Jewish state housed and fed and educated millions of Jewish immigrants from all around the world, defended itself against hostile neighbors, and still managed to achieve an economic growth rate of about 10 percent—a triumph matched only by Japan, Taiwan, and South Korea. Income went up steadily; inflation never went highter than 10 percent.

Israel accomplished this without much in the way of U.S. government aid. Between 1948 and 1973, the U.S. provided Israel with only $2.7 billion in economic and military aid in the form of grants and loans. Israel's economy, however, benefited from a vast amount of private foreign aid from Jews and other supporters around the world—about $2 billion from Jewish charities and another $2 billion from the sale of Israel bonds. Israel also received $6 billion in reparations from West Germany (violently opposed by Menachem Begin and his followers).

The Israeli economy prospered with plenty of outside capital and a level of education unique among developing countries. But that foreign money covered up some structural flaws in the economy, the most serious being the nation's constant balance of payments deficit. Israel began life importing more than it exported, a surplus financed by Diaspora charities, German reparations, along with foreign loans and investments. The extra cash made a lot of domestic investment possible, investment that never cut into private or public spending. "This is the national equivalent of having one's cake and eating it," wrote the economist Nadav Halevi, director of Israel's Falk Institute of Economic Research. "As the balance of payments deficit persisted, its negative implications became more obvious: growing reliance on foreign finance, an increasing burden on foreign debt, and most disturbing, the fear that the economy was not preparing for the time when it would have to live within its own means."[16]

Israel badly needed a real economy, one that wasn't totally dependent on outside money. A balance of payments deficit of $500 million in 1965 frightened the government into reducting imports and increasing exports. This helped Israel's balance and payments position, but the resulting recession and unemployment cut into Israel's most precious resource: Jews. People started emigrating. In 1967, the government switched back to its goals of growth and full unemployment, helped along by the Six-Day War, which was not only a public-relations bonanza for Israel, but also gave a huge boost to its economy. Incredible amounts of money poured in from Jews abroad.

But as the economy grew rapidly, prosperity, inevitably, was not every Israeli's birthright. By 1973, the issue of "two Israels"—the relatively prosperous and politically dominant European Jews *versus* the poor Jews from Asia and Africa—had become *the* major political issue. The major industry seemed to be tax evasion; relative to its GNP, Israel had one of the biggest "underground economies" in the world. And then the Yom Kippur War hit, pushing economic and social problems, once again, onto the back burner. Defense became the top priority, gobbling up greater and greater chunks of Israel's total resources. Israel spent 8.2 percent of its total resources on defense in 1960, by 1975 the percentage was more than 20. It was also the same period when U.S. military aid increased exponentially, to $700 million, a huge infusion of cash for buying arms considering the size of Israel's income.

But Israel's old economic problems had not disappeared: those import surpluses, that foreign aid and charity, had led workers into jobs handling that money and spending it. By the mid-1970s fully half of Israel's labor force was working in finance, trade, and public and private service areas. It was not the most creative way to build a solid, independent future.

With the 1976 election coming up, the Labor Party seemed serious about confronting these economic problems by increasing taxes and cutting subsidies as well as reining in wages and prices. Such measures actually seemed to be cutting private spending. The growing defense budget, however, remained sacrosanct. The most promising economic policy was peace, though no one seemed to be moving too fast in that direction. Tax reform was in the offing, though no one was sure how readily Israelis would comply. The balance of payments remained unaffected.

Israel had real economic problems. The government recognized it; so did the public. "But," as Halevi noted at the time, "the public response to these measures has not been encouraging . . . there seems to be a failure to grasp that a successful economic policy cannot mean anything other than an extended departure from the trend of rising living standards." The Israeli economist noted with some frustration, "Each new step in the economic policy designed to curb the standard of living is widely denounced for the very reason it is adopted."

Israelis were unwilling to tighten their belts. Worse, the government did not manage to spread the burden of the new austerity. The poor Oriental Jews who were now finding their place in the economy were not about to see it shrink just when they were readying to grab their share of Israeli affluence.

It was precisely that bitterness that Menachem Begin's election campaign capitalized on in 1976–1977. The "Other Israel" chose Begin as its savior and boosted him to the premiership after more than a quarter century of opposition. "Begin King of Israel," they cheered.

Economics, however, was not the king's strongpoint. And when the prime minister resigned in 1983, the Israeli economy was not much to cheer about.

BEGIN had promised an "economic revolution." Instead, he only weakened the Israeli economy further. The path was paved with good intentions, but whenever political issues collided with good economic sense, politics won every time.[17]

"The Likud will strive to establish a free economy based on efficiency, initiative and competition," the party platform declared. Begin's coalition offered a complete break with the past. Labor's system was, the platform charged, "an abortive mélange between capitalism, socialism and anarchy designed to perpetuate the ruling class."[18]

Seven years later, one could make precisely the same charge. But now the economy was even worse off than Labor had left it. Inflation had jetted into the stratosphere of 500 percent, and according to his successor, Shimon Peres, "the state coffers [were] empty . . . The banks were empty."[19] Instead of being independent, the Israeli economy was now an absolute ward of the U.S. Treasury.

Begin was not much interested in economic matters. His priorities were the political goals of Greater Israel and keeping his constituency happy, particularly the Oriental Jews. The Likud would leave the economy up to the finance minister—all four of them. And each tried to live within the paradox of the economic need for budget, wage, employment, and food subsidy cuts and the political reality of keeping the electorate happy with bread and videos. It was an unpopular, and finally impossible, job. Neither the Israeli government nor the people had become any more eager for austerity than during Labor's hard times.

Begin's first finance minister was Simha Ehrlich, a member of the Liberal branch of Begin's Likud coalition made up of mainly small-business men and the self-employed; the Liberals had been Labor's most vocal critics in economic matters. Ehrlich boldly sought to build an economy that could cut its dependence on U.S. aid. His goals were to move government-owned companies into the private sector, cut government spending and subsidies, and allow foreign currency exchange rates to be determined by market forces instead of the Byzantine controls and restrictions that had ruled exchange for years. The regulations had only encouraged exporters to keep their earnings stashed abroad, even though in Israel it was illegal to have foreign currency or, with exceptions, bank accounts abroad. Even Labor officials had recognized that the currency controls had to be changed.

Ehrlich floated Israeli currency—it was still the pound—on the foreign-exchange market and lifted currency controls. The foreign currency that Israelis had buried outside the country came flowing back into the economy. It was his first move, his first success, and his last. The budget and subsidy cuts Ehrlich wanted would not fly among his coalition partners. The Herut vowed to maintain full employment and social welfare programs.

Nor could Begin cut defense spending, which, along with government social services, made up half the nation's budget. With most of the rest of the budget accounted for in repaying the interest on loans at fixed rates, there was little else to cut. Raising taxes was politically taboo. Nor were there enough capital funds in the private sector to buy out companies from the government. Meantime, inflation moved toward triple digits fueled by the Central Bank's loans on the Eurodollar market and the printing of money to meet the deficits not covered by foreign loans, grants, bonds, and taxes. To speed ahead of inflation, the unions pressed for wage increases.

The "anti-Socialist" Begin government was now more involved in the economy than before, owning more companies, employing more workers, and spending more on subsidies than ever. No real review of the budget à la Ronald Reagan had ever taken place. The labor unions were as intimidating as ever, and real wages, the balance of payments deficit, and inflation all increased.

Second at bat, in 1979, was a member of the Likud coalition's smaller La'am Party, Yigal Hurwitz. An entrepreneur who specialized in turning failing businesses around, Hurwitz promised to run the economy on sound business practices—and political consequences be damned. For some reason, Hurwitz had forgotten that his boss—the "Boss," as Begin's disciples had called him since the old days in the Irgun—never ignored the political consequences of any act.

Hurwitz started slashing the budget in an all-out effort to reduce, or at least stop, government spending and increases in the bureaucracy. The press soon tagged him with the nickname "Mr. Ein-Li." When other Cabinet ministers or interest groups lobbied budget increases or subsidies, Hurwitz's standard reply was *"ein-li"*—"I haven't any." Hurwitz prodded the Cabinet to cut the budget and seemed ready to demand sacrifices from an Israeli public largely insulated from their nation's moribund economy by subsidies, indexation, and the tax-free good life in the underground economy. Though Begin's own ministers had approved Hurwitz's budget cuts, few went so far as to implement them. Begin was no help either. As his biographer, Eric Silver writes, "Begin remained the dominant personality. The Cabinet could do nothing without him, but for much of the time it could do nothing with him either."[20] Silver contends that by late 1980 Begin had fallen into one of his "troughs of depression." His ministers were complaining about lack of leadership. Rumors circulated (confirmed by Silver) that the prime minister was falling asleep during briefings with the general staff, that he didn't recognize old friends. On one occasion as he entered the Knesset, Begin walked straight for the seat of the leader of the opposition where he had sat until 1977.[21]

In 1980–1981, as Hurwitz's austerity measures took hold, for the first time in the history of the Jewish state, the number of Israelis leaving the country—called *yordim*, those who descend—outstripped the number of immigrants. This alerted even Begin to the economy, and the political problems it was creating for his coalition. Nineteen eighty-one was an election year, and the polls showed him trailing Shimon Peres. Begin had six months and finance minister number three to catch up. The new financial wizard was Yoram Aridor, a Herut member and Hurwitz's loudest critic within the coalition. Billed as Begin's first finance minister with an academic background in economics, Aridor soon proved himself a loyal Herutnik. Politics once again took precedence over economics. The Likud economic platform of 1981 had abandoned the promises of free competition and now advocated an economy of "modern and progressive social liberalism."[22]

Aridor went after the politically safest target, inflation, and reversed the policies of his two predecessors. He *increased* subsidies, lowered the prices of basic goods, and cut tariffs on high-ticket consumer imports. Tax cuts reduced the cost of television sets upwards of 15 percent; cars were going for 10 to 17 percent less. VCRs, washing machines, and furniture were equally affordable. Aridor's Finance Ministry swept any doubts that Likud economic theory was closely tied to getting out the vote with its candid announcement that the tax on sweet wine would be cut 50 percent—until the day after election day. Aridor also depreciated Israeli currency—the pound during the age of Begin, a man devoted to Israel's Biblical traditions, had become the *shekel*—at a rate slower than what inflation called for. The upward spiral of the prices controlled by the government also slowed, as did inflation. Their confidence in the economy restored and the prices right, Israelis did what they had been wanting to do all along: they went on a shopping spree that peaked just before the election. Within a month, Israelis had ordered eight thousand new cars—a 400 percent increase—and sixty thousand color television sets, all imported.[23]

The results of Aridor's policies soon showed up in the opinion polls, and then at the polling booths. "Begin made the biggest comeback since Lazarus," writes his biographer Eric Silver.[24] The economy, however, was going down for the count. In Begin's second term, the Israeli public continued spending at a dangerous rate, and by 1982 consumption was still up, while output remained flat. "In terms of policy goals," writes the Israeli economist Yoram Ben-Porath, "it appears that without achieving either economic growth or price stability, the policies led to greater economic dependence on the outside world, serving unwarranted improvement in the standard of living, at a time when world prices were coming down and the inflationary pressures from the import side were reversed."[25]

Exports failed to grow, while imports did. Proof that the Israeli worker assumed inflation would rise came in a series of small strikes, including a doctors' work stoppage, which got wide publicity around the world. No one was eager to take less in his pay envelope. "The choices facing the government," wrote the State Department economist Kenneth Stammerman, "were a return to the Hurwitz policy of fiscal restraint and currency depreciation or a radical revision of the entire indexing system."[26] Rather than admit defeat—and the ire of voters—Aridor chose to change the indexing system. It turned out to be political suicide.

Aridor worked up a secret plan to cut the budget, depreciate the shekel, and then tie it to the dollar instead of the Consumer Price

Index. The dollar would eventually replace the shekel, as the Israeli economy became a Middle East outpost of the U.S. Federal Reserve System. Interest and inflation rates would parallel those of the U.S. The plan made sense; with triple-digit inflation, most Israelis had been forced to think in dollar terms (and still do) in order to figure out what anything was worth. But the real defect in Aridor's "dollarization" plan was that by facing up to reality it abandoned any pretense of economic independence. The Central Bank would yield all its discretion to the U.S. Federal Reserve Bank, and Israel's balance of payments would dominate the economy: if the country spent more than it made, then dollars would flow out of the economy, reducing bank reserves and credit; an increase in production would increase dollars in Israel and thus generate economic activity.

It was a simple system, but Aridor never got a chance to put it all into effect. Israelis smelled a devaluation and began getting liquid by selling off bank shares on the stock exchange in order to buy dollars. The "Crisis of October" 1983, as it became known, shook the country, which had yet to recover from Begin's inexplicable resignation only a month before. It was not an ideal time for another economic revolution. When the dollarization plan leaked to the press, the loyal Herutnik Aridor was attacked as a virtual traitor. The head of the Histadrut charged that dollarization was "a deep blow to the people's prestige, to the national honor." Geula Cohen, a leader of the right-wing Tehiya Party, which was part of the Likud coalition, declared that Israel "might as well put Abraham Lincoln on the face of its currency."[27] The rhetoric and posturing were predictable. Cabinet members threatened to resign. The finance minister was right, but he also knew he was beaten. Aridor decided to pack it in.

The new prime minister, Yitzhak Shamir, devalued the shekel and slashed basic food subsidies. He then went to the bank—Washington, D.C. The Begin government had received $17 billion in U.S. economic and military aid between 1977 and 1983. In spite of his irritation with Begin's efforts to annex the West Bank and Gaza, Jimmy Carter promised not to use U.S. aid as "a weapon" to pressure Israel into complying with U.S. interests in the Middle East. In 1981, after the AWACS Battle, the Reagan Administration, in an effort to patch up the wounds caused by the Senate battle over the Saudi plane deal, authorized another $300 million in military aid to Israel. Reagan too was not eager to force Israeli policy in his direction—in spite of

Begin's attack on the Iraqi reactor, bombing of Beirut, annexation of the Golan Heights. In spite of Sharon's invasion of Lebanon. In spite of Begin's rejection of the Reagan Plan.

In late November, Shamir visited Washington, carrying along his shopping list. After a chat with Shultz and an hour lunch with the President, the Israeli premier returned home with the store. U.S. military aid for the next fiscal year would drop from $1.7 billion to $1.3 billion, but it would be an outright gift, no interest attached. Reagan promised Israel another $910 million in economic aid, also a total grant. Unlike every other recipient of U.S. military aid, Israel would not have to spend it all in the U.S.; 15 percent could be spent in Israel on Israeli-made weapons. Reagan also agreed with Congress that Israel needed $550 million to produce the Lavi and expressed support for a more defined "strategic cooperation" with Israel and duty-free trade between the two nations.

What did the Reagan Administration get from Shamir in return? "Nothing," Shamir told the Israeli press. "We did not pay for whatever we got from the Americans." There was no commitment to the Reagan Plan, which Shamir had opposed; nothing said about freezing settlements on the West Bank, which Reagan was known to think might help the peace process. There was definitely no agreement between the two on U.S. arms sales to the Jordanians, which Reagan was keen on. And there were certainly no admonishing words from the President about Israel repairing its economy. *Time* magazine reported that American officials would be happy if Shamir, unlike Begin, didn't "throw a tantrum" every time the Administration sought to woo moderate Arab states. *Time* also quoted an unnamed Pentagon official who summed up Shamir's visit: "They went over us like a steamroller."[28]

Reagan had his own political reasons for getting steamrolled. Nineteen eighty-four was a presidential election year. Yet it seemed that the President and his secretary of state—and AIPAC's friends in Congress—were genuinely eager to help Israel through its hard economic times. The Americans had been watching the Erhlich, Hurwitz, Aridor follies with alarm. (Aridor began talking to the State Department about a bailout.) There was no evidence that American policy makers noticed Ehrlich's efforts to make the Israeli economy less dependent on the U.S.; they didn't seem to listen to the finance minister's argument that U.S. aid was only hurting Israel. Nevertheless, with promises of more aid in direct grant form, which of course would not add to Israel's already burdensome debt to the U.S., it was time for the Likud's fourth finance minister to go into action. He was Yigal Cohen-Orgad, another Herut member and a former Treasury economist who was head of his own economic consulting firm.

Cohen-Orgad had his work cut out for him. Polls showed that more than 80 percent of the public reckoned the government had lost control of the economy. Shamir's finance minister came up with a budget featuring real reductions in spending for defense and social programs. He even pushed through a cut in the estimated $400 million the Likud was spending on those controversial settlements in the West Bank. But, like his predecessors, Cohen-Orgad ran into resistance among his fellow ministers for whom the theory of budget cuts was more appealing than the practice. The public too continued to spend. By 1984, the government, like too many Israelis, was still operating beyond its means. Inflation kept going up, and the public sensed another devaluation. Currency was again being stashed outside the country.

This was the state of affairs that Shimon Peres found when he finally put together his National Unity Government in the fall of 1984. Politically, he was in a bind. That the economy was near collapse was obvious enough. But the culprit was the Likud of Begin and Shamir—now his partner in the new coalition government. The economy cried out for austerity. Both the Likud and Labor halves of the government admitted that. But how much austerity would the people take? A billion dollars needed to be cut from the budget. In three months' time, less than $400 million had been slashed. It was more of the same. Neither the government nor the public was willing to do what had to be done. Peres turned to the Israeli government's time-honored solution—the U.S. government: he estimated $4.8 billion in U.S. aid would be required over the next two years. The Israeli economy was in the balance.

That huge number freaked even Israel's most loyal supporters in the U.S. Tom Dine told Peres that Congress would not pay; there were limits on even what AIPAC could deliver when a budget battle was shaping up between Reagan and Congress, when U.S. politicians were gnashing their teeth over the mammoth U.S. deficit. Hyman Bookbinder was also concerned about the repercussions: "I think we can get the aid from Congress, but whether it will be worth the costs in public opinion I'm not sure," he said in an interview.[29]

In fact, congressmen were less concerned about the figure than were the lobbyists. Dine and Bookbinder had trained their politicians even better than they could have hoped.

But would additional U.S. aid do the trick? Economists in the U.S. and Israel warned that without fundamental changes in the economy, without real austerity, painful cutbacks, and a lower standard of living, Israel would gobble up billions of U.S. aid in a matter of months and be in the same pickle. "The economic crisis gripping Israel today, if not swiftly and effectively addressed by the new unity government," warned a Senate Foreign Relations staff bipartisan report on the Israeli economy in November 1984, "could pose as serious a threat to the security of Israel as any hostile neighbor." The report also pointed out that U.S. aid would not solve the problem. The only solution was for the Israelis to institute austerity and reform their economy.[30] AIPAC pressed for more aid.

In Israel, Prime Minister Peres was searching for a way to sell austerity politically. He solicited various plans for economic recovery from experts in and outside government. Three economists at Tel Aviv University offered a plan to, in the words of one of them, "rebuild the financial structure of the Israeli economy." The proposal included a $2 billion budget cut, a 60 percent cut in subsidies across the board, and an unheard-of proposal in Israel—a surcharge on business taxes. "Businesses here are not very good at paying taxes," explained Assaf Razin, dean of the social sciences faculty at Tel Aviv University and an economic adviser to Peres.[31]

But Peres had already run into opposition from the unions and the Likud half of his government. In November, he initiated the first of two "package deals" to try to drag inflation down from its 500 percent annual rate promising to cut the budget by $1 billion. According to experts in the U.S. and Israel, the prime minister was applying a Band-Aid where a tourniquet was needed. One of them—Secretary of State George Shultz, a professional economist—sent what reports described as "a strong letter" to Peres at the end of December 1984 warning that unless drastic reforms were adopted, the U.S. would not be kicking in the $800 million in emergency aid for 1985 and 1986 that Peres had requested in addition to the $2.6 billion Israel had already received for 1985.

In an op-ed piece in *The New York Times*, Razin encouraged the

U.S. to resist pressure to aid Israel immediately. "With no American bailout in sight, Israel's policy makers may now be able to take the decisions needed to impose a tough economic program." Razin pointed to reducing Israel's trade deficit—$3.5 billion for 1983–and slowing down the borrowing of money from foreign commercial banks.

The only way Israel could avoid a "debt crisis," Razin explained, was by "drastically reducing public and private spending." To that old bromide, Razin added a different—indeed radical—twist, one that certainly no American Jewish leader would utter in public. Israel had benefited from U.S. aid since its birth, but it was economic assistance, Razin notes, "with no strings attached." The economist declared, "Now the time has come for a change.... If Washington took an active role by attaching strings to its aid, Israel could take the painful but necessary steps required to return to solvency and, even-tually, prosperity."[32]

Razin suggested "matching accounts"—that is, for every dollar of U.S. aid in excess of its usual aid in the past several years—$2.6 billion—Jerusalem would be required to reduce its own spending by a dollar. The U.S. would thus perform the same kind of close vigi-lance on the Israeli economy as the International Monetary Fund does on the delinquent nations under its watch. Aware that both Americans and Israelis would find this "unpalatable," Razin insisted that without such "prodding" there was no way that Israel's "weak coalition gov-ernment" would risk budget cuts beyond the $1.5 billion it proposed.

There emerged a surprising amount of support for U.S. pressure on Israel to repair its economy, even among Israel's strongest boosters in the American press. Both William Safire, the *New York Times* colum-nist, and the *New Republic* magazine wagged their fingers at the Peres government. During Peres's October 1984 visit, Safire had ad-vised the Israeli premier that Washington was not the place to get help for Israel's economic problems; instead he had to return home to his people with "a message of universal pain." Only some serious belt tightening, privately and publicly, would end what the headline of his column referred to as Israel's "Masada Economy."[33] In a sec-ond column, two months later, Safire ragged Shamir for having brought Israel "to the brink of ruin and vassalhood," and advised that before Israel could expect American funds, it ought to cut the budget by $3 billion (double what Shultz was recommending and a billion more than Razin), end "narcotic indexation," cut real wages, and peg the shekel—was Aridor smiling?—to the dollar. "An economic war of survival was underway," noted Safire, "and unless Israeli leaders faced that reality, Israel's government of national unity threatens to become a government of national disgrace."[34]

An editorial in the pro-Israel *New Republic* agreed that there were good strategic reasons to give Israel $4 billion, "but," the unsigned article noted, "the United States has no reason to subsidize stupidity and cowardice." The magazine concluded: "The coalition government of Prime Minister Shimon Peres hasn't even begun to do what is necessary to put Israel's house in order." The *New Republic* advised the U.S. to "pressure" Peres into doing what he knew he had to do. "Only the United States, in short, can make the Israelis swallow their medicine," the magazine advised.[35]

The U.S., or at least the State Department, was trying to dole out that medicine. In March 1985, W. Allen Wallis, undersecretary for economic affairs, warned a congressional subcommittee that the emergency aid would "disappear quickly" because Israel had yet to face up to its financial problems. Budget cuts were being ignored by the very ministries they were supposed to affect, Wallis explained, pointing out that "the basic problem is that [the Israelis] are consuming quite a lot more than they are producing." Until that changed, until there were some legitimate structural reforms in the Israeli economy, Wallis declared, the $800 million of supplemental aid for 1985 "will disappear and their economy won't be any better off, and they'll face bigger problems later on, they'll be back for more money with worse problems."[36]

Wallis's message was clear, though the committee did not enjoy its implications: someone had to persuade Israel that it had to mend its spendthrift ways. If the U.S. did not use its economic leverage to force Israel to act in U.S. interests in the Middle East, it could at least force Israel to act in Israel's own interests.

Safire weighed in with a third column a few weeks later, using the kind of language the man from State might have liked and warning what had been true for a decade: Israel was too dependent on U.S. aid. "America is not 'selling out Israel,'" Safire noted, "rather, it seems to be buying Israel."[37] Once again, Safire counseled the Israelis to protect their "political freedom" and "diplomatic independence" by sorting out their economy, with U.S. help.

It was strong stuff indeed, particularly from such staunch friends of Israel as Safire and the *New Republic*, whose editor-in-chief/owner, Martin Peretz, was a self-confessed obsessive on the matter of U.S. support for Israel. Yet neither analyst seemed to have probed far enough. Was it only Begin's cynical politicking that had ruined the economy? More to the point, why U.S. "pressure" now and not before?

THE American position toward the Israeli economy tends to be as politically motivated as that of any Israeli prime minister. U.S. economic aid to Israel increased sevenfold—from $51.5 million to $353.1 million—to help Israel, the argument went, recover from the 1973 war and that year's oil crisis, both of which had raised Israel's balance of payments deficit. The economy continued its slide, and Israeli economic experts warned that the remedy was either austerity or inviting the International Monetary Fund to step in to supervise some structural changes. Austerity would provoke political instability, the Israelis argued, and the U.S. agreed. Bringing in the IMF would be embarrassing. The Israelis claimed $700 million would keep austerity and the IMF at bay.

There were good political reasons for the U.S. to agree. Though Henry Kissinger has been criticized by the American Jewish community for his efforts to get Israel to pull out of the Sinai as part of his shuttle diplomacy in 1975, the secretary of state made sure Israel was well compensated for its cooperation. President Ford doubled aid to Israel to $793 million—the largest amount of economic aid Israel had received since its birth and a figure that also happened to equal Israel's balance of payments deficit. Congress passed it. To encourage the Labor Party's economic reforms in 1976–1977, the high levels of aid were renewed. And then came the Likud.

"Some people [in government] thought that because of Begin, donations from American Jews would drop; they thought more government aid would be required," notes another State Department economist familiar with the motives for aid to Israel. But American Jews kept paying, and so did the U.S. "Suddenly, aid to Israel was locked in at more than $700 million," says the U.S. economist. "Politically, everyone knew it wouldn't change. Carter said he wouldn't use aid as a stick," recalls one government economist about the 1980 bill. "Israel would always come in for an increase. They wanted a billion. Our number was no way near a billion. So the magic number we came up with was $786 million. It was a purely political decision."[38]

The numbers remained in that magic region during the Carter and Reagan years: 1977—$742 million, 1978—$791.8 million, 1979—$790 million, 1980—$786 million, 1981—$764 million, 1982—$806 million, 1983—$785 million.[39]

In 1984, the Reagan Administration proposed $785 million. Congress voted $910 million. And while in previous years, U.S. aid to Israel had been paid out in one-third loan, two-third grant payments, Congress now voted to make it all grants.

Military aid too was raised for political reasons. After the AWACS vote, President Reagan boosted Foreign Military Sales assistance (FMS) to Israel another $300 million to $1.7 billion. For the next FMS package, the $1.7 billion figure became the measure. According to a 1983 General Accounting Office analysis of U.S. aid to Israel, "State Department officials say that it is not politically possible to submit to the Congress, as an administration proposal, a lower FMS for Israel than the previous fiscal year." The report pointed out that many State Department and Pentagon officials reckoned that in order to get Congress to pass FMS assistance to any country, increased aid to Israel was required. The Pentagon, in fact, was convinced that Israel did not require additional military aid.*

While Congress and the President were competing to see how much aid they could send to Israel, Begin's political opponents were suggesting that U.S. aid to Israel be cut. With American aid propping up Begin's adventures in Lebanon and the West Bank, his political opponents worried that they'd never get back into power. In 1982, they sent their message to the Reagan Administration and American Jews via *The New York Times*. After a visit to Israel, *Times* editorial page editor Max Frankel reported that Begin's opposition was "reduced to begging America to break Mr. Begin's political power. And it now advocates means that would have been unthinkable even a few

---

*This information comes from excised sections of the GAO Report, which some claim had been "censored." Informed sources contend that the so-called "censored" report was merely an earlier draft of what was eventually published. Nevertheless, a quick look at what was removed shows that the "editors" were inclined to remove remarks that were most critical of U.S. aid to Israel.[40]

weeks ago. The startling plea of many leading Israelis is that the
United States *reduce* its economic aid to their nation."[41] According to
Frankel, Begin's critics were advising "sharp cuts" in U.S. economic
aid, otherwise, Frankel reported them saying, "Mr. Begin will go on
bribing the electorate . . . until his West Bank ambition—underwritten
by the American taxpayer—is finally achieved."

Frankel's article ignited protests from American Jews. Suddenly,
no one could be found among Begin's opposition who would admit
publicly to what Frankel had written. Little wonder, given the enor-
mity of their request. But Frankel stuck with his story, and no one
who knew anything about Israeli politics doubted he was reporting
the truth.

Apart from internal political battles between the Likud and Labor,
Frankel's report offered evidence for two things: (1) that U.S. money,
which was supposedly not to be spent in the Occupied Territories,
was being used to subsidize Begin's efforts to annex the West Bank
and Gaza (if only to free up Israeli funds that could be directed into
settlement projects); (2) Begin's opposition believed that less U.S.
money would not necessarily endanger the Israeli economy.

And when, after the invasion of Lebanon, the Begin government
claimed it would not ask the U.S. for additional aid to pay for the
war, U.S. analysts reported to the Administration their suspicion that
Israel's requests for increased U.S. grants had the costs of the Lebanese invasion factored in. Israel, in fact, admitted that bond sales and
UJA money would be used to cover $350 million in war-related
costs.*[42]

By 1985, Israeli opposition to U.S. aid had spread from the economic journals onto the editorial pages and became a matter of public
debate. The movement spanned the political spectrum from right to
left, Likud to Labor. It was rooted in the Zionist Dream of a truly
normal and independent Jewish state. Newspaper commentators, par-

---

*This was one item that slipped by the editors of the GAO report, though they did cut out the
opinion that requests for increased economic and military aid reflected the expense of Lebanon. As the authors pointed out, again in the published version, "the United States is faced
with the possibility of indirectly supporting Israeli actions, with which it does not necessarily
agree, through the bolstering of Israeli budget needs."[43] The "possibility" became quite real on
the West Bank and in Lebanon, which by mid-1983 Israeli military sources figured had cost
Israel $4 billion.

ticularly Mier Merhav, the economics editor of the Jerusalem *Post*, called for an independent economy, so Israel would no longer have to take American advice, on the economy or anything else. There was even a new party in Israel devoted to economic independence called, appropriately, Atzmaut (Independence). In March 1985, just when it looked as if the Americans were satisfied with the coalition government's economic reforms and willing to go along with the $800 million in emergency funds, Atzmaut organized a demonstration in front of the U.S. Embassy in Tel Aviv against U.S. aid to Israel.[44]

Government critics charged that the reforms looked good only on paper. A *Wall Street Journal* editorial reported that "according to Daniel Doron of the Israel Center for Social and Economic Progress, the budget contains hidden and potentially substantial overruns." Doron pointed out that the effort to ease government out of the business sector was still largely talk, and that the Central Bank was still required, by law, to print money to cover the government's debts. Economic reformers in Israel were afraid that U.S. congressmen would be competing to see who could push the aid package through faster, thus endangering any real chance for reform and future prosperity.[45]

The *Journal* concluded, "It's never going to be easy to break the habit of foreign aid and subsidies Israel acquired during its first turbulent generations. That's all the more reason for Congress not to flinch now."

The Reagan Administration and Congress flinched the first chance they got. The House Appropriations Committee voted for the emergency aid 12 to 0. The Administration, however, seemed genuine about pressing Israel into austerity, and Shultz warned that there would be no emergency aid unless Israel proved it was ready to cut its standard of living and create a real economy. Then there was a change of mind. That the Administration's inclination to lean on Israel vanished at the same time the President was beating off a barrage of criticism from American Jewish leaders for his plans to visit a German cemetery in Bitburg where Nazi SS officers were buried did not lessen speculation that, once again, it was politics and only politics that called the shots in the special U.S.–Israeli financial relationship.

Nevertheless, George Shultz seemed eager from the start to help Israel; the word out of the State Department was that the economist serving as secretary of state was eager to go down in history as, if not the man who made peace in the Middle East, then the man who saved the Israeli economy. As early as fall 1983, when it looked as if Israel was going to have trouble meeting its quarterly roll over of its short-term commercial loans and needed a quick fix, Secretary Shultz was reportedly considering a one-time $2 billion bailout, as one Congressional analyst put it, "not wrapped up in the foreign aid flag." The idea was abandoned when it was pointed out that such a remedy would injure Israel's reputation among bankers to such a degree that it might never be able to borrow a cent from anyone else but the U.S. government again. Shultz set up a "secret" group in the State Department to study the Israeli economy, and predictably ran into the same old problems. "When the State Department economic experts presented the list of our things and the list of their things, and went down the list with [Israeli finance minister] Aridor, he said, 'no, no, no.' The reason was always 'politics,'" recalls this Capitol Hill source. "It was always the old 'it won't happen on my watch' attitude."[46]

Others talked about the possibility of the U.S. absolving Israel of all its debt, though they were persuaded that that too would have disastrous consequences for Israel's image as a worthy borrower and make the government of Israel more beholden to the U.S. than it would ever like to be. Some Israeli policy makers—and AIPAC—even argued that U.S. aid to Israel should not even be debated. "It's a bargain," says Knesset member, Dan Meridor. "What's $2.6 billion to Israel when compared to the $500 million we pay to NATO?" became another favorite AIPAC rationale. "It's an investment in our strategic asset, in democracy, in the stability of that democracy, in the future of the Middle East. . . ."[47] And so it goes.

In the U.S. budget, $2.6 billion is indeed a relatively low figure—less, in fact, than the 1986 budget for the M-1 tank.[48] And that is part of the problem. A senator can easily justify the trade off for Jewish support or peace and quiet. No matter how often members of Congress were told by State Department and other economists that more aid to Israel would only increase Israel's problems, they refused to listen.

In the summer of 1985, the Senate and House agreed to pass a $12.6 billion foreign-aid bill for programs in fiscal 1986 and 1987—the first foreign-aid bill approved by the Congress since 1981. Israel was down for $3 billion in aid plus an extra $1.5 billion, allegedly to help it survive its financial crisis. The bill also reaffirmed the 1984 ban on recognition of the PLO until it recognizes Israel.[49] Conservatives supported the bill because they were happy with the Reagan Administration's efforts to, as one House member put it, "support resistance movements around the world." Liberals supported it reportedly because of the $4.5 billion for Israel.

THE House foreign-aid budget was passed by a voice vote; no one apparently was eager to be on the record. "The worry is," explains an aide (who happens to be Jewish) to an eminent senator, "that if the U.S. slides into a serious recession and Israel simultaneously needs a huge infusion of emergency aid, there will be a backlash out there like no one has ever seen, and too many people around here will be on the record for giving billions of aid to Israel, without debate."[50]

It was the same thought that AIPAC and other Jewish groups had when Peres first asked the U.S. for $4.8 billion. "There are a lot of people in this country who will not think kindly of the Jews when they see Israeli farmers getting money and American farmers going broke," noted Hyman Bookbinder.[51]

But caught up in their own big economic story at home, Americans had been insulated from the economic story in Israel. The Israeli press, however, had been following the government's every move with relish since the Americans had started to press Israel toward austerity in the fall of 1984. In July 1985, the prime minister and his Cabinet sidestepped a useless and inevitably unproductive Knesset debate, and used emergency powers to impose austerity measures on the economy. Finally. "We are in a life and death war," declared Peres. "There is no choice but to opt for this plan to fight inflation. I found the state coffers empty when I took over. The banks were empty. For the past seven years the government printed and borrowed money, and I found myself having to save the State of Israel from ruin."[52]

The Israel public and their politicians reacted strongly, and predictably. Deputy Prime Minister David Levy, a leader of the Likud, opposed the government program, which his own party boss, Shamir, had supported, and disappeared from the Knesset during the vote. Finance Minister Yitzhak Moda'i and Histadrut Labor Federation secretary general Yisrael Kessar appeared on Israeli television to discuss the emergency program and fell into what the press called "a ferocious shouting match" in which a shaken TV moderator had to keep them from coming to blows. The Histadrut called a general strike.[53]

The "life and death struggle" continued. To Peres's credit—and more to the credit of his finance minister, Yitzhak Moda'i—the National Unity Government tended to the nation's economic problems. In fact, that task may have been the only thing that kept this odd-couple government from crumbling over the first petty political insult from one side to the other. Within the year, inflation did fall back down to double digits. Nevertheless, rumors still persisted that in 1985 Israel had informed Shultz that over the next three years it would require $12 billion in U.S. economic and military aid to survive. All grants.

How long will Congress put up with it? How long will the American voter put up with a Congress that is so eager to finance Israeli spending sprees? As one U.S. economist put it, "As chorus girls used to say, 'Even sugar daddies die.'"

In 1985, the National Association of Arab Americans had initiated an ad campaign attacking U.S. aid to Israel as money that could be better spent at home. Why should U.S. Jews leave the economic issue up to their enemies? Why haven't American Jews been more concerned about the future of the Israeli economy? What could be more of a strategic liability to Israel and thus to the U.S. if the Israeli economy goes belly up?

Again, politics is at issue. AIPAC is committed to U.S. aid to Israel; it was its *raison d'être* in the 1950s and remains a main priority today. AIPAC will continue to oppose arms to Arab states, even if a prime minister of Israel desires otherwise; the lobby will continue to block U.S. recognition of the PLO in spite of a growing number of Israelis who believe that peace can never be achieved without dealing with the enemy; AIPAC will continue to press for increased U.S. aid to Israel, even if that aid deprives Israeli governments of the incentive to remedy, indeed restructure, their ailing economy.

In 1986, in the face of congressional efforts to slash the deficit and cut foreign-aid programs, Prime Minister Peres proposed a "Marshall Plan" for the ailing economies of the Middle East. Shultz, apparently still eager for a policy success in the region, seemed enthusiastic. For critics of U.S. aid to Israel, in the U.S. and in Israel, there was suddenly a longing for the good old days of the annual $2.6 billion package. The price tag on Peres's Marshall Plan was in the neighborhood of $20 billion to $30 billion.

Clearly, a debate on the future of U.S. aid to Israel was in order. No member of Congress seemed in the mood. Few Jewish leaders would even discuss the prospect.

REDISCOVERING THAT "TWO-WAY STREET"

BY the fall of 1985, four years after the AWACS battle, AIPAC seemed to have won the War for Washington. The pro-Israel lobby had proved Reagan could live with Begin—in spite of the bombing of the Iraqi nuclear reactor, the bombing of Beirut, the annexation of the Golan Heights, the rejection of the Reagan Plan, and the invasion of Lebanon. After Begin left office in 1983, AIPAC succeeded in bringing the Reagan Administration and the governments of Shamir and Peres so close through trade and strategic cooperation deals that Egypt and Jordan attacked America for abandoning its traditional role of peace broker in the Middle East—and lashed out at AIPAC for its restraints on U.S. policy. As the Arabs (and AIPAC) knew well, Reagan was heading the most pro-Israel government since the Johnson Administration. Israel had also won the heart of Secretary of State George Shultz, who had taken a personal interest in salvaging the Israeli economy and personal pride in building a *de facto* strategic alliance between the two old friends.

AIPAC had certainly achieved its organizational goals. With its membership increasing in every congressional district and on college campuses, the lobby had become the [kind of] "mass movement" Dine had promised and was pursuing the "agenda for a citizen lobbyist" with speed and ease. AIPAC now dominated the issue of Israel in the American Jewish community, to the annoyance and envy of other major groups. Thanks to the lobby, the U.S. had no flexibility in dealing with the Palestinian issue. Nor had the dissent that had been brewing among Jewish leaders over the decade following

Begin's election boiled over in public to embarrass Israel or its lobbyists. AIPAC was also deftly assuring that the next generation of
Jewish activists and leaders would be alumni of the lobby's aggressive college campaign. An organization that had been created to
counter the Eisenhower Administration's apparent U.S. tilt toward
the Arabs, the pro-Israel lobby was now flourishing in Ronald Reagan's Washington where few "pro-Arab" politicians or officials were
to be found. (In Middle East diplomacy, even the term "evenhanded"
had turned into code for "anti-Israel.")

In American domestic political terms, AIPAC had become a symbol of the final arrival of the Jews as Americans. They had quickly
succeeded in business, banking, and the arts, and now politics. U.S.
representatives and senators feared and cultivated "Jewish muscle";
few ambitious American politicians could even dream of higher office without the prospect of Jewish money. And thus AIPAC's policies affected the politics of America, and the policies of the U.S.
government. AIPAC's role was not only impressive, it was phenome-
nal.

But what were the consequences of this for the American Jewish
community, Israel, and, most important, peace in the Middle East?

THE Arab-Israeli conflict is a *political* problem, as the peace with
Egypt, despite its icy moments, has proved. A major American political force, organized American Jewry might play a role in the solution of that conflict—but only if it is willing to abandon its role as a
rubber stamp of Israeli policy or as its enforcer, the part that AIPAC
has filled so well. During the Begin years, the American Jewish community's subservience to Israel committed it to policies millions of
America Jews disapproved of, and encouraged religious nationalist
fantasies and rejectionism among Israel's far right. Politics is the
art of the possible, and the leaders of Zionism, from Herzl to Ben-
Gurion, used their artistry to turn the dream of a Jewish state into a
reality. Herzl was willing to settle for a Jewish state in Uganda; Ben-
Gurion, for the partition of Palestine. The Likud of Begin, Shamir,
and Sharon, along with the rest of Israeli right, is willing to settle
only for the impossible, the Biblical Land of Israel. Meantime, Likud
policies have encouraged the racism of Rabbi Meir Kahane and the
Jewish terrorism of the religious nationalist organization Gush
Emunim (The Bloc of the Faithful), two well-publicized trends in

Israel that have frightened American Jewish leaders. But Kahane's political success and the Gush's political power in Israel are genies Begin let out of the bottle. By encouraging Begin, Jewish leaders also encouraged his genies.

In 1986, the people best informed about the Middle East seem the most pessimistic about the region's prospects for peace. Over the past twenty years since the Six-Day War, a moderate consensus in Israel to trade land for peace has evolved into the rejection of any partition of Palestine, either for Revisionist Zionist or religious nationalist reasons. The last three elections in Israel show the rejectionists gaining in political power. The "facts" are on their side. As Conor Cruise O'Brien, Irving Kristol, and others have pointed out, any peace plan that requires withdrawal (and every one has) is up against the reality of fifty thousand Jews living in the new suburbs on the West Bank.[1] O'Brien and Kristol conclude that a stalemate is inevitable.

But what is complex, difficult, even maddening is not necessarily impossible. American Jewish leaders are in a position to encourage the possible. Yet they—and the U.S. government—must consider that the "peace process" has been moribund since Camp David. Its future hangs on solving the Palestinian problem. Its present, however, has been mired in the rejectionist camps of both sides, Arab and Israeli. Jewish critics of Israeli intransigence must withstand their anger and press toward peace. In September 1985, two of the most progressive Jewish organizations in the U.S. tried to give the moribund peace process a nudge, and were attacked by Israel's foreign minister, Yitzhak Shamir, for meddling in affairs "best handled by the Israeli government." The American Jewish Congress sent a twenty-man delegation to the Middle East for an unprecedented series of talks with Mubarak and Hussein. "Who elected them?" asked Shamir in an interview in Jerusalem. The Israeli foreign minister derided the American group as a "peanut-sized organization" that was being used "as instruments [sic] in the hands of the Arabs to score points against us."[2] Howard Squadron, the New York attorney who has served as president of the American Jewish Congress and as chairman of the Conference of Presidents, demanded that the Israeli foreign minister apologize to him and the organization. Singled out in Shamir's attack, Squadron noted that he had not been a member of the Middle East tour.

No one, however, asserted, in public at any rate, the right of Jews outside of Israel to encourage peace. No one challenged Shamir's condescending attitude toward American Jewry's concern about the future of Israel.

Shamir also attacked Edgar Bronfman, chairman of Seagram, his family's $2.8 billion liquor, real estate, and chemical business, and president of the World Jewish Congress. Bronfman had been invited to Moscow to discuss with the new Soviet leader, Mikhail Gorbachev, the prospects of Jewish emigration. The Israeli foreign minister was furious. Bronfman's group should stay out of international affairs and stick to "philanthropic frameworks," Shamir declared.

It was one more example of the growing tensions between U.S. Jewish leaders and Israel—and between Shamir and his coalition partner, Shimon Peres. Peres refrained from criticizing the Americans, particularly Bronfman, an old friend who has contributed generously to Peres's campaigns. The prime minister also knew the Seagram's chairman was carrying a message to Gorbachev from Peres about Jewish emigration. But then Shamir, scheduled to replace Peres as prime minister in the fall of 1986, would probably have preferred that the current prime minister refrain from international affairs.

Peres was not obliging. During the fall of 1985, he and King Hussein tried to inject some life into the peace process. At the end of September, Hussein declared he and the PLO were ready to negotiate with Israel "promptly and directly" under the international auspices. The Reagan Administration and Peres congratulated Hussein for his, in the Israeli's words, "vision of peace." Likud leaders derided it as a diplomatic ploy to assure U.S. arms to Jordan.

A few days later, Palestinian terrorists killed three Israelis in Cyprus. On October 1, Israel retaliated: American-built Israeli fighter planes flew fifteen hundred miles to Tunis and bombed the PLO headquarters there, killing at least thirty people. PLO Chairman Yasser Arafat, who escaped injury, vowed retaliation. A week later, four Palestinian terrorists hijacked an Italian cruise ship, held its passengers hostage, murdered one American, a Jewish invalid—and set back the PLO public-relations machine a decade.

Peres saw the opportunity to eject Arafat from the peace process. Hussein was reportedly furious that the PLO had scuttled his own peace initiative; the king proceeded with talks with the Syrians, who were hostile to Arafat, and who, after their own successes in Lebanon, were becoming increasingly important to any resolution of the

Arab-Israeli conflict. Israel and the Soviets were discussing resuming diplomatic relations.

Later that same month, again at the U.N., Peres proposed a "new diplomatic initiative" that recalled, as the Israeli prime minister pointed out, Sadat's historic trip to Jerusalem: Peres was now willing to meet King Hussein in an "international forum" that could precede direct talks; he would even be willing to travel to Amman if necessary.[3] It was a hopeful move, as spokesmen for the U.S. and Jordan publicly stated. In Israel, members of Peres's coalition attacked their prime minister's peace plan (reportedly even before reading it); the far right called for a vote of no confidence, which Peres survived easily.

IT was an extraordinary period in Middle East diplomacy. The extremists on both sides, the PLO and the Likud, proved their power to frustrate the peace process. Where did the American Jewish community stand? Hardly in the forefront of the peaceniks. Eager to encourage Hussein's efforts to get negotiations off the ground, the Reagan Administration earlier had proposed, again, to send arms to Jordan. And again AIPAC opposed the sale, persuading a majority of representatives and senators to do the same. Again, the White House backed down, agreeing to postpone the sale until March. Congress wanted King Hussein to prove his commitment to peace. Once again.[4]

In the midst of the wild events of September and October, U.S. Jewish groups remained uncharacteristically silent. All asserted they were for peace, yet there was no public criticism of right-wingers in Israel bent on blocking a rapprochement between Hussein and Peres. Silence ruled even in the face of reports that Jewish settlers on the West Bank were threatening civil disobedience—even civil war—if their prime minister dared to exchange any occupied land with Jordan.[5] Surely American Jewish leaders who supported some kind of negotiations on the future of the West Bank—70 percent of them, according to polls—knew that if the Likud returned to power that would be the end of the prospect of any talks between Jordan, Israel, and any Palestinians. Instead of support for Peres, there were rumblings on the neo-conservative aisle over the sudden emergence of the Soviets in the diplomatic process. By the end of October rumors circulated through New York Jewish circles that there would be a right-wing attack on the prime minister should he get too cozy with the Russians.

The prospect of Jews fighting Jews, in Israel, in the Israeli Cabinet, and in the American Jewish community over a peace proposal made by the prime minister of Israel was bizarre, and troubling. Peace was again possible, but the prime minister needed support, and some prodding, particularly in his inability to recognize that whether he or Hussein or Reagan liked it or not, as Arafat said at the time, "There will be no peace in the area without the PLO."[6]

The Reagan Administration too embraced the illusion that "moderate" Palestinians were preferable to *representative* ones. No one seemed to recall that Herzl himself had believed that the "sensible anti-Semite" had a positive role to play in Zionism. If Herzl could meet with the Russian anti-Semite Plehve, if Weizmann could talk to Mussolini, if German Zionists could negotiate with the Nazis in the 1930s, surely Shimon Peres could sit down with Yasser Arafat, or whomever else the Palestinian people elect as their "legitimate" representative. Rejection of the PLO has been an axiom of both Labor and Likud policy. Yet even former hardliners other than Peres are now recognizing that after Arafat's military defeat in Lebanon, the time has come to talk to the PLO.

"I am ready to meet with Arafat if he's ready to recognize Israel," Ezer Weizman told an Israeli reporter in early 1985.[7] In a later interview, Weizman, the Israeli government's minister overseeing Arab affairs, declared:

> We [Israelis] have to undergo some sort of psychological transformation before we can believe in peace and move ahead. We of the military raised an entire generation to be fighters. The generations to come will have to educate the people of Israel, in an intelligent and rational manner, to believe in the necessity of peace agreements between us and the Arabs. That's a lot harder than doing battle. . . .[8]

Once one of Israel's most vocal hawks, Weizman, an Israeli war hero, former Air Force chief of staff, nephew of Chaim Weizmann,* and the man who engineered Begin's campaign victory in 1977, has become one of Israel's most outspoken doves. One Israeli commenta-

---

*To avoid the shadow of his famous uncle, Ezer dropped the final *n* of the family name.

tor has pointed out that "Weizman's entire universe, both public and private, has, in recent years, revolved entirely around one axis . . . the idea of peace."[9]

American Jewish leaders would do well to enter Ezer Weizman's universe, and face the logic of war and peace. "You can only make peace with your enemies," says Weizman. The only American Jewish leader who has publicly agreed, and called for Israel to talk to the PLO, is Philip Klutznick. In return, the former president of B'nai B'rith and cofounder of the Presidents' Conference has been vilified by fellow Jews. Embittered by the personal attacks on his motives since his first public criticism of Israeli policies in 1981, Klutznick went even further in 1985 and called for a Palestinian state on the West Bank, "in one form or another."[10] Other dissenters may be unwilling to go so far, but Klutznick has made an honest—and courageous—call for peace that requires the crucial psychological leap that Weizman is promoting.

That an American Jew who has devoted his life, and a good part of his fortune, to working on behalf of Jewish interests in the U.S. and Israel is willing to criticize Israeli policy should be taken as a hopeful hint of what lies beneath American Jewish silence. As we have seen, in 1966, 1971, 1973, 1976, and after the invasion of Lebanon, serious, though minority, efforts arose to reclaim the American Jewish community's rightful role as an equal partner in Israel's future. Wars and events overtook those dissident movements. And though the dissidents remain relatively few in number, their disparate group features some of the best-known and respected Jewish leaders in America. In the 1980s, Klutznick was joined by the repentant Beginite Alexander Schindler and Arthur Hertzberg, the latter holding the American Jewish record for most anti-Begin articles, op-ed–page pieces, book reviews, and speeches.

Unfortunately, these American Jews, no matter how impressive their credentials, have no organized constituency, and so no political power. Policy makers have heard their remarks but do not dare to listen lest they pay AIPAC's price. In 1983, a group of eighteen American rabbis traveled to Washington to meet with fifteen well-known pro-Israel legislators, including the Indiana Democrat Lee Hamilton, now chairman of the House Foreign Relations Subcommittee on the Middle East; Stephen Solarz, a member of that same committee whose Brooklyn district is predominantly Jewish; and Carl Levin, a senator from Michigan. It was an extraordinary event, and received no coverage in the major media. The rabbis lobbied members of Congress to *oppose* policies of the government of Israel. The group, which included such veterans of the Breira wars as Balfour Brickner and Arnold Wolf, explained that they were in favor of a freeze on West Bank settlements; they also said that they were eager for the U.S. to devise a way of getting the Israelis and the Palestinians together to negotiate an end to the craziness in the Middle East.

Their audience was sympathetic; some went so far as to agree with their criticisms of Israeli policies. "But they kept saying to us," Rabbi Wolf recalled, "'Show us the names of your constituents. Where is your organization?'"[11]

The Israeli peace movement too has been wondering where the American counterparts have been hiding. Peace Now leaders cannot fathom why American Jews, the most progressive segment in American life, do not rush into their arms. "I had great hopes of capturing the young people of the United States, or making great inroads in the Jewish community," recalled Janet Aviad, a Peace Now leader, of her visit to the U.S. after the invasion of Lebanon. "I wanted to show the Israeli government that the American Jewish community was not a rubber stamp."

Aviad walked right into a rubber stamp. A patriotic Zionist group, its core young Israeli intellectuals, kibbutzniks, and combat army officers, Peace Now quickly discovered that American Jews perceived them as "very left wing," as a kind of Israeli lunatic fringe. After gaining a hearing among only a small group of American Jewish intellectuals and what Aviad describes as "peripheral Jews not part of the organized community," she concedes, "I gave up."[12] And turned the field over to AIPAC. Unlike most Israelis, American Jewish leaders have been unable to choose sides. Before the 1984 Israeli election, Kenneth Bialkin, a New York attorney and the new chairman of the Presidents' Conference, told an Israeli reporter, "If the [Labor] Alignment wins and changes Israel's policies, we will support them; if the Likud wins and pursues a strong line in the West Bank, we will get behind them."[13]

In spite of the possibility of jeopardizing the Jewish and democratic character of Israel? And if Sharon should win? Or Kahane? Is that a Jewish leader speaking or a rubber stamp? Peace Now has been more successful in Israel. After Peres took over as the National Unity Government's first prime minister in the fall of 1984, he proceeded to surround himself with young aides in their early thirties, most of them known to be sympathizers with Peace Now.[14]

To be fair, the psychological leap that Weizman is promoting is no easy jump for American Jews, because the tie that binds them to Israel is psychological. "Anyone who doesn't understand that will not understand American Jews," says Barry Chazan, an American-born sociologist at the Hebrew University who has studied the attitudes of American Jews toward the Jewish state. Israel has served American Jews as a symbol of the vitality of Judaism, proof that Judaism has a future; it has been their most important philanthropy—the Israel of refugees, Israel besieged. After 1967, the Jewish state became the "old country." Suddenly, Israel emerged as the "religion" of America's secular Jews. Since Louis Brandeis had argued that "every American who aids advancing the Jewish settlement in Palestine . . . will be a better man and better American for doing so," American Jews have pressed the notion that Israel is an American surrogate in the Middle East—our kind of democracy there—the good guys among the bad guys. The most recent manifestation of the view is the "strategic asset" argument.

While all these images of Israel play a crucial psychological role in the lives of American Jews, they bear no resemblance to the Israel most Israelis see. Weizman's psychological switch will be quite impossible until American Jews face up to what Israel is—and is becoming. In 1984, the San Francisco Federation of Jewish Charities ran a fund-raising ad that featured a photograph of an automatic clothes-washing machine: "To you this is a washing machine," the copy read. "To the people of Kiryat Shmona, this is a miracle." When Professor Chazan showed the ad to residents of Kiryat Shmona, an Israeli development town, "They laughed at it," he recalls. "And then they got angry. They are not living in some primitive society."[15]

But the society they are living in is one that American Jews might have more difficulty identifying with in the future. Already, when they look at Israel, they see the face not of their European and Russian cousins but of Jews from Arab countries, the Sephardim. Today the population of Israel is almost two-thirds Sephardic. "American Jews are obsessed with the view that Israel is the West in the East.

We are not," explains Shlomo Ben-Ami, a professor of history at Tel Aviv University and a leader of Israel's Sephardim. "Israel is a Mediterranean country. Most of our population is not committed to democratic values."[16]

Even many Israeli Establishmentarians were stunned by the results of a poll in 1984 declaring that upwards of 50 percent of the Israeli teen-agers interviewed, most of them "Eastern Jews," displayed antidemocratic attitudes "toward non-Jews in general and to Arabs in particular." According to the poll, commissioned by the Van Leer Jerusalem Foundation, a privately financed research institute, about 25 percent of the sample held "consistently antidemocratic views." Almost a third of the teenagers were against giving Arabs the vote if Israel annexed the West Bank and made them Israeli citizens. Forty-seven percent were for reducing the rights of the one out of six Arabs who are already Israeli citizens; 60 percent believe that Arab citizens of Israel "are not entitled to fully equal rights."[17] (Even Begin had argued for the civil rights of all Israeli citizens.)

It is little wonder that these kids support the openly racist, anti-Arab views of Rabbi Meir Kahane, who has publicly called for transferring all Arabs out of Israeli territory. (Another Van Leer poll found that 40 percent of all Israeli secondary-school pupils support the views of Kahane's party.)

The Israeli Ministry of Education has responded with special programs to "deepen democratic consciousness" among Israel's young people. So far American Jews have not been very supportive. "Americans still have this image of Israel as a perfect democracy," says Alouph Hareven, a sociologist at Van Leer who is the author of *Every Sixth Israeli*, a book about Israel's 100,000 Arab citizens (as opposed to the 1.3 million Arabs under occupation who are not citizens). "They have not followed the gradual erosion of Israeli democracy among our youth."[18]

Hareven himself ran into incontrovertible evidence of this in 1984 when he traveled to the U.S. to raise money for Israel's first school curriculum, supported by the Ministry of Education, "to develop among young Arabs and young Jews in Israel an understanding of each other, on the basis of equality and respect." Hareven was flabbergasted, and then embittered, by the American Jewish community's "total unresponsiveness to the subject." According to the Israeli sociologist, "The UJA rejected it, the American Jewish Congress, the American Jewish Committee, the Anti-Defamation League, all of them were totally uninterested in it." The first American group to donate money was the Ford Foundation with an initial grant of $75,000, a fraction of the amount required by such a major undertaking.

"For the purpose of fund raising," Hareven has concluded, "American Jews are not interested in the image of Israel making friends with her Arab citizens and Arab neighbors. They want a beleaguered Israel—Israel on the brink. Making friends with Arabs is anathema to them." Hareven waved a hand in the air, as if to dismiss these Americans from his view, and added, "There is a basic refusal to face reality."

For decades Israel's critics have urged her to shed her European pretensions and become a proper Middle Eastern country. That is now happening—the result, ironically, of the Likud's success as a political party. In the last three elections, more than half of Israel's Oriental Jews have voted Likud. The real Israel is now more "Arab," due to its increasing population of Arabs and Jews from Arab countries. That Israel is likely to be less democratic, more chaotic, more unpredictable, and—what is worrying many Israelis and American Jewish leaders—a harder sell to American voters, Jewish and non. AIPAC speakers have already admitted little enthusiasm for the Israel of a Prime Minister Sharon. The prospect of Kahane gaining a Cabinet position in a future Likud government, not out of the question given his popular support, is a recurrent nightmare for the pro-Israel lobby.

Yet AIPAC has been instrumental in recent years in breeding ignorance about political and social trends in Israel. The lobby has worked so hard at focusing American Jews—and politicians—on supporting Israel that few in either camp are paying attention to what is actually going on there. Indeed, Arthur Hertzberg and a few other Jewish leaders have argued that American Jewish life has become so centered around Israel that Jews are paying little attention to what is going on in their own communities.

At least one Jewish organization has noticed this unhappy trend, and raised the red flag. According to a report published in 1985 by the American Jewish Congress:

> . . . there is a tendency toward the self-ghettoization of Jewish public life. Connected to that trend is the tendency to develop "one-issue" organizations and mentalities. And connected to that trend also is the tendency to constrict

—or at least not to provide the process for broadening—the kind of "Jewish discussion" of issues, relating to Israel or America, which is necessary to the complexities of this new era.[19]

In other, and fewer words, American Jews have become so obsessed with Israel that they have forgotten the other kinds of political activism and coalition building that made them politically influential. The report criticized the growth of "single-issue PACs" and the "ominous narrowing" of Jewish interest and contributions away from a broader agenda that included such issues as civil rights, unions, and social and economic justice for the poor. What the report avoided mentioning was that this narrow view of Jewish interests and failure to consider Palestinian rights had already cut off Jewish organizations from labor, blacks, feminists, and mainstream Christian groups.

Was anybody listening to such complaints? The 1984 U.S. presidential election at least proved that Jews still had a strong liberal-progressive tendency despite the efforts of Jewish neo-conservatives, particularly Irving Kristol and Norman Podhoretz, editor of the Jewish monthly *Commentary*, to pull them into the Reagan camp. In 1980, Ronald Reagan had won 39 percent of the Jewish vote; no more than 35 percent of American Jews voted for Reagan in 1984. Why did America's most affluent ethnic group vote against its economic interests, and a strong supporter of Israel? Partly because most Jews of middle age and up have not forgotten how crucial New Deal programs were to their own success as Americans, and still identify with the blacks, Hispanics and Orientals, who are eager to repeat the Jewish success story.

Jewish voters, too, were uncomfortable with Reagan's attraction to a "Christian America," according to the gospel of such popular fundamentalist Protestant preachers as Jerry Falwell and Pat Robertson, who, two years later, would announce his own ambitions for the Presidency. An ABC News exit poll indicated that 23 percent of Jews sampled—as opposed to 7 percent of the general population—voted against Reagan because he "mixes politics with religion." In another poll, 78 percent of the Jews cited their distaste for Falwell, who, it turned out, bothered them more than Jesse Jackson.[20] That Jerry Falwell had been seen by the Begin government—and apparently AIPAC—as a major ally of Israel in the U.S. was lost on them. Their memory of red-neck anti-Semitism was too strong.

There is little evidence though that such discomfort with Ronald

Reagan will translate into a renaissance of the kind of Jewish social activism preferred by the American Jewish Congress.

Is it good for the Jews? The report thinks not. "What we don't want to see is for the American Jewish community to become a single-issue community," declared Theodore Mann, the Congress's president. Though the report is careful not to attack AIPAC outright—"none of this is meant to disparage one-issue organizations such as AIPAC and its efforts"—AIPAC is the prime progenitor of the kind of "self-ghettoization" the report laments. The lobby's task, as Tom Dine has said on several occasions, is to become a "mass movement" that dominates American Jewish life. Since AIPAC's only issue is Israel, Israel is bound to continue to dominate American Jewish life, if AIPAC has its way. "We are single-minded about being single issue," said Tom Dine in response to the AJC report.[21] And as its authors concede, "The fastest-growing American Jewish organization by far has been AIPAC."

Proof that Dine was succeeding in bringing American Jewish political activists around to his way of thinking was that in the first half of 1985, pro-Israel PACs gave more money to Republicans than Democrats. The only criterion for Jewish support—more than $300,000 worth in only half of a nonelection year—was support for Israel. And so a senator like Robert Kasten, chairman of the Senate Appropriations Subcommittee and a loyal friend of Israel, received the most Jewish PAC money, in spite of the unsettling fact that he votes *for* prayer in public schools, *against* abortion, and has been less than forceful on the issue of legal enforcement of civil rights, placing him on the wrong side of every domestic issue the Jews care most about. At least traditionally. PACs were even encouraging two Jewish congressmen not to run for the Senate against two powerful, and pro-Israel, senators, Robert Dole and Bob Packwood.[22] In 1985 and 1986, Democratic leaders in New York, eager to find an opponent to challenge the Republican senator Alfonse D'Amato, were grumbling about the lack of support among Jewish leaders who claimed they were satisfied with the GOP senator; D'Amato, after all, had proved a vigorous supporter of Israel (as if any U.S. senator from New York could be otherwise).

Other Jewish leaders warned that tying support for Israel to PAC money was a much too narrow and shortsighted way to nourish the "pro-Israel" coalition. Franker critics noted that it was buying support for Israel instead of winning it on the merits. They are right to worry.

It is as if AIPAC is daring members of Congress and top policy makers to backslide on Israel. Given the growing resentment of the lobby's hardball methods on Capitol Hill, it is a high-risk strategy.

An even more worrisome trend is the concerted efforts of Jewish conservatives to force pro-Israel lobbying on Capitol Hill to take a sharp rightward turn, because AIPAC, they charge, is "too liberal," too closely tied to the Democratic Party, and not ideological enough. The National Jewish Coalition, a group of Republican Jews, has been working closely with the Republican leadership in Congress trying to "sensitize" party members to the concerns of Israel and American Jews.[23] The Americans for a Safe Israel, a New York–based group with ties to the Likud and religious right in Israel, and the Herut Zionists of America, linked to Begin's party, have set up Washington offices. Both are against Israel yielding any of the West Bank and Gaza, the issue most central to support of Israel, they argue. AFSI and Herut have been romancing conservative Democrats and Republicans, and building up pro-Israel support among former ideological foes of foreign aid like North Carolina senator Jesse Helms.

In the midst of the Hussein-Peres efforts to get the peace process in gear again in the fall of 1985, the Jerusalem *Post* reported that AFSI was supporting an antipeace "crusade" in the U.S. by the secretary general of Gush Emunim, a group that is a prime instigator of anti-Arab violence on the West Bank. The Gush official was in Washington informing Helms and "anyone else who will listen," according to the *Post*, that the group spoke for "half of Israel's electorate." The paper also reported that word had gone out from Shamir's Foreign Ministry to the embassy in Washington to cooperate with the Gush representative, whose trip was paid for by the Aliyah Department of the Jewish Agency, headed by a member of the Herut Party.[24]

The implications are outrageous and troubling: a right-wing Israeli rejectionist bad mouths the prime minister of Israel to right-wing senators on a trip paid for by the Jewish Agency, which is funded by *tax-deductible* money donated to the United Jewish Appeal, presumably by some Jews who support neither the Gush Emunim nor the Americans for a Safe Israel. If Peace Now set up a lobbying operation in Washington to build support against Jewish settlements on the West Bank or for trading territory for peace, Jewish organizations would erupt in protest. (Peace Now has a New York office, and has never raised more than $250,000 in a given year from American Jews.)

• • •

BUT how successful and powerful can a lobby be before the backlash strikes? More to the point: How powerful can a *Jewish* lobby be before the anti-Semites come out of the woodwork?

The Jewish leader Nahum Goldmann, who lived in the U.S. for twenty years, often warned of "the greatest danger for a people that, after centuries of persecution and lack of power, comes to a position of strength, wealth, and power within one short generation."[25] During the last years of his life, Goldmann had become a nagging critic of what he viewed as the abuses of Jewish power, particularly the efforts of the pro-Israel lobby against the Jarring Mission and the Rogers Plan, which, he charged, kept the U.S. from exploiting the opportunities to initiate a full settlement in the Middle East. Conceding that special-interest lobbying is "a normal element of any democracy," Goldmann often wondered aloud whether American Jews were not pushing it a bit.

> The Jews have always been a people of superlatives, inclined to think in extremes. The support of America under the pressure of American Jewry, has been precious for Israel, but it is now slowly becoming something of a negative factor. Not only does it distort the expectations and political calculations of Israel, but the time may not be far off when American public opinion will be sick and tired of the demand of Israel and the agressiveness of American Jewry.[26]

Resentment against Jewish power is already festering in Washington. A former official in the Pentagon and the White House is not atypical in his grudging admiration for AIPAC's lobbying skills and his concern about the potential results.

> It's not that AIPAC is too powerful. The problem is that it's out of control. It is a self-stimulating machine with no corrective device. If you don't agree, you get savaged. That's the problem with activists [like AIPAC]; they want 100 percent cooperation, or else, they claim, there will be another Holocaust. But they can't get 100 percent. The Administration is bound to disagree on some things. The system doesn't work if a group goes only for 100 percent. No one is supposed to win all the time.[27]

• • •

ABOUT Middle East matters there is virtually no debate, and even some American politicians enjoy a good debate. "No intellectual curiosity is being tolerated," notes one former Senate aide. "Too many senators are playing along out of fear or expediency. If I were the Israelis, or the lobby, I would not want my support built on fear and political expediency."[28]

Arthur Hertzberg, who considers himself a disciple of Goldmann, asks, "If a lobby pushes the American consensus beyond its limits, when does the push evoke a counterpush?" Hertzberg's own critics have belittled his predictions of an anti-Semitic backlash; more Jewish power than ever, they point out, has not met with any significant resistance. "I answer," Hertzberg says, "not as a Cassandra but as a long-term politician and historian. You can only push so far. The first President who says, 'I'm going to treat Israel like any other country,' the first President who says that is going to reverse the anti-Semitic issue, because then the AIPACs of this earth will have to say, 'But we don't want you to treat Israel like any other country.' And then the President will say, in effect, 'If you raise the issue that way, then *you* are creating an opening for anti-Semitism.'" Hertzberg charges that because the young AIPACers have never experienced anti-Semitism, they believe it no longer exists.

Top aides in the State Department complain that lobby pressure has become an obstacle to analyzing Middle East policy. The Reagan Administration, they argue, is lamentably short on Middle East experts, which leaves the professional Middle East specialists at the State Department no one to sit down and argue things out with, to analyze policy. Others argue that young officers worried about their careers are unwilling to suggest policies that they know will run into a stone wall in Congress. "As a result, a lot of real analysis is not even getting off peoples' desks for fear of what the lobby will do. It's crazy," says one top State Department official who retired not long ago.[29] More significant still is Secretary of State George Shultz's transformation into a major supporter of Israel. During AIPAC's 1986 annual policy conference, Tom Dine reported that Shultz had said that the goal of U.S.–Israeli strategic cooperation—AIPAC's pet project of 1984–1985—was "to build institutional arrangements so that eight years from now, if there is a secretary of state who is not positive about Israel, he will not be able to overcome the bureaucratic relationship between Israel and the U.S. that we have established."[30]

The situation has gotten so twisted around that now some of the main American advocates for dissent and critics of the Jewish lobby are card-carrying Zionists. Goldmann begged Carter to "break the lobby"; Hertzberg has publicly called for AIPAC to be disbanded. And an American Zionist leader has attacked the attitude of American fund raisers to Israel as anti-Zionist. Writing in the Zionist magazine the *Jewish Frontier*, Howard Addison, a Chicago rabbi and national vice president of the Labor Zionist Alliance, praised the commitment of Jewish fund raisers to Israel but criticized "the vision of Jewish life" that motivates them. But Rabbi Addison noted:

Seeing the local federations as the central Diaspora Jewish institutions, they believe that the primary mode of Jewish association is ethnic in nature and is best expressed through philanthropy and communal service. Israel, for them, is a symbol of Jewish unity and revitalization, a common platform upon which all Jews can stand. Therefore, in their view, the symbol should not be sullied nor the platform weakened by partisan political struggles. Their vision of the Jewish future would probably show all elements of the community growing ever more united and expressing that unity through ever-increasing levels of Jewish philanthropy. . . .[31]

This "lovely fiction," Addison rightly points out, raises questions about the commitment of American Jews to Israel. And because the federations' view of Jewish activism is also AIPAC's view of the "new" Jewish politics, it raises questions about the role of the pro-Israel lobby in Jewish life. Addison formulates one unavoidable question: "If ethnic solidarity is the essential mode of Jewish communal expression, are religious and ideological approaches to Judaism to be relegated to the periphery of private taste and public inconsequence?"

According to AIPAC, yes. Ideological concern raises debate, debate spoils the fund-raising image of unity; worse still, debate increases the possibility of dissent, and dissent provides the ammunition, so the AIPAC argument goes, for "the enemies of Israel." To the fund raisers, Israel has been reduced to a symbol that will keep the donations flowing. For AIPAC, the stakes are even higher—more than $2.5 billion in U.S. economic and military aid a year, in fact.

Yet Addison argues persuasively that the only alternative a committed Jew has is to join in the scuffle. "If one chooses to leave the haggling over 'what type Israel' to the Israelis alone," Addison argues, "then perhaps one is making an admission that he or she will never be affected personally and directly by the decisions made."

Addison suggests that Jews must play a role in shaping the State of Israel, preferably as Zionists. But only if—and it's a big if—American Zionism abandons "a guarded, 'we all love Israel' stand and is willing to highlight diversity and invite the Jewish public to join in the debate."

DURING the 1950s, in the face of Ben-Gurion's efforts to dominate World Jewry and to persuade Jews in the Diaspora, particularly America, to move to Israel, American Jewish leaders stood their ground. The American Jewish Committee's Jacob Blaustein informed the Israeli government that the relationship between American and Israeli Jews would be "a two-way street." Three decades later, Israeli politicians were begging Americans to stick to that promise; the peace movement in Israel needed their support. "Those who ask world Jewry to maintain silence are relegating the Diaspora to a grave loss of dignity," Abba Eban declared in an interview in the Jerusalem *Post* in 1985. "They are saying, in effect, that Jewish support of Israel should have a material and political dimension, but not an intellectual dimension. If we impose this limitation, the Jewish world will slide into non-involvement, leaving the Israeli cause diminished."[32]

A few weeks later in an article in the Jerusalem *Post* criticizing Israel's religious establishment for demanding that the recently arrived Ethiopian refugees from famine in effect prove their Jewishness, Eban took a swipe at Jews outside of Israel unwilling to criticize what he called "the growing defacement of [Israel's] image and vision" by Israel's own leaders. The former foreign minister also had in mind the efforts of the current foreign minister (and past and future prime minister), Yitzhak Shamir, to gain a public pardon for the Israeli fanatics who had terrorized Arabs on the West Bank and who were planning to blow up the Dome of the Rock, Jerusalem's Arab mosque and the third most sacred spot in the Arab world. (Shamir had called them "fine fellows who have gone too far.") "Some Diaspora Jews renounce any analytical role and give blind endorsement to any doctrine or practice that comes out of Israel," Eban charged. "They are thus for everything—and its opposite—according to the rise and the fall of the electoral seesaw."[33]

No Israeli is more popular in the United States than Abba Eban; for many American Jews, Eban is Israel, which, of course, is only more evidence of how little Americans Jews know about Israel. Eban is near the bottom of the Israeli's list of most popular politicians. Nevertheless, the success of *Civilization and the Jews* in 1985, a public television series on the history of the Jews hosted by Eban, made the famous diplomat familiar to a new generation of Jews, and gentiles. What many of them did not realize is that a number of wealthy Jews had refused to donate money to the series because they resented Eban's criticisms of the Begin and Shamir governments, particularly the Likud's policies to settle the West Bank.

It was incredible, and most ironic: in the War for Washington, even the most famous Israeli in the American mind, one of the Jewish state's Founding Fathers, its greatest diplomat and most effective PR man—even Abba Eban had become the enemy.

FOR American Jews, the situation in 1986 could not have been better, or worse. American support for Israel was at the highest level in history, an achievement of the pro-Israel lobby that even the Arabs admired and envied. At the same time, however, the success of the Zionist Dream was in doubt as Israel battled a troubled economy and divided society, legacies of the Begin Revolution. Hanging over all this was the ever-present danger of war. And while Israeli politicians and intellectuals of the center and left wanted the Diaspora to face up to Israel's problems, and help solve them, the American Jewish community, its leadership, and its lobby were so devoted to maintaining the special relationship between the U.S. and Israel that they had ignored the consequences of their political pressure.

The Reagan Administration still had no clear policy for the Middle East. Eager to save the Israeli economy and build up its role as a strategic asset through strategic cooperation, the White House persisted in its delusion that it could have that and Arab friends. By the early spring of 1986, Reagan's efforts to sell more weapons to Jordan had been postponed indefinitely, the victim of a Congress well tuned to AIPAC's arguments against selling arms to Arabs and the curious belief that the man most actively in pursuit of peace in the Middle

East—King Hussein—was not doing enough. They were driving Jordan into the arms of French, and Russian, arms salesmen. In May, both houses of Congress voted overwhelmingly against the Administration's proposal to sell $354 million worth of arms, mostly missiles, to the Saudis, again, the argument went, because Saudi Arabia had given financial support to Syria and the PLO and had not supported Hussein's peace moves. (The same Hussein whom Congress had spurned only months before for not speeding toward peace.) Few seemed to recognize that Saudi Arabia, regardless of its actions, was because of its oil a genuine "strategic asset" to U.S. interests in the region and throughout the rest of the world. Should Iran attack the Saudis, the U.S. would be hard pressed not to intervene. What would the Israelis do? The congressional vote did not seem in the long-term interest of either the U.S. or Israel.

Almost five years after the battle over selling five AWACS to Saudi Arabia, it was significant that neither Israel nor AIPAC had to oppose the latest Saudi sale in public. AIPAC had trained Congress well.[34] Congress agreed that the Saudis had not proved that they had been cooperating in the search for peace.

But what peace? The real victim of the Reagan Administration's nonpolicies in the Middle East was the peace process itself. All sides had been talking a good game for years, but the peace process was a charade. The U.S. wanted negotiations, and so did Israel and Jordan, they claimed; but neither the U.S. nor Israel would negotiate with the PLO, and Jordan argued that it could not negotiate without Arafat, who remained vague over his commitment to recognizing Israel and U.N. 242. The PLO's rejectionist stance so frustrated Hussein that in early 1985 he publicly split with Arafat. The tiff seemed to mean little, however, because the PLO maintained the support of the West Bank Palestinians, and Jordan still needed Arafat. And what did it matter? The Likud half of the Israeli government was still opposed to trading land for peace—and thus, in effect, was no more committed to 242 than Arafat. Worse, the head of the Likud, Yitzhak Shamir, was scheduled to take over as prime minister in October 1986, and was unlikely to change his mind. The peace process seemed more lifeless than it had in years. U.S. policy was positively incompatible with Likud policy on the West Bank.

During the second half of 1986, the Middle East peace process—indeed the issue of the Middle East—seemed to vanish in the mire of politics and scandal in the U.S. and Israel. As he prepared to take over as prime minister of Israel in the fall, Yitzhak Shamir spent a good part of the summer fending off charges by a former head of the Shin Bet, the Israeli FBI, that as prime minister in 1984 he had authorized the murder of two Palestinians apprehended in a bus hijacking by Shin Bet agents. Critics in the Knesset and the Israeli press also raised questions about how much Shamir, a former top official in the Mossad, Israel's intelligence service, had known about the recruitment of an American to spy for Israel in the United States. And when Prime Minister Peres held a two-day summit meeting with Egypt's Mubarak in September, discussing, among other things, preliminaries for an international conference, his Likud coalition partners, notably Shamir and Ariel Sharon, derided the Israeli-Egyptian talks as, in Sharon's words, so much "PR gimmickry."

In Washington, Ronald Reagan's foreign policy advisers concentrated on his upcoming summit in Iceland with the Soviet leader Mikhail Gorbachev, while Middle East matters were limited to the nagging, emotional issue of how to free American hostages still held in Lebanon. After the summit, hardly a success for the Reagan camp, the President campaigned (unsuccessfully, as it turned out) to preserve the Republican majority in the Senate. In late November, however, proof that the Reagan Administration, almost six years into its tenure, was still operating without a comprehensive (or comprehensible) Middle East policy emerged in the scandal over revelations that in an effort to gain help in freeing the remaining hostages in Lebanon, members of the Reagan Administration had secretly sold more than $12 million worth of arms to Iran, a nation that the U.S. had repeatedly attacked as an exporter of terrorism.

The Iranian connection left Egypt's President Mubarak and Jordan's King Hussein confused and then angry. Both nations were struggling with home-grown versions of Islamic fundamentalism which was bound to be encouraged by the success of Iran's Ayatollah Khomeini. The State Department had assured the moderate Arab states that the U.S. would not interfere in Iran's war with Iraq, the Arab favorite. And Mubarak and Hussein's dismay only increased when the world soon learned that Israel had acted as the middleman in the U.S.-Iran arms sale at the "request" of the Reagan Administration, and that the profits of the transaction ended in Swiss bank accounts belonging to the leaders of anti-government guerrillas—the Contras—in Nicaragua.

For Israeli critics of a formal "strategic cooperation" agreement

between the Americans and their government, the Iran mess became
an unwelcome confirmation of their worst fears that Israel's role as a
"strategic asset" for the U.S. would eventually turn into a diplomatic
—and public-relations—liability for Israel. Once again, the special
relationship between the U.S. and Israel had served up some hard
times for both sides. Arab leaders were more convinced than ever
that the U.S. was not serious about acting as a broker for peace in the
region; and Israel, in its eagerness to please the Americans (and be-
devil its neighbors who supported Iraq and feared Islamic fundamentalism), had entangled itself in an American political scandal of
potentially bigger than Watergate proportions.

The Israeli government's reluctant admission that it had cooperated
in the transfer of arms to Iran (in fact, had been selling weapons to
the Khomeini government for years) was also a public-relations disaster for the American Jewish leadership which had believed that
both Jerusalem and the Reagan Administration were committed to
stamping out the kind of state terrorism that the Iranians specialized
in. That the money from the arms sale had ended up in the war chests
of the Contras only doubled the embarrassment to the progressive
Jewish groups who supported Congress's opposition to U.S. aid for
the Contras.

But the biggest victim, once again, was peace in the Middle East.

WHAT could American Jews do? The answer brings us to the end,
and the shortest section, of this analysis of relations between American Jews and Israel. Any discussion of the following proposals might
fill another book. For now, however, my goal is discussion. It is time
to debate the future relationship between American Jews and Israel.

The prime requirement for that debate is for American Jewish
leaders to pay attention to what their constituencies (and they themselves) have been saying for years. (Those on Capitol Hill who complain about "Jewish pressure" might do themselves a favor and listen
very carefully, too.) In survey after survey by the major U. S. polling
groups, as well as by Jewish organizations, for at least a decade,
American Jews and their leaders have insisted that, by and large,
they tend to be doves on Israeli policy, particularly the touchy issues
of the future of the West Bank and the role of the PLO in peace
negotiations. (See page 206.) They have simply failed to broadcast
that fact, mainly for fear of giving ammunition to the anti-Semites.

Instead, by their silence, the dissenters have allowed AIPAC to sell a neoconservative version of the American Jewish community to the White House and Congress. This picture needs to be corrected. "When fellow Jews attack me as a dissenter," explains Arthur Hertzberg, "I tell them that my views represent almost half the Jewish public in the U.S. and Israel. It is the Likud that is out of line with Jewish opinion."

The facts—if not always the perception—bear Hertzberg out. It cannot be stressed enough that American Jews, according to the polls, oppose annexation of the West Bank and are for sitting down with the PLO at the peace table, provided Arafat can recognize Israel and renounce terrorism. They are even willing to consider the possibility of a Palestinian state, a thought that sends shivers up the spines of Presidents and members of Congress.

Yet such notions are not that surprising once one considers that Jewish voters have hung on to their progressive and liberal reputations. The much discussed metamorphosis of American Jews into Republicans has yet to occur. The fact is—and a striking fact it is—Jewish voters resoundingly rejected Ronald Reagan, a proven friend of Israel whose economic policies were in the financial interests of the Jewish community and whose notion that Israel was an important "strategic asset" to U.S. foreign policy has become a favorite AIPAC refrain. In the 1984 presidential election, Reagan received only 21 percent of the Jewish vote; Walter Mondale, the Democratic candidate and Jimmy Carter's vice president, won 71 percent. Indeed Jews were so eager to vote against the Republican Reagan that, according to a study by the American Jewish Congress (*The Jewish Vote in the 1984 Presidential Election*), they were not even swayed by charges that the other Democrat in the race, Jesse Jackson, had indulged in some old fashioned anti-Semitism. Jews made it clear that they were more concerned about Reagan's efforts to make religion a major issue in the campaign. The vote against Reagan might even be interpreted as another silent demonstration against the Likud whose leaders made no secret about preferring the President to his opponent.

Such views, of course (and unfortunately), remain largely "in house." But they are the views of a huge and influential segment of the American Jewish community, and commentators and politicians serious about debating the issues of the Arab-Israeli conflict might keep them in mind. AIPAC represents an active and outspoken con-

stituency, but there are literally millions of American Jews who disagree. It is time for the dissenters to make their move, before it is too
late. The signs from the Middle East are dispiriting to those who care
about the future of Israel: the "peace process" is stalled, the leader of
the Likud is once again heading the government of Israel, and Israel's
democratic and Jewish future is threatened.

The pro-Israel lobby has pursued its "agenda for a citizen lobbyist"
aggressively and successfully. And in public. Here are some of the
pressing issues that ought to be on an agenda for citizen dissenters,
pro-Israel branch:

(1) The American Jewish community must face up to its obligation
to help shape the Jewish state and finally construct the "two-way
street" between Israel and American Jews that Jacob Blaustein called
for in the early 1950s. Israel was founded by the World Zionist Organization for Jews everywhere. The Diaspora has a right to affect its
future. Some political moderates and doves, such as Abba Eban,
would welcome the help; indeed, some, like Professor Ben-Ami,
think the Americans owe Israel more involvement.

> By their silence, American Jews are not playing a constructive role in Israeli
> society. Since whatever their differences, they always support an Israeli gov-
> ernment, they cannot be viewed as a constructive pressure group. Relations
> between American Jews and Israel have always been expressed through ma-
> terial help. Giving money has always been a good alibi for not coming to
> Israel. But we have to challenge them to come to Israel and help build this
> nation. Moreover, they can't just give money without exerting some influ-
> ence or some pressure for the good. Israel as a "strategic asset"? We used to
> be morally right and a democracy like America. To be supported only be-
> cause we are a strategic asset, that's a devaluation of our image, isn't it?[35]

(2) Jews outside Israel must feel free to criticize Israeli policy. "If
American Jews are worried about the consequences of settlements on
the West Bank or annexation, then they not only have a right to
dissent, they have an obligation to do so, as Jews," says Charles
Liebman, the Israeli sociologist. But for such dissent to be effective,
it will have to be institutionalized. The success of American Jews has
rested in their ability to organize. It is now time to redefine "American Jewish community." For too long the title has been the property
of only the professional and voluntary leaders who run Jewish organizations. But "organized" Jewry represents less than half the total
Jews in America. The other half, which includes hundreds of thou-

sands of Americans who believe that something has gone wrong with the Zionist Dream, are waiting to be organized.

Already there are dissident groups, like the New Jewish Agenda, a 1980s version of Breira, and the New Israel Fund, a left-of-center answer to the UJA, which have been trying to tap the growing number of dissidents. Yet they are relatively tiny and underfinanced. (In 1985, the New Israel Fund raised only $1.25 million.) If they are to provide a focus of a real "new Jewish agenda," then they will require the support of the top leaders of American Jewry. Those who sympathize with their views will have to come out of the closet to argue that it is in the best interests of Israel, the American Jewish community, and peace in the Middle East for Israel to learn to live with—and listen to—her American critics.

Including members of Congress. Support for Israel and peace is too important to stifle political debate on both subjects. The muzzle has to come off. Politicians who have been voting annually more than $2 billion of American taxpayers' money to Israel for more than a decade ought to be able to debate the issue of how much aid Israel really needs.

(3) To assure that American Jewish criticism is not ignored, as it has been in the past, a Jewish forum should exist outside Israel. A kind of "Diaspora Parliament" or "Jewish House of Lords" ought to be created where the top leaders of World Jewry can debate Israeli policy and make *public* recommendations that will be difficult to be ignored. One virtue of this suggestion is that at various times during the past fifteen years or so such a body has been suggested by Nahum Goldmann, Arthur Hertzberg, Alexander Schindler, and Menachem Begin (before he was elected prime minister). (According to one former Begin aide, the prime minister "would have been less enthusiastic about his settlements policy if American Jews had threatened to cut off all support to Israel."[36])

The first issues such a group might study are: (a) Israel's security needs for the 1990s; (b) how much foreign aid its economy really requires to become self-sufficient; (c) the role of the PLO in the peace process; (d) the U.S. position toward moderate Arab states, a delicate issue that has created distrust between the government and the Jews since Eisenhower—and the pro-Israel lobby.

(4) Jewish leaders often pledge their commitment to Camp David. They must now reread the agreement, study it, and debate it. Only then perhaps will they recognize that there will be no peace without

the Palestinians, and no Palestinians in the peace process without the approval of that people's "legitimate representative," which, like it or not, happens to be Yasser Arafat's PLO. Stipulating that the Palestinians, along with Egypt, Jordan, and Israel will determine the future of the West Bank and Gaza as well as giving the Palestinians veto power over any agreement, Camp David is a more pro-Palestinian document than anyone has been inclined to admit (including the PLO, which rejected it).

(5) As part of the treatment for their Palestinian problem, American Jewish groups might press for an international peace conference under the auspices of the U.S. and the U.S.S.R. Variations of such a forum are now acceptable to Shimon Peres, King Hussein, and the Reagan Administration, which has also said that the PLO will be invited provided it recognizes Israel and the appropriate U.N. resolutions. The subject should be the future of the West Bank, Gaza, *and* the Golan Heights. Syria ought to be invited, mainly because she is bound to discredit any peace party she is not invited to. Such a conference might provide an opportunity to force both sides to prove how serious each is about peace, under the gaze of their bankers and main arms suppliers, the U.S. and the Soviet Union. Superpower pressure also offers all parties to any compromise a fail-safe excuse in the face of the rejectionists on their side: "The Americans (or the Soviets) made us do it."

There already seems to be a starting point for negotiations. The Hussein-Arafat agreement of February 1985 indicates that the PLO is willing to settle for something less than a Palestinian state in conjunction with Jordan; the Reagan Plan sought a fully autonomous Palestinian "entity" linked to Jordan on the West Bank; and Peres has discussed the possibility of Palestinian "autonomy" on the West Bank under a Jordanian-Israel "condominium."

(6) Within days of stepping back into Israel's top job in October 1986, Yitzhak Shamir once again proved how disunited Israel's National Unity Government was. While Peres had put a freeze on Jewish settlement activity on the West Bank, Shamir reasserted his support for it; while new Foreign Minister Peres declared that lack of interest in the peace process he had set rolling was the one thing that would provoke him to break up the Likud-Labor coalition, the new prime minister was insisting that he was willing to negotiate with the Arabs—but only in "direct talks." Since Jordan and Egypt have said repeatedly that they can meet Israel across the table only at an inter-

national peace conference that includes the Soviets and the Palestinians as well as the Americans, Arab leaders and Israeli doves read Shamir's familiar refrain of "direct talks" as Likud code for "no talks."

American Jewish leaders should encourage Peres to keep the pressure on Shamir. They should also dissent loudly from the settlement policy of the Likud and make sure none of their donations are used to further efforts to absorb the West Bank into Israel. Should there be new elections in Israel, the American Jewish leadership must throw its support back to the Labor Party, and separate itself from the Likud's impossible dreams of a Greater Israel. The Americans must make it clear that their support depends on peace being the primary issue in any Israeli election campaign.

(7) American Jewry once produced great leaders like Brandeis, Wise, Silver, and the nationalized Goldmann. The Jewish community must now turn its considerable energy and genius to generating new leaders (and paying attention to a few of the wiser old ones) who can understand their complex role as Americans and Jews and press their constituents into a mature relationship with Israel.

American Jews no longer have to prove that they care about Israel. They do, however, have to prove that they care enough to listen to all sides in the Arab-Israeli conflict. The debate must begin anew. In public. Only then will the interests of Israel, American Jews, and U.S. foreign policy be served.

ACKNOWLEDGMENTS

THIS is a book shaped from a daunting amount of reading, research, and reporting. Its success rests on its sources, particularly my interviews with the best players and expert observers of the lobbying game. Happily, I had close to 200 interviews, too many to list here. Indeed many people preferred not to be named and agreed to be interviewed only for "background" or "off the record," and I have kept their confidences. Those who agreed to be interviewed on the record are cited either in the text or in the notes.

But I would like to give special thanks to some of the people without whom this book would have never have come to be. In the beginning there was the idea, and that came compliments of my friend Steve Schwartz, who originally suggested that the political influence of American Jews—the famed "Jewish lobby"—might make a book. We intended to collaborate, but when Steve decided to pursue some other projects, he generously allowed me to be the sole proprietor of the idea, no strings attached. I also thank him for his comments and corrections on the manuscript, and hope I have done his idea justice.

Sheila Rogers, Andy Davis, and Mary Neznek did a great deal of excellent research for me during the early stages of this project. Their work made a hard job easier, and my only regret is that I couldn't afford to use them more. My luckiest find was the Blaustein Library at the American Jewish Committee, where all the books, journals, and reference works I seemed to need were right there on the shelves. What wasn't in sight was quickly dug out for me by the librarian

Cyma Horowitz and her associate, Michele Anish. I thank them for their hospitality, not to mention their "extra copies" of pamphlets and documents.

The most fascinating and productive series of interviews I did for this book was in Israel in the fall of 1984. That success was due to Drora Kass who runs—who *is*—the New York office of the International Center for Peace in the Middle East. In addition to the Israeli politicians and intellectuals I was eager to talk to, she suggested others from every location on the Israeli political spectrum from left to right. And then to assure that I actually got to meet these people, she recommended that Hedva Weiner make the arrangements in Israel. The result was a miracle of organization and diplomacy and good connections: Hedva lined up twenty or so of Israel's most eminent politicians, scholars, and journalists, and—much to my amazement—every one of the interviews came off right on schedule. But the most incredible thing about all these interviews was the candor of my subjects; not one of them, including cabinet ministers and former ambassadors to the U.S., asked to speak "off the record." If only American politicians—and Jewish leaders—were as self-confident and secure in their opinions.

I would also like to thank Jerry Nadler, a United Press correspondent based in Jerusalem during my visit, for sharing the insights of four years covering Israeli politics as well as some of his sources. Back in the U.S., Carl Bernstein also generously suggested some people to interview and kindly wrote letters of introduction to each of them to get me through their doors.

In the early months of my research, my old friend Dan Twomey and his family extended their hospitality to a budget-conscious New York writer who had to spend time in Washington. Phil Taubman of *The New York Times* and his wife, Felicity Barringer, did the same, even though they were learning to live with a second child and preparing to ship off to Moscow. In the final stages, Larry Lucchino always had a room for me in his townhouse off Dupont Circle, even when he himself was on the road.

But this book would still be an idea without the strong support and editorial skill of my editor, Alice Mayhew, who helped me turn a manuscript distinguished mainly by its heft into a real book. Her associate, Henry Ferris, was always available on the other end of the phone, and I thank him for his support and suggestions. My enduring gratitude and relief go to Patricia Miller, who copyedited the manuscript and saved me from making silly errors. There's more to publishing books than writing and editing them, and for knowing about those mysteries and making them work on my behalf, I thank my agent, Amanda Urban, of International Creative Management.

Above all, I thank my wife, Marilyn Bethany, whose encouragement and patience helped me finish this book before we both grew old and poor. It could not have been easy living day to day with a growing encyclopedia of minutiae about U.S.-Israeli relations.

The success of this book is due to all of the above; its failures are all mine.

NOTES

INTRODUCTION

1. Arthur Hertzberg, ed., *The Zionist Idea* (New York: Atheneum, 1969), p. 48; see p. 23 for his summary of the intellectual history of Zionism.

2. Cited in Peter Grose, *Israel in the Mind of America* (New York: Knopf, 1983), p. 44.

3. Walter Laqueur, *A History of Zionism* (New York: Schocken Books, 1972), pp. 107–108.

4. Grose, *Mind of America*, p. 44.

5. Laqueur, *A History of Zionism*, p. 159; Grose, *Mind of America*, p. 48.

6. Louis Dembitz Brandeis, "The Jewish Problem and How to Solve It," in *The Zionist Idea*, ed. Hertzberg, pp. 518–519.

7. Sheila Stern Polishook, "The American Federation of Labor, Zionism and The First World War," *American Jewish Historical Quarterly*, March 1976, pp. 228–244; see also Grose, *Mind of America*, p. 67.

8. *The Arab-Israeli Conflict: Readings and Documents*, ed. John Norton Moore (Princeton, N.J.: Princeton University Press, 1977), p. 885.

9. Cited in Conor Cruise O'Brien, "Israel in Embryo," *New York Review of Books*, March 15, 1984.

10. Isaiah Berlin, *Personal Impressions* (New York: Viking, 1981), pp. 46–47.

11. Laqueur, *A History of Zionism*, p. 459.

12. Grose, *Mind of America*, pp. 74–75.

13. See Jabotinsky's speech before the Peel Commission: Colonial No. 134, *Palestine Royal Commission*, Minutes of Evidence, pp. 370–371; also collected in Hertzberg, *The Zionist Idea*, p. 562; see also Joseph Heller, "Weizmann, Jabotinsky and the Arab Question: The Peel Affair," *Jewish Quarterly*, No. 26, Winter 1983, pp. 109–126.

14. Joseph B. Schechtman and Yehuda Benari, *History of the Revisionist Movement*, vol. 1 (Tel Aviv, 1970), p. ix.

15. Laqueur, *A History of Zionism*, pp. 350–353.

16. Joseph B. Schechtman, *Rebel and Statesman* (New York: T. Yoseloff, 1956); Schechtman and Benari, *History of the Revisionist Movement*, p. ix.

17. See Simha Flapan, *Zionism and the Palestinians* (London: Croom Helm; New York: Barnes & Noble Books, 1979), p. 116.

18. Joseph B. Schechtman, *Fighter and Prophet* (New York: T. Yoseloff, 1961), p. 453; cited also in Laqueur, *A History of Zionism*, p. 375.

19. Laqueur, *A History of Zionism*, p. 550.

20. Grose, *Mind of America*, p. 172; see also Melvin I. Urofsky, *We Are One!: American Jewry and Israel* (New York: Anchor Press/Doubleday, 1978), p. 20ff.; interview with Philip Klutznick in Chicago, April 4, 1984.

21. Grose, *Mind of America*, p. 172.

22. Ibid., pp. 174–75; see also Drora Brierbrier, "The American Zionist Emergency Council: An Analysis of a Pressure Group," *American Jewish Historical Quarterly*, September 1970.

23. Michael J. Cohen, "Truman, the Holocaust and the Establishment of the State of Israel," *Jerusalem Quarterly*, No. 23, Spring 1982; cited also in Grose, *Mind of America*, p. 217.

24. Grose, *Mind of America*, p. 229.

25. Howard M. Sachar, *A History of Israel* (New York: Knopf, 1976), p. 265.

26. Cited in *New York Times*, November 30, 1947.

27. Abram L. Sachar, *The Redemption of the Unwanted* (New York: St. Martin's/Marek, 1983), p. 192. The following biographical information on Niles is taken from Sachar's chapter "Truman, Niles, and the American Effort," p. 190ff.

28. Nahum Goldmann, *The Jewish Paradox* (New York: Grosset & Dunlap, 1978), p. 27ff.

CHAPTER 1: THE PRO-ISRAEL LOBBY COMES TO WASHINGTON

1. Melvin I. Urofsky, *We Are One!: American Jewry and Israel* (New York: Anchor Press/Doubleday, 1978), pp. 265–266.

2. Ibid., p. 271.

3. Ibid., p. 279.

4. *Commentary*, January–June 1949, p. 341ff.

5. Ibid., p. 523ff.

6. Urofsky, *We Are One!*, p. 267.

7. See appendix of "In Vigilant Brotherhood: The American Jewish Committee's Relationship to Palestine and Israel," American Jewish Committee Institute of Human Relations, May 1964.

8. Ibid., p. 57.

9. Seymour Leventman, "From Shtetl to Suburb," in *The Ghetto and Beyond*, ed. Peter I. Rose (New York: Random House, 1969), pp. 33–56.

10. Charles Liebman, *The Ambivalent American Jew* (Philadelphia: Jewish Publication Society, 1973).

11. See National Community Relations Advisory Council Annual and Plenary Reports for 1949 and ff.

12. Amnon Rubinstein, *The Zionist Dream Revisited: From Herzl to Gush Emunim and Back* (New York: Schocken Books, 1984); see Chapters 2 and 8.

13. Jay Y. Gonen, *A Psychohistory of Zionism* (New York: Mason/Charter Books, 1975), p. 308.

14. I. L. Kenen, *Israel's Defense Line* (Buffalo: Prometheus Books, 1981), pp. 66–67.

15. Ibid., Chapter 7.

16. Ibid., p. 68.

17. Ibid.

18. Ibid., Chapter 7.

19. Cited in Joyce and Gabriel Kolko, *The Limits of Power* (New York: Harper & Row, 1972), p. 242.

20. See Howard M. Sachar, *A History of Israel* (New York: Knopf, 1976), p. 444; also Kenen, *Israel's Defense Line*, pp. 101–102.

21. See Sara M. Averick, *U.S. Policy Toward Jerusalem the Capital of Israel*, AIPAC Papers on U.S.-Israel Relations: 6, 1984.

22. Kenen, *Israel's Defense Line*, p. 105.

23. Ibid., p. 106.

24. Stephen Green, *Taking Sides* (New York: William Morrow and Company, 1984), p. 83ff. Green cites the documents and U.N. reports on Kibya.

25. The Dulles story is part of the oral tradition of U.S.-Israeli relations. Goldmann too gave his version often in conversation and interviews. See Etta Zablocki Bick, "Ethnic Linkage and Foreign Policy: A Study of the Linkage Role of American Jews in Relations Between the United States and Israel 1956–1968," an unpublished doctoral dissertation, City University of New York, 1983, p. 218; Kenen, *Israel's Defense Line*, p. 111.

26. Interview with Israel Singer, August 20, 1984.

27. Philip M. Klutznick, *No Easy Answers* (New York: Farrar, Straus, Cudahy, 1961), p. 45; also interview with Klutznick in Chicago, April 4, 1984.

28. Livia Rokach, *Israel's Sacred Terrorism* (Belmont, Mass.: Association of Arab-American University Graduates, Inc., 1980), p. 18.

29. Green, *Taking Sides*, p. 99.

30. Maurice Orbach, *New Outlook Magazine*, Tel Aviv, October and November-December, 1974, a two-part series; also cited in Green, *Taking Sides*, p. 103.

31. Green, *Taking Sides*, p. 119.

32. *American-Israel Relations: Addresses and Statements to the Conference of Major Jewish Organizations*, March 5–6, 1955, Shoreham Hotel; in the files of the Blaustein Library of the American Jewish Committee, p. 27.

33. Memorandum from Eliezer Greenberg to Dr. John Slawson, May 23, 1955, p. 7, Blaustein Library.

34. Ibid., p. 9.

35. Rokach, *Israel's Sacred Terrorism, passim*.

36. Ibid., p. 16.

37. Ibid., p. 17.

38. Ibid.

39. All the details of the Lavon Affair are still not known. What is known is fairly compiled and reported in H. M. Sachar's *A History of Israel*, pp. 481 and 543ff, and in Green's *Taking Sides*, p. 107ff.

40. Abba Eban, *An Autobiography* (New York: Random House, 1977), p. 213.

41. Ibid., p. 217.

42. Ibid., p. 218.

43. Interview with Klutznick.

44. H. M. Sachar, *A History of Israel*, p. 509.

45. *New York Times*, October 13, 1958.

CHAPTER 2: "TURNING ON THE SPIGOT": LOBBYING JFK AND LBJ

1. Etta Zablocki Bick, "Ethnic Linkage and Foreign Policy: A Study of the Linkage Role of American Jews in Relations Between the United States and Israel 1956–1968," an unpublished doctoral dissertation, City University of New York, 1983, p. 190.

2. I. L. Kenen, *Israel's Defense Line* (Buffalo: Prometheus Books, 1981), p. 156.

3. Melvin I. Urofsky, *We Are One!: American Jewry and Israel* (New York: Anchor Press/Doubleday, 1978), p. 333; Kenen, *Israel's Defense Line*, p. 155.

4. Kenen, *Israel's Defense Line*, p. 155.

5. Ibid., p. 156.

6. Urofsky, *We Are One!*, p. 332.

7. George Thayer, *Who Shakes the Money Tree?* (New York: Simon and Schuster, 1973, pp. 26–27.

8. Stephen D. Isaacs, *Jews and American Politics* (New York: Doubleday, 1974), p. 121; see also all of Chapter 8.

9. Confidential interview.

10. Kennedy's request is famous and often quoted. See Urofsky, p. 333. It and the Ben-Gurion response are cited by Etta Zablocki Bick, "Ethnic Linkage", p. 191. She found it in the Hebrew edition of Bar-Zohar's biography *Ben Gurion* (Tel Aviv: Am Oved, 1977), p. 417. The new edition of Bar-Zohar's biography celebrating Ben Gurion's centennial (New York, Adama Books, 1986) includes the story on pages 274–275.

11. Bick, p. 145ff.

12. Kenen, *Israel's Defense Line*, p. 161.

13. David Polish, *The Eternal Dissent: A Search for Meaning in Jewish History* (London: Abelard-Schuman, 1961), pp. 147–149; briefly discussed in Urofsky, *We Are One!*, p. 339.

14. Kenen, *Israel's Defense Line*, p. 173.

15. Lyndon Johnson, Presidential Papers, Washington: Government Printing Office.

16. White House logs, LBJ Library at the University of Texas.

17. Donald Neff, *Warriors for Jerusalem* (New York: Linden Press/Simon and Schuster, 1984), pp. 157–158.

18. Abba Eban, *An Autobiography* (New York: Random House, 1977), p. 355.

19. Bick, "Ethnic Linkage and Foreign Policy," p. 81; confirmed by author's interviews with members of the Knesset and former Israeli Cabinet ministers.

20. Bick, "Ethnic Linkage and Foreign Policy," p. 111.

21. Confidential interview.

22. Income and anti-Semitism data cited in Urofsky, *We Are One!*, p. 324.

23. Discussed in ibid., pp. 340–341; Jakob Petuchowski, *Zion Reconsidered*, (New York: Twayne Publishers, 1966).

24. Cited in Nadav Safran, *Israel: The Embattled Ally* (Cambridge, Mass: The Belknap Press of the Harvard University Press, 1981), p. 389.

25. Merle Miller, *Lyndon: An Oral Biography* (New York: G. P. Putnam's Sons, 1980).

26. *Commentary*, August 1967.

27. Shlomo Avineri, *The Making of Modern Zionism* (New York: Basic Books, 1981), p. 219.

28. Neff, *Warriors for Jerusalem*, p. 217.

29. Ibid., p. 107.

30. "Rabin: Nasser Wanted Gains Without War," *New Outlook*, Tel Aviv, June/July 1977. Translation of an article that had appeared in the Israeli daily *Yediot Ahronot*.

31. Summary of Resolution of Arab Summit Conference, Khartoum, Sudan, September 1, 1967, in *The Arab-Israeli Conflict: Readings and Documents*, ed. John Norton Moore (Princeton, N.J.: Princeton University Press, 1977), p. 1081; United Nations Security Council Resolution 242 Concerning Principles for a Just and Lasting Peace in the Middle East, November 22, 1967, in ibid., p. 1083.

32. Bick, "Ethnic Linkage and Foreign Policy," p. 65.

33. Eban, *An Autobiography*, p. 460.

34. Bick, "Ethnic Linkage and Foreign Policy," p. 166.

35. Lyndon Johnson, *The Vantage Point* (New York: Holt, Rinehart and Winston, 1971), p. 483.

36. Bick, "Ethnic Linkage and Foreign Policy," p. 167.

CHAPTER 3: PEACE IN THE MIDDLE EAST: THE YEARS OF INDECISION

1. Jon Kimche, *There Could Have Been Peace* (New York: The Dial Press, 1973), p. 270.

2. Steven L. Spiegel, *The Other Arab-Israeli Conflict* (Chicago: University of Chicago Press, 1985), p. 185.

3. Henry Kissinger, *White House Years* (Boston: Little, Brown, 1979), pp. 370–371.

4. Yitzhak Rabin, *The Rabin Memoirs* (Boston: Little, Brown, 1979), p. 154ff.

5. I. L. Kenen, *Israel's Defense Line* (Buffalo: Prometheus Books, 1981), p. 239.

6. Interview with Simha Flapan, Jerusalem, October 30, 1984.

7. Interview with Arthur Hertzberg, April 11, 1984.

8. Kenen, *Israel's Defense Line*, p. 238.

9. Kimche, *There Could Have Been Peace*, p. 286.

10. Ibid., p. 297.

11. Rabin, *The Rabin Memoirs*, p. 165.

12. See Conor Cruise O'Brien, *The Siege* (New York: Simon and Schuster, 1985), p. 496ff.

13. Anwar el-Sadat, *In Search of Identity* (London: Collins and Fontana, 1978), p. 263. According to O'Brien, Sadat did not actually mention the peace agreement until he sent confirmation of his plans to the U.N. on February 14 (O'Brien, *The Siege*, p. 707 n. 15).

14. Cited in Noam Chomsky, *The Fateful Triangle* (Boston: South End Press, 1983), p. 64.

15. See O'Brien, *The Siege*, p. 510.

16. *Newsweek*, February 14, 1971.

17. *Newsweek*, February 23, 1971.

18. Cited in Chomsky, *The Fateful Triangle*, p. 65.

19. Melvin I. Urofsky, *We Are One!: American Jewry and Israel* (New York: Anchor Press/Doubleday, 1978), p. 402.

20. Rabin, *The Rabin Memoirs*, p. 229.

21. *Facts on File*, September 27, 1972, pp. 773, 844.

22. Kenen, *Israel's Defense Line*, p. 285ff.

23. Rabin, *The Rabin Memoirs*, pp. 230–231.

24. Interview with Hertzberg, April 11, 1984.

25. Leonard Fein, "Israel or Zion," *Judaism* 22 (Winter 1973).

26. See O'Brien, *The Siege*, Chapter 10.

27. Urofsky, *We Are One!*, p. 405.

28. Confidential interview.

29. Kenen, *Israel's Defense Line*, p. 320.

30. Interview with Morris Amitay, November 28, 1986; confidential interview with former AIPAC staffer.

31. Ibid.

32. Figures compiled by G. William Domhoff, *Fat Cats and Democrats: The Role of the Big Rich in the Party of the Common Man* (Englewood Cliffs, N.J.: Prentice-Hall, 1972), pp. 42–44.

33. Stephen D. Isaacs, *Jews and American Politics* (New York: Doubleday, 1974), Chapter 8.

34. See Hauser's remarks in "Liberalism and the Jews," a symposium in *Commentary*, January 1980.

35. Norman Podhoretz, "The Abandonment of Israel," *Commentary* 62, July 1, 1976, pp. 23–31.

36. Edward R. F. Sheehan, *The Arabs, Israelis, and Kissinger* (New York: Reader's Digest Press, 1976), p. 162.

37. Confidential interview with former Kissinger associate.

38. Gerald Ford, *A Time to Heal* (New York: Harper & Row, 1979), pp. 246–247.

39. Sheehan, *Arabs, Israelis, and Kissinger*, pp. 164–174.

40. Full text in ibid., p. 175; also see Seth P. Tillman, *The United States in the Middle East* (Bloomington: University of Indiana Press, 1982), p. 67.

41. Russell Warren Howe and Sarah Hayes Trott, *The Power Peddlers* (Garden City, N.Y.: Doubleday, 1977), pp. 272–273.

42. Interview with ex-Senator James Abourezk.

43. *Foreign Affairs*, Summer 1981, p. 993.

44. The following information on Breira is from Paul Foer, "The War Against Breira," *Jewish Spectator*, Summer 1983, based on his unpublished undergraduate thesis at Hampshire College, "The Attack on Breira: Dissent and Repression in the Jewish Community"; from interviews with former Breira leaders Arthur Samuelson, Rabbi Balfour Brickner, and Rabbi Arnold Wolf, who confirm many of Foer's facts; from Carolyn Toll, "American Jews and the Middle East Dilemma," *Progressive*, August 1979, pp. 28–35; and from various reports in the Israeli press, which I will cite when appropriate.

45. Cited in George E. Gruen, "Solidarity and Dissent in Israel-Diaspora Rela-

tions," in *Forum*, a publication of the American Jewish Committee, Spring/Summer 1978.

46. Mattityahu Peled, "American Jewry: 'More Israeli Than the Israelis,'" *New Outlook*, May/June 1975, pp. 18–26.

47. Ibid.

48. Cited in Gruen, "Solidarity and Dissent."

49. See Foer, "The War Against Breira," p. 21.

50. See Toll, "Middle East Dilemma," p. 34.

51. Interview with Arthur Samuelson, September 1983.

52. See Foer, "The War Against Breira," p. 21.

53. "Interview with Rabbi Alexander Schindler," *New Outlook*, April/May 1976, p. 53.

54. Confidential interview with one of the professors.

55. Interview with Hertzberg.

CHAPTER 4: JIMMY CARTER'S "JEWISH PROBLEM"

1. *Time*, June 21, 1976.

2. *Statement by Governor Carter on the Middle East*, June 6, 1976, released by the New York Citizens Committee for Jimmy Carter.

3. Cited in Richard Reeves, "Is Jimmy Carter Good for the Jews?" *New York*, May 24, 1976.

4. Cited in Mark Bruzonski, "Carter and the Middle East," *The Nation*, December 11, 1976, p. 617.

5. *New York Times*, January 15, 1977.

6. To the World Affairs Council of Northern California, June 17, 1977.

7. Zbigniew Brzezinski, *Power and Principle* (New York: Farrar, Straus, Giroux, 1983), p. 86.

8. Ibid., p. 88.

9. Brzezinski, *Foreign Policy*, New York: Summer 1975.

10. "Toward Peace in the Middle East," Washington, D.C.: The Brookings Institute, December 1975.

11. Confidential interview.

12. Cyrus Vance, *Hard Choices* (New York: Simon and Schuster, 1983), p. 172.

13. In a recent summary of U.S. policy in the Middle East, the historian Bernard Reich attributes the "intellectual" (his quotation marks) origin of Carter's policy to Brzezinski's writings and "the Brookings Report." See Reich, *The United States and Israel: Influence in the Special Relationship* (New York: Praeger, 1984), pp. 43–44; and "Mark Siegel Reveals White House Rivalries," *Israel Today*, June 23–July 6, 1978.

14. Interview with Cyrus Vance, New York, September 26, 1984.

15. *Weekly Compilation of Presidential Documents*, March 21, 1977, p. 361.

16. *New York Times*, March 18, 1977.

17. Brzezinski, *Power and Principle*, p. 91.

18. Confidential interview.

19. Jimmy Carter, *Keeping Faith* (New York: Bantam Books, 1982), p. 280.

20. Brzezinski, *Power and Principle*, p. 90; Vance, *Hard Choices*, p. 173.

21. Brzezinski, *Power and Principle*, p. 90; for the Israeli prime minister's appraisal of Carter, see Yitzhak Rabin, *The Rabin Memoirs* (Boston: Little, Brown, 1979), pp. 298–300.

22. Carter, *Keeping Faith*, p. 280.

23. Rabin, *The Rabin Memoirs*, p. 300.

24. Ibid., p. 294.

25. *Time*, June 27, 1977.

26. Ibid.

27. Carter, *Keeping Faith*, p. 282.

28. Vance, *Hard Choices*, pp. 173–174.

29. Rabin, *The Rabin Memoirs*, p. 300.

30. Carter, *Keeping Faith*, p. 284.

31. Ibid., p. 288.

32. Vance, *Hard Choices*, p. 29.

33. "Lunatic dictator" reported in *Facts on File*, June 23, 1948, p. 198; on the *Altalena* affair, see original reports *New York Times*, June 23 and 25, 1948; also Howard M. Sachar, *A History of Israel* (New York: Knopf, 1981), pp. 329–330; and for its curious role in Israeli history, see Sidney Zion, "Begin from the Beginning," *Harper's*, November 1983, pp. 25–31; Einstein and Arendt letter, *New York Times*, December 4, 1948.

34. Interview with Rabbi Alexander Schindler, New York, April 26, 1984.

35. Quotations cited in Eric Silver, *Begin: The Haunted Prophet* (New York: Random House, 1984), p. 166.

36. Dan V. Segre, *A Crisis of Identity: Israel and Zionism* (Oxford: Oxford University Press, 1980), p. 147.

37. Cited in George E. Gruen, "Solidarity and Dissent in Israel-Diaspora Relations," in *Forum*, a publication of the American Jewish Committee, Spring/Summer 1978. See files on "Dissent" in AJC's Blaustein Library.

38. Silver, *Begin: The Haunted Prophet*, p. 161.

39. Confidential interview.

40. Interview with MK Dan Meridor in Jerusalem, October 23, 1984.

41. Confidential interviews.

42. Confidential interview with a prominent Israeli academic who is very familiar with American Jewish politics, October 26, 1984.

43. Confidential interview with former Begin aide.

44. Ezer Weizman, *The Battles for Peace* (New York: Bantam Books, 1981), p. 118.

45. Simha Flapan, "Begin and the Diaspora," *New Outlook*, Tel Aviv: June/July 1979, p. 17.

46. Cited in Silver, *Begin: The Haunted Prophet*, p. 167.

47. Interview with Arthur Hertzberg in Englewood, N.J., March 16, 1984.

48. J. Bowyer Bell, *Terror out of Zion* (New York: St. Martin's Press, 1977).

49. Confidential interview.

50. Moshe Dayan, *Breakthrough* (London: Wiedenfeld and Nicolson, 1981), p. 21.

51. Ibid.

52. Silver, *Begin: The Haunted Prophet*, p. 168.

53. Ibid., p. 164.

54. Jimmy Carter, *Presidential Papers*, July 30, 1977, pp. 1393–1394; August 23, 1977; *Department of State Bulletin*, August 22, 1977, p. 233.

55. See Sol Stern, "Menachem Begin vs. the Jewish Lobby," *New York*, April 24, 1978; I also discussed Schindler's differences with Begin in an interview with Schindler, April 26, 1984.

56. Cited in Sol Stern, *New York*, April 24, 1978; see Annual Report, Conference of Presidents of Major American Jewish Organizations, 1977.

57. Brzezinski, *Power and Principle*, p. 108.

58. Interview with Vance.

59. Dayan, *Breakthrough*, p. 64.

60. *Middle East Contemporary Survey*, ed. Colin Legum, vol. 1, 1976–77, p. 30.

61. See Stern, *New York*, April 24, 1978, who, as far as I know, was the only journalist to report this extraordinary story; associates of Goldmann and Vance have confirmed its accuracy to me in interviews.

62. Interview with Vance.

63. Sadat's Knesset Address as translated for ABC News; also cited in *Peace-making in the Middle East*, ed. Lester A. Sobel, (New York: Facts on File, Inc., 1980), p. 173.

64. Weizman, *The Battle for Peace*, pp. 142–143.

65. Yoel Marcus, "American Jewry: Between Power and Perplexity," *Ha'aretz*, February 24, 1978. Translated by Israel Shahak. A slightly different translation appears in Arthur Samuelson, "The Dilemma of American Jewry," *The Nation*, April 1, 1978.

66. Samuelson, *The Nation*, April 1, 1978.

67. Interview with a Jewish leader, who was sent the results of the unpublished Ruder & Finn poll.

68. *Newsweek*, March 20, 1978.

69. *Peace-making in the Middle East*, ed. Lester A. Sobel, p. 204.

70. See Stern, *New York*, April 24, 1978; also *Newsweek*, March 20, 1978; also Mark Siegel, *Israel Today*, June 23–July 6, 1978.

71. Interview with Schindler.

72. Interview with Vance.

73. Stephen D. Isaacs, *Jews and American Politics* (New York: Doubleday, 1974), p. 122.

74. Confidential interview with former McGovern aide.

75. Carter, *Keeping Faith*, p. 315.

76. Cited in Gruen, "Solidarity and Dissent."

77. Confidential interview.

78. *New York Times*, August 1, 1979.

79. *Peace-making in the Middle East*, ed. Lester A. Sobel, p. 279ff.

80. Sharon remark cited in Paul Findley, *They Dare to Speak Out* (Westport, Conn.: Lawrence Hill & Co., 1985), p. 134.

81. Confidential interview.

82. Confidential interview with a close associate of President Carter and a top member of his Administration.

CHAPTER 5: "REAGAN OR BEGIN?"—THE AWACS BATTLE

1. Interview with Leonard Davis, Jerusalem, November 4, 1984.
2. Interview with Fred Dutton, Washington, March 1984.
3. Confidential interviews with a Senate aide and former AIPAC staff member.
4. From AIPAC official biography of Thomas A. Dine.
5. Confidential interview.
6. *Facts on File*, June 16, 1980, p. 450.
7. Interview with Thomas A. Dine, January 1985.
8. *Facts on File*, February 22, 1981, p. 121.
9. Ibid., February 19, 1981, p. 122.
10. Interview with Dine.
11. Confidential interview.
12. Carl Bernstein, "Is He All There?" *New Republic*, February 4, 1985.
13. Interviews with Fred Dutton, Washington, March 1984 and January 1985.
14. Ibid.; see also *Wall Street Journal*, March 29, 1982.
15. Steven Emerson, "Dutton of Arabia," *New Republic*, June 16, 1982.
16. Interview with Dutton, Washington, January 1985.
17. *Facts on File*, March 18–19, 1981, p. 169; see also "Middle East Regional Security," Washington, D.C.: Bureau of Public Affairs, Department of State, March 23, 1981.
18. Ronald Reagan, "Recognizing the Israeli Asset," Washington *Post*, August 15, 1979.
19. Thomas A Dine, "A Primer for Capitol Hill," *New York Times*, April 4, 1975.
20. *Facts on File*, April 10, 1981, p. 229.
21. Interview with Dine, January 1985.
22. *Facts on File*, April 24, 1981, p. 265.
23. Confidential interview with member of Baker entourage.
24. Confidential interview.
25. Confidential interview with former aide to Begin.
26. Cited in the Washington *Post*, June 10, 1981.
27. *Department of State Bulletin*, August 1981; *New York Times*, June 10, 1981.
28. See Steven Emerson, "The Petrodollar Connection," *New Republic*, February 17, 1982.
29. *The American House of Saud* (New York: Franklin Watts, 1985).
30. Emerson, *New Republic*, February 17, 1982.
31. Confidential interview.
32. Confidential interview with former AIPAC staffer.
33. Facts on File, September 20, 1981, p. 705.
34. Ibid.
35. Ibid., October 1, 1981, p. 706.
36. Confidential interview.
37. Confidential interview.
38. *Facts on File*, October 16, 1981, p. 743.
39. Interview with Dine.
40. Washington *Post*, October 30, 1981.
41. Confidential interview.

CHAPTER 6: AIPAC: "THE WAR FOR WASHINGTON"

1. From copy of the letter to a senator kindly supplied by Bookbinder which he discussed in an interview in Washington, January 14, 1985.

2. Thomas A Dine, Speech to the Council of Jewish Federations in Toronto, November 1984.

3. Interview with Tom Dine in Washington, March 23, 1984.

4. Confidential interview.

5. Interview with Dine in Washington, March 23, 1984.

6. Confidential interview.

7. Confidential interview.

8. Arthur Hertzberg, "American Jews and Israel," speech at the American Enterprise Institute, Washington, D.C., June 12, 1985.

9. Confidential interview.

10. Interview with Arthur Hertzberg.

11. See Steven L. Spiegel, "U.S. National Interests in the Middle East," and Les Janka, "U.S. National Interests in the Middle East: A New Approach for the '80s," collected in *The National Interests of the United States in Foreign Policy*, edited by Prosser Gifford, Woodrow Wilson Center for Scholars, 1981. Though Spiegel, a historian at the University of California at Berkeley, is a staunch advocate of Israel as a major strategic plus for U.S. policy (see his "Israel as a Strategic Asset," *Commentary*, June 1983, pp. 51–55), and Janka, a former assistant secretary of defense and academic specialist in the Middle East, contends that as long as there is no peace in the region Israel is bound to be a destabilizing influence, both seem to agree on this list of interests. See also Seth P. Tillman, *The United States in the Middle East* (Bloomington: University of Indiana Press, 1982), Chapter 2. Expanding the notion of "national interest" to include moral concerns, Tillman adds to the list "the inadmissibility of the acquisition of territory by force, and the right of peoples to self-determination."

12. Washington *Post*, August 15, 1979.

13. Cited in Tillman, *United States in Middle East*, p. 52; from Department of State Memorandum of Conversation, Meeting with Jewish leaders, Hotel Pierre, New York, June 15, 1975, p. A9.

14. Text cited in *New York Times*, December 1, 1981.

15. *New York Times*, December 21, 1981.

16. "Israel Moves to Smooth Ties with the United States After Golan Action," Washington *Post*, December 15, 1981.

17. See Ze'ev Schiff and Ehud Ya'ari, *Israel's Lebanon War* (New York: Simon and Schuster, 1984), for a detailed account of Sharon's grand plan. The authors are considered two of Israel's best military correspondents.

18. Alexander M. Haig, Jr., *Caveat: Realism, Reagan, and Foreign Policy* (New York: Macmillan, 1984), p. 323ff.

19. See Schiff and Ya'ari, *Israel's Lebanon War*.

20. Arye Naor, "Begin 'misinformed on war,'" Jerusalem *Post*, June 29, 1985.

21. Cited in George Ball, *Error and Betrayal in Lebanon* (Washington, DC: Foundation for Middle East Peace, 1984), p. 45.

22. *Newsweek*, February 20, 1984.

23. Philip Klutznick, Los Angeles *Times*, June 10, 1982.

24. Confidential interview with former *Near East Report* staffer.

25. Reagan Plan can be found in Department of State, Current Policy No. 417, Sept 1, 1982.

26. Cited in *New York Times*, September 2, 1982.

27. Foreign Broadcast and Information Service (FBIS), September 7, 1982.

28. See *New York Times*, September 15, 1982.

29. *New York Times*, September 6, 1982.

30. Arthur Hertzberg, "Begin Must Go," *New York Times*, September 26, 1982.

31. See Arthur Hertzberg, "The Tragedy and The Hope," *New York Review of Books*, October 21, 1982, pp.22–27; "Israel and the West Bank," *Foreign Affairs*, Summer, 1983, pp. 1064–1077; "The Present Position of Jews in America," *Christianity and Crisis*, March 7, 1983, pp. 53–60.

32. Cited in Michael Kramer, "American Jews and Israel: The Schism," *New York*, October 18, 1982.

33. Ibid.

34. Report of Rabbi Alexander Schindler, President of the Union of American Hebrew Congregations, to the Board of Trustees, December 3, 1982, Denver, Colorado.

35. Confidential interview.

36. Interview with Dine, March 23, 1984.

37. Interview with Martin Indyk in Washington, August 20, 1984.

38. Cited by William Safire, *New York Times*, March 24, 1980.

39. Interview with Dine, March 23, 1984.

40. Ibid.

41. See AIPAC Papers on U.S.–Israel Relations monograph series 1, 2, 4, 5: Steven J. Rosen, *The Strategic Value of Israel*; Martin Indyk, Charles Kupchan, Steven J. Rosen, *Israel and the U.S. Air Force*; W. Seth Carus, *Israel and the U.S. Navy*; Stephen P. Glick, *Israeli Medical Support for the U.S. Armed Forces* (Washington, D.C., 1982 and 1983).

42. Rosen, *The Strategic Value of Israel* (AIPAC Papers on U.S.–Israel Relations: 1, 1982).

43. Glick, *Israeli Medical Support for the U.S. Armed Forces* (AIPAC Papers on U.S.–Israel Relations: 5, 1983), p. 8.

44. Carus, *Israel and the U.S. Navy* (AIPAC Papers on U.S.–Israel Relations: 4, 1983), p. 20.

45. Confidential interview.

46. "Power, Glory—Politics," *Time* cover on TV preachers, February 17, 1986.

47. Interview with Minister Without Portfolio Moshe Arens in Jerusalem, October 23, 1984.

48. Nathan and Ruth Ann Perlmutter, *The Real Anti-Semitism in America* (New York: Arbor House, 1982), p. 145.

49. Amy Kaufman Goott and Steven J. Rosen, *The Campaign to Discredit Israel*, AIPAC Papers on U.S.–Israel Relations, ed. Steven J. Rosen (Washington, D.C., 1983).

50. Anthony Lewis, "Protocols of Palestine," *New York Times*, January 15, 1984.

51. "Pro-Arab Propaganda in America: Vehicles and Voices," Anti-Defamation League of B'nai B'rith (New York, 1983).

52. *The AIPAC College Guide: Exposing the Anti-Israel Campaign on Campus*,

ed. by Jonathan S. Kessler and Jeff Schwaber, AIPAC Papers on U.S.–Israel Relations: 7 (Washington, D.C., 1984), p. v.

53. Ibid., p. vi.

54. Notes taken by a participant in the AIPAC National Leadership Conference in Washington, D.C., July 28, 1984.

CHAPTER 7: PRO-ISRAEL PAC POWER

1. See John Fialka, "Pro-Israel Lobby: Jewish PACs Emerge As a Powerful Force in U.S. Election Races," *Wall Street Journal*, February 26, 1985.

2. Confidential interview.

3. "'84 PACs Gave More to Senate Winners," *New York Times*, January 6, 1985.

4. Ibid.

5. Confidential interview.

6. Confidential interview.

7. Fialka, *Wall Street Journal*, February 26, 1985; see also Fialka, *Wall Street Journal*, August 3, 1983.

8. Washington *Post*, June 28, 1975.

9. Interview with Percy aide Scott Cohen, October 1983; see also Paul Findley, *They Dare to Speak Out* (Westport, Conn.: Lawrence Hill & Co., 1985), pp. 109–113.

10. From a mailing by Corcoran's campaign committee.

11. Speech by Tom Dine to the Council of Jewish Federations in Toronto, November 1984.

12. Newsletter Washington Political Action Committee, February 1983.

13. "Jewish PACs Emerge As a Powerful Force in U.S. Election Races," *Wall Street Journal*, February 26, 1985; see also Washington *Post*, December 7, 1984; *Citizens for Percy* vs. *Federal Election Commission*, U.S. District Court for the District of Columbia, No. 84–2653, November 19, 1984.

14. *Wall Street Journal*, February 26, 1985.

15. Speech to the Council of Jewish Federations in Toronto, November 1984.

16. Mailing sent out by Harkin supporter in Iowa, Gary Rubin; cf. Amitay's criticism of Harkin, Newsletter Washington Political Action Committee, February 1983.

17. Interview in Jerusalem, October 22, 1984.

18. Mark Green, "Using PACs to Reform PACs," *Congress Monthly*, published by the American Jewish Congress, June 1983.

19. Morris Amitay, "A Field Day for Jewish PACs," *Congress Monthly*, June 1983.

20. Amitay, "Report from Washington," Jewish Press, October 15, 1982.

CHAPTER 8: "AN AGENDA FOR A CITIZEN LOBBYIST"

1. Thomas A Dine, "An Agenda for a Citizen Lobbyist," a speech to the UJA Young Leadership Biennial Conference in Washington, March 12, 1984.

2. American Israel Public Affairs Committee, "The Israel Airforce New Aircraft 'Lavi'," 1984 press release; also see Duncan L. Clarke and Alan S. Cohen, "The Lavi Fighter," *The Middle East Journal*, vol. 40, No. 1, Winter 1986, pp. 16–32.

3. Interview with Tom Dine, March 24, 1984.

4. *New York Times*, March 30, 1984.

5. Ibid.

6. *New York Times*, March 11, 1984.

7. "Hussein Rules Out Talks with Israel and Bars U.S. Role," *New York Times*, March 15, 1984.

8. Cited in *New York Times*, March 20, 1984.

9. "U.S. and Israel Set Pact to End Tariffs by 1995," *New York Times*, March 5, 1985.

10. "FBI Investigates Leak on Trade to Israel Lobby," Washington *Post*, August 3, 1984.

11. Dine interview, March 24, 1984.

12. Interview with Dr. Akram Barakat, Washington, July 18, 1984.

13. Karen Elliot House, "King Had U.S. Pledges on Peace Talks but Met a Maze of Arab Foes," *Wall Street Journal*, April 15, 1983.

14. John B. Oakes, "Arafat's Card," *New York Times*, March 18, 1984.

15. *Le Nouvel Observateur*, May 4, 1984.

16. Cited in Philip Geyelin, " 'Presidential Flexibility' and the PLO," Washington *Post*, May 8, 1985.

17. Interview with Cyrus Vance in New York, September 26, 1984.

18. See Steven M. Cohen, *Attitudes of American Jews Toward Israel and the Israelis*, The 1983 National Survey of American Jews and Jewish Communal Leaders, Institute of American Jewish–Israeli Relations, American Jewish Committee, October 1983; see also similar poll done in Israel by the Israeli pollster Hanoch Smith, *Attitudes of Israelis Toward America and American Jews*. Institute of American Jewish–Israeli Relations, American Jewish Committee, October 1983. Similar results had already been found in Cohen's poll for the American Jewish Committee, *The 1982 National Survey of American Jews*; Cohen summarizes it in "What American Jews Believe," *Moment*, July/August 1982. See also "Attitudes toward Israel since June 1982," American Jewish Committee Information and Research Services, November 1982, AJC Blaustein Library file "Israel-Arab Conflict Reaction/Public Opinion"; also see the Gallup poll on American attitudes toward Menachem Begin, September 22, 1982.

19. Interview with Mordechai Virshubski in Tel Aviv, November 2, 1984.

20. Meron Benvenisti, *The West Bank Data Project* (Washington and London: American Enterprise Institute for Policy Research, 1984), p. 64.

21. *New York Times*, February 24, 1985.

22. Pinchas Inbari, "Arafat's Disengagement from the PLO," *Al Hamishmar*, March 14, 1985, translated by the Center for International Peace in the Middle East in Tel Aviv; see also "The Peace Initiative Is Still Alive," *Ma'ariv*, March 26, 1985; see also Matti Steinberg, "The PLO: the Natural Alternative," *Ha'aretz*, March 8, 1985; see also David Richardson, "Name Dropping," Jerusalem *Post*, International Edition, week ending June 8, 1985.

23. See Cyrus Vance and Jimmy Carter memoirs for text of Camp David peace accord; also see *Peace-making in the Middle East* (Facts on File: Washington, D.C. 1980).

24. Meir Merhav, *New York Times*, March 31, 1985; see also Merhav, "A Con-

sensus of Nonsense," Jerusalem *Post*, March 10, 1985; also collected in *Facing the PLO Question* (Washington, D.C.: 1985), Foundation for Middle East Peace.

25. Ibid.

26. Matti Steinberg, "The PLO: The Natural Alternative," *Ha'aretz*, March 8, 1985; see also David Shaham, "Discreet American Pressure Would Help Peres," *New York Times*, April 7, 1985; reprinted in the Jerusalem *Post*, April 8, 1985.

27. "Hussein Says PLO Agrees on Parley with the Israelis," *New York Times*, May 30, 1985.

28. "Are the Palestinians Ready to Seek Peace?" *New York Times*, June 2, 1985.

29. Ibid.

30. "Jordan Arms Curbs Called Dangerous," *New York Times*, June 5, 1985.

31. "A Retreat on Arms for Jordan," *Newsweek*, June 24, 1985.

32. Confidential interview.

33. See Secretary Shultz's testimony before the Committee of Foreign Affairs House of Representatives in "Arms Sales to Jordan and the Middle East Peace Process," First Session on H.J. Resolution 428 and S.J. Resolution 228, October 17, 1985.

34. See "Terror Aboard Flight 847," *Time*, June 24, 1985; see also "Israel and U.S. Apparently Resolve Some Differences on Hostage Crisis," *New York Times*, June 23, 1985; "Pressure Is on Israel for a Swap," Jerusalem *Post*, International Edition, week ending June 29, 1985; "The Quandary for Israel," *New York Times*, June 22, 1985.

35. Confidential interview.

36. Confidential interviews.

37. Confidential interview.

38. Interview with Arthur Hertzberg, June 20, 1985.

39. Confidential interview.

40. Interview with Tom Dine.

41. David Silverberg, "AIPAC at the Crossroads: Elite Team or Mass Movement," *Washington Jewish Week*, April 4, 1984.

42. Interview with Fred Dutton, Washington, January 14, 1985.

CHAPTER 9: U.S. AID: HELPING ISRAEL TO HURT ITSELF

1. Figures compiled from Agency for International Development, *U.S. Overseas Loans and Grants from International Organizations*, Annual Reports. Prepared by Lawrence Potter, Foreign Affairs and National Defense Division Congressional Research Service, Library of Congress, for *Time* magazine, June 1984; see also Mohamed El-Khawas and Samir Abed-Rabbo, *American Aid to Israel: Nature and Impact* (Brattleboro, Vt.: Amana Books, 1984), p. 1.

2. Thomas L. Stauffer, "U.S. Aid to Israel: The Vital Link," *Middle East Problem Papers* No. 24 published for the members of the Middle East Institute, Washington, D.C., 1983.

3. El-Khawas and Abed-Rabbo, *American Aid to Israel*.

4. Mark Segal, "Public Faces" column, Jerusalem *Post*, International Edition, week ending July 20, 1985.

5. Senate Foreign Relations staff report on the Israeli economy cited in *New York Times*, November 21, 1984.

6. Confidential interview with State Department economist.

7. "Foreign currency reserves dip $73 million," Jerusalem *Post*, International Edition, week ending July 20, 1985.

8. "Dun and Bradstreet 'Blacklist,'" Jerusalem *Post*, International Edition, week ending March 30, 1985; "More firms in trouble in June," Jerusalem *Post*, International Edition, week ending July 20, 1985.

9. Cited in Assaf Razin, "U.S. Foreign Aid to Israel," *Jerusalem Quarterly*, No. 29, Fall 1983, p. 16.

10. "U.S. Says Israelis Show Little Gain in Economic Plan," *New York Times*, March 7, 1985.

11. Interview with the Georgetown economist Thomas Stauffer, who had already cited these figures in testimony before the House Appropriations Committee in 1985.

12. Cited in Amos Elon, "Letter from Jerusalem," *New Yorker*, July 29, 1985, pp. 68–69.

13. I thank Jerry Nadler, correspondent for the United Press in Jerusalem in 1984, for the anecdote.

14. Cited in "Business as Usual: Congress Increases Aid to Israel," *Voice*, March/April 1984, the magazine of the National Association of Arab Americans.

15. Stauffer interview, August 1985.

16. Nadav Halevi, "The Economy of Israel: Goals and Limitations," *Jerusalem Quarterly*, No. 1, Spring 1976.

17. This section is based on interviews with several economists in the U.S. and Israel who are experts in the history—and mysteries—of the Israeli economy. The American economists are still working in government, and asked for anonymity. I will cite Israeli sources, interviews, and articles where relevant. Useful summaries of the Likud years are found in Peter Grose, *Changing Israel*, a Council of Foreign Relations Book (New York: Vintage Books, 1985), Chapter 4; Kenneth Stammerman, "Israeli Economic Policy Under the Likud: A Guide for the Perplexed," a paper presented to the Middle East Institute symposium "Israel After Begin," January 20, 1984. Stammerman is a State Department economist with five years' experience at the U.S. Embassy in Israel. He took the trouble to preface his speech with the disclaimer that the views in the paper were his own and not necessarily the State Department's. From the Israeli side, also useful is Yoram Ben-Porath, "The Conservative Turnabout That Never Was," *Jerusalem Quarterly*, Number 29, Fall 1983, pp. 3–9.

18. Ben-Porath, "The Conservative Turnabout," pp. 3–9.

19. Jerusalem *Post*, International Edition, week ending July 13, 1985; also "Peres Orders Shock Therapy," *Newsweek*, July 15, 1985.

20. Eric Silver, *Begin: The Haunted Prophet* (New York: Random House, 1984), p. 212.

21. Ibid., p. 213.

22. Ben-Porath, "The Conservative Turnabout," p. 6.

23. Cited in Silver, *Begin: The Haunted Prophet*, p. 214.

24. Ibid., p. 215.

25. Ben-Porath, "The Conservative Turnabout," p. 7.

26. Stammerman, "Israeli Economic Policy," pp. 13–14.

27. "Israeli Resigns as Dollar Plan Sets Off Furor," *New York Times*, October 14, 1983.

28. "Steel and Muscle," *Time*, December 12, 1983.

29. Interview with Hyman Bookbinder in Washington, January 1985. See also David Silverberg, "American Jews Balk at Israeli Aid Requests," *Washington Jewish Week*, January 3, 1985.

30. "Senate Report Is Pessimistic on Israel's Plight," *New York Times*, November 21, 1984.

31. Assaf Razin, "Ways of Repairing the Israeli Economy," *New York Times*, December 28, 1984.

32. Interview with Assaf Razin in Tel Aviv, November 1, 1984.

33. William Safire, "The Masada Economy," *New York Times*, October 8, 1984.

34. William Safire, "Passing the Shekel," *New York Times*, December 27, 1984.

35. "Dr. Shekel and Uncle Sam," *New Republic*, January 28, 1985.

36. "U.S. Says Israelis Show Little Gain in Economic Plan," *New York Times*, March 7, 1985.

37. Safire, "Israel for Sale?" *New York Times*, April 11, 1985.

38. Confidential interview with U.S. government economist.

39. Figures compiled from Agency for International Development, *U.S. Overseas Loans and Grants from International Organizations*, Annual Reports. Prepared by Lawrence Potter, Foreign Affairs and National Defense Division Congressional Research Service, Library of Congress, for *Time* magazine, June 1984.

40. *American Assistance to the State of Israel*. General Accounting Office, June 1983. The Arab-American Anti-Discrimination League published a version of the GAO Report called "The Uncensored GAO Report." The same document was included in El-Khawas and Abed-Rabbo, *American Aid to Israel*, p. 123ff. The latter has printed the edited remarks in bold type, and I have referred to that text for this information.

41. Max Frankel, "Looming over the West Bank," *New York Times*, November 16, 1982.

42. See the official version of the GAO Report *U.S. Assistance to the State of Israel* under the section "Economic Impact of Lebanon." See also El-Khawas and Abed-Rabbo, *American Aid to Israel*, p. 151.

43. GAO Report, Chapter 3, "Israel's Economy and U.S. Assistance"; cf. El-Khawas and Abed Rabbo, *American Aid to Israel*, p. 141.

44. Meir Merhav, "Why U.S. economic advice won't work," Jerusalem *Post*, International Edition, week ending March 2, 1985.

45. "Israeli Independents," editorial in *The Wall Street Journal*, March 29, 1985.

46. Confidential interview.

47. See Steven L. Spiegel, "Israel's Economic Crisis: What the U.S. Can Do." *Commentary*, April 1985, pp. 22–28; Leon Hadar, "Wisely Aiding Israel," op-ed–page piece in *New York Times*, February 20, 1985; Isaac Cohen, "Aid to Israel: A bargain . . ." Chicago *Tribune*, October 24, 1984.

48. "The Butter That's Traded Off for Guns," *New York Times*, April 22, 1985.

49. "House Approves Foreign Aid Bill," *New York Times*, July 12, 1985.

50. Confidential interview.

51. Interview with Hyman Bookbinder in Washington, January 1985. See also Silverberg, "American Jews Balk."

52. "Quest for compromise on economic plan," Jerusalem *Post*, International Edition, week ending July 20, 1985.

53. "A bitter fight over economic austerity," Jerusalem *Post*, International Edition, week ending July 13, 1985.

CHAPTER 10: REDISCOVERING THAT "TWO-WAY STREET"

1. Conor Cruise O'Brien, "Political Reality in the Middle East," *Atlantic*, October 1985; Irving Kristol, "America's Doomed Mideast Policy," *New York Times*, August 11, 1985.

2. Cited in "Squadron Rips Shamir for Blast at U.S. Jews," New York *Post*, September 15, 1985.

3. "Peres at U.N., Proposed to Go to Jordan for Talks," *New York Times*, October 20, 1985; see also, "Israeli Cabinet Debates Peres's Peace Proposal," *New York Times*, October 28, 1985.

4. "Reagan Notifies Congress of Arms Sale to Jordan," *New York Times*, September 28, 1985; "Hussein Assails Arms Delay," *New York Times*, November 3, 1985.

5. "Settlers on the West Bank Threaten Disobedience," *New York Times*, November 6, 1985.

6. "Warning by Arafat: Peace Will Not Exist Without the PLO," *New York Times*, October 29, 1985.

7. "Weizman Ready to Meet Arafat," *Ha'aretz*, February 1985; translation in *Israel Press Briefs*, No. 32, March 1985, published by the International Center for Peace in the Middle East, Tel Aviv.

8. "Ezer Weizman on the Peace Process," *Yediot Ahronot*, November 2, 1984; translation in *Israel Press Briefs*, No. 30, December 1984.

9. "Weizman: 'It will be a different PLO at the negotiating table,'" *Yediot Ahronot*, July 19, 1985; translation in *Israel Press Briefs*, No. 37, August 1985.

10. Philip Klutznick, "Negotiations with the PLO: When? Now!" *Facing the PLO Question*, Foundation for Peace in the Middle East, 1985.

11. Interview with Rabbi Arnold Wolf, in Chicago, April 1984.

12. Interview with Janet Aviad, Jerusalem, October 29, 1984.

13. Bialkin's remarks are cited in Jerusalem *Post*, International Edition, July 8–14, 1984; according to Yehuda Hellman, the executive director of the Presidents' Conference, Bialkin said much the same in a meeting with the editors of *The New York Times* a year later.

14. See Amos Elon, "Letter from Jerusalem," *New Yorker*, July 29, 1985, p. 61.

15. Interview with Professor Barry Chazan, Jerusalem, October 30, 1984.

16. Interview with Professor Shlomo Ben-Ami, Tel Aviv, October 31, 1984.

17. "Attitudes of Adolescents with Regard to Democratic Values," Mina Tzemach and Ruth Tzin; findings of survey of attitudes conducted by the Dahaf Research Institute at the request of the Van Leer Jerusalem Foundation, September 1984, unpublished paper.

18. Interview with Alouph Hareven, Jerusalem, October 28, 1984; see also *The*

Comprehensive Educational Project on Relations Between Arabs and Jews and Between Israel and Her Neighbours, a project directed by the Van Leer Jerusalem Foundation for the Israeli Ministry of Education and Culture, July 1984.

19. Earl Raab and Seymour Martin Lipset, *The Political Future of American Jews*, American Jewish Congress, March 1985.

20. William Schneider, "The Jewish Vote in 1984: Elements in a controversary," *Public Opinion*, Vol. 7, No. 6., December/January 1985. ABC News put the figure at 31 percent, CBS/*New York Times* poll put it at 33 percent, and NBC at 35 percent.

21. "Pro-Israel PACS Giving More to GOP," Washington *Post*, November 4, 1985.

22. Ibid.

23. "Fire on the Right," *Washington Jewish Week*, May 16, 1985; "AFSI Links with New Right," *Washington Jewish Week*, February 7, 1985.

24. "Gush Goes West," Jerusalem *Post*, International Edition, week ending November 16, 1985.

25. Nahum Goldmann, "The Present Chance for Mideast Peace," *Worldview*, March 1980.

26. Ibid.

27. Confidential interview.

28. Confidential interview.

29. Confidential interview.

30. Notes taken by a member of the audience and confirmed by others.

31. Howard Addison, "Zionism, Democracy, and the Fundraisers," *Jewish Frontier*, January, 1985.

32. See Etta Zablocki Bick, "An Ongoing Dialogue," Jerusalem *Post*, International Edition, week ending July 4, 1985.

33. Abba Eban, Jerusalem *Post*, International Edition, week ending July 27, 1985.

34. *New York Times*, May 7, 1986; see also May 8, 1986.

35. Interview with Ben-Ami.

36. Confidential interview.

37. See Israel-Egypt summit coverage in the Jerusalem *Post*, International Edition, week ending September 13, 1986.

38. "The White House Crisis: The Israeli Stake," *New York Times*, November 27, 1986.

INDEX